Q&A
Land Law

Routledge Questions & Answers Series

Each Routledge Q&A contains questions on topics commonly found on exam papers, with comprehensive suggested answers. The titles are written by lecturers who are also examiners, so the student gains an important insight into exactly what examiners are looking for in an answer. This makes them excellent revision and practice guides.

Titles in the series:

Q&A Company Law
Q&A Commercial Law
Q&A Contract Law
Q&A Criminal Law
Q&A Employment Law
Q&A English Legal System
Q&A Equity and Trusts
Q&A European Union Law
Q&A Evidence
Q&A Family Law
Q&A Intellectual Property Law
Q&A Jurisprudence
Q&A Land Law
Q&A Medical Law
Q&A Public Law
Q&A Torts

For a full listing, visit www.routledge.com/cw/revision

Q&A
Land Law

Martin Dixon and Emma Lees

Routledge
Taylor & Francis Group

LONDON AND NEW YORK

Ninth edition published 2015
by Routledge
2 Park Square, Milton Park, Abingdon, Oxon OX14 4RN

and by Routledge
711 Third Avenue, New York, NY 10017

Routledge is an imprint of the Taylor & Francis Group, an informa business

First edition published by Cavendish Publishing 1993
Eighth edition published by Routledge 2013

British Library Cataloguing in Publication Data
A catalogue record for this book is available from the British Library

Library of Congress Cataloging in Publication Data
Dixon, Martin (Martin J.) author.
Q&A land law / Martin Dixon and Emma Lees. – Ninth edition.
  pages cm. – (Routledge Q&A series)
  1. Land tenure–Law and legislation–England–Examinations, questions, etc. 2. Land titles–Registration and transfer–England–Examinations, questions, etc. 3. Real property–England–Examinations, questions, etc. I. Lees, Emma, author. II. Title. III. Title: Question and answer land law.
  KD833.D593 2015
  346.4204'3–dc23   2014026141

ISBN: 978-1-138-78230-3 (pbk)
ISBN: 978-1-315-76924-0 (ebk)

Typeset in TheSans
by Wearset Ltd, Boldon, Tyne and Wear

MIX
Paper from
responsible sources
FSC
www.fsc.org   FSC® C013056

Printed and bound in Great Britain by
TJ International Ltd, Padstow, Cornwall

Contents

Table of Cases

Table of Legislation

■ Statutes

■ Secondary legislation

Guide to the Companion Website

www.routledge.com/cw/revision

Visit the Law Revision website to discover a comprehensive range of resources designed to enhance your learning experience.

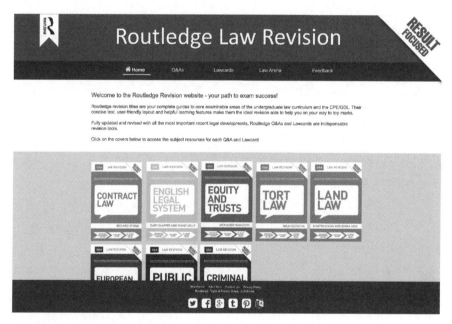

The Good, The Fair, & The Ugly

Good essays are the gateway to top marks. This interactive tutorial provides sample essays together with voice-over commentary and tips for successful exam essays, written by our Q&A authors themselves.

Multiple Choice Questions

Knowledge is the foundation of every good essay. Focusing on key examination themes, these MCQs have been written to test your knowledge and understanding of each subject in the book.

Bonus Q&As

Having studied our exam advice, put your revision into practice and test your essay writing skills with our additional online questions and answers.

Introduction

Land law holds a certain fascination for the student: usually one of dread. We do not deny that it can be a difficult subject, and students face conceptual and practical problems of a kind not always found in other branches of the law. The fact that the subject is often composed of statutory provisions overlaying ancient principles of common law and uses a vocabulary that can be, to say the least, unusual does not make things easier. However, with the correct approach – both as to how the subject is studied and revised and how questions are tackled in examination – many of the perceived problems and pitfalls can be identified and avoided. The new edition of this book is designed to help you to find and develop that approach with consequent success in your examinations.

At the outset, you need to be aware that an examination in land law cannot be treated as a series of separate questions, nicely compartmentalised. Anyone who attempts to understand land law in this manner is in for a rude awakening, as the subject can be viewed only as an integrated whole. What the student learns in their first week of study may well be relevant in a question set on work they cover in their last week. This is not a subject in which topics can be picked from a menu and eaten piecemeal in the examination. Land law has a clear structure. If you can understand the principles of land law and how they relate to each other, most students will see the picture fall into place and be able to answer the practical problems raised by land law in an examination setting. For that reason, the questions in this edition are presented in a logical order – an order that gives the student a slowly developing but clear picture of the subject as a whole. Of course, the answers can be taken on their own for what they are: an aid to revision and examination performance. However, this book can also be used as a teaching aid.

There are a number of new questions in this edition, and every one has been updated to reflect legislative changes and the addition of new and recent case law. In particular, there are now a number of cases interpreting and applying the **Land Registration Act 2002** and the importance of these, and this statute, cannot be overestimated. Likewise, the Supreme Court has been active in matters of property law, with significant cases in co-ownership and leases, and there have been very many cases on a range of topics decided in the Court of Appeal.

ESSAYS, PROBLEMS AND EXAMINATIONS

Although a feature of many land law courses over recent years has been the introduction of a variety of assessment strategies, in the vast majority of cases it is your performance in written examinations that counts most. Consequently, it is most important that you develop a proper approach to legal writing. Not only is it one of the skills expected of a practising lawyer but, more immediately, it is the foundation for your examination success. Many students fail to do themselves justice in the examinations through lack of a technique that they could and should have learned in their written work during the year.

The essay is used in most disciplines for general exposition and analysis of a topic, looking down and over it from a vantage point. In land law, you may be asked to explain, illustrate or discuss a particular doctrine or institution (proprietary estoppel, or the impact of the **Land Registration Act 2002**), or to analyse recent developments or proposed reforms in a particular area (e.g. human rights and property, easements or Law Commission Reports), or to comment critically on a quotation (e.g. 'Interests which override are in no more a satisfactory state now than they were prior to the 2002 legislation. Discuss.'). Where imaginary facts are given and your advice is sought, this is called a problem question. In what follows, guidance is offered first on essay-writing and then on tackling problems, although answers to both types of question require similar skills of analysis and discussion.

ESSAYS

In answering essay questions, it is vital to read and consider carefully the question before plunging into your actual writing. Whatever you do, do not waste time writing out the quotation or whatever else comprises the question. You should start with an idea of the general area in which the question falls – and this is especially important where the question is in the form of a quotation – but you should not simply repeat your lecture notes or study notes. The question almost certainly will require an answer different from the general exposition given in a lecture and simply repeating lecture notes tells an examiner that you do not really understand the question. So think what further depth or breadth is required (more detail? more history? more comparison? more criticism?) and let your own opinion develop, as to both the treatment of the topic and its content, and then concentrate on these aspects. Otherwise you may well find you have not answered the actual question but have written a 'tell me all you know about' response. You should always be prepared to come to some sort of conclusion: something, however tentative, should follow logically from your discussion of the topic. If the question was in the form of a quotation, look back at it and say how valid it was. Remember that attributed quotations are often selected for discussion because they are thought to be provocative and not necessarily sound, whilst unattributed quotations are often concocted by the question-setter. It is perfectly acceptable to agree with the quotation, provided that you have given reasons. As always, you must support what you say by reference to, and discussion of, cases, statutes and, where appropriate, academic or judicial opinion. In land law, you hardly ever will need to repeat the facts of a case. Cases stand for points of law and a good technique will give a case – just the name, not the facts – for every point of law made. Absence of cases, even in essay answers, inevitably means a weak mark.

PROBLEMS

The purpose of problem questions is to see how you are able to apply legal rules and principles to a given set of facts. These rules and principles are derived from cases and from statutory provisions. Rules derived from cases necessarily may be dependent on the facts of the particular case but very often in land law they stand for important general statements of principle: e.g. 'that proprietary estoppel is established by assurance, reliance and detriment in circumstances of unconscionability' (*Thorner v Majors* (2009)). Nevertheless, one set of facts in Case A may be very like the facts in Case B – so much so that the judges' decision in Case A will be applied by the judges to the facts in Case B in order to reach a decision. Thus, when you are presented with a problem question, you are being asked to apply rulings from previous cases and pieces of statute law to the facts before you in order to decide what the solution to the legal problem is.

It is important to remember that the first step is to analyse the problem in order to determine the particular legal issues involved. One possible approach is as follows:

❖ Consider what legal issues are posed by the factual circumstances presented in the problem.
❖ Locate and discuss the law relevant to such issues (i.e. case law, statutes).
❖ Suggest an appropriate answer based on your application of relevant legal principles to the facts you have before you.
❖ If you are asked to give advice, do so. Remember, however, it is not your job to tell your client that everything is well. The advice must be accurate, even if the advice is not what your client would like to hear.
❖ Remember that the answer must be supported by cases and statutes wherever possible.

It must be emphasised that there is not really any such thing as a 'model answer'. Rarely is it possible to provide an answer that is the only acceptable or authoritative one. As suggested above, what is important is that law students should develop an ability to highlight the main legal issues to which a particular set of facts gives rise and then arrive at a conclusion that is accurate, comprehensive and justifiable in the light of those facts.

EXAMINATIONS

Much 'advice' on examination technique is, in fact, little more than common sense and the following points are obvious, but easily forgotten.

❖ Make sure you have the correct date, time and place for the examination. It may not be the same venue as your last examination.
❖ Do you have all you need, e.g. pens, statutes, watch etc.? If you are permitted to take in materials – e.g. a statute book – make sure that you do. Materials are not permitted just for fun. The examiner will deduct marks if you fail to follow a statute correctly when you are meant to have a statute book in front of you.
❖ Read the paper thoroughly: how many questions need you answer? Decide on your choice of questions and quickly plan your answer; divide your time. You *must* answer the correct number of questions.

❖ You will *not* get any generosity for answering three questions really well if you should have answered four. Examiners will be fair to all candidates and that means applying the rules equally.

❖ Do not be 'smart'. Little 'notes' to the examiner about your personal circumstances at best are ignored and at worst irritate the examiner.

❖ Do *not* expect to know the answer to every question. You get no extra marks by being able to answer all questions. You get marks for producing good answers to the required number of questions.

Dr Martin J Dixon
Emma Lees
June 2014

Common Pitfalls

The most common mistake made when using Questions & Answers books for revision is to memorise the model answers provided and try to reproduce them in exams. This approach is a sure-fire pitfall, likely to result in a poor overall mark because your answer will not be specific enough to the particular question on your exam paper, and there is also a danger that reproducing an answer in this way would be treated as plagiarism. You must instead be sure to read the question carefully, to identify the issues and problems it is asking you to address and to answer it directly in your exam. If you take our examiners' advice and use your Q&A to focus on your question-answering skills and understanding of the law applied, you will be ready for whatever your exam paper has to offer!

1

Registered Land

INTRODUCTION

Land lawyers in England and Wales fall into two broad groups. First, there are those who believe that the 1925 property legislation and, specifically the **1925** and **2002 Land Registration Acts (LRA)**, established new machinery for controlling the creation and transfer of land and interests in land, but did not radically alter the nature of property law. Thus, some textbooks will explain in detail the nature of, say, easements or mortgages, and add a section at the end of each chapter on the implications of 'registered land'. Others take the view that the system of registered conveyancing has produced fundamental changes in the nature of the rights and interests falling within the concept of 'land law'. Thus, on this view, a detailed understanding of the *mechanics* of registered land is necessary *before* a student can fully appreciate substantive property concepts such as easements or mortgages. There is, of course, merit in both views, but even without the powerful theoretical arguments that could be used, there are practical advantages for the student in following the second approach and this is the course adopted in this edition of Questions & Answers.

Since 1 December 1990, all of England and Wales has been designated as an area of compulsory registration of title and it is now estimated that over 80 per cent of all potentially registrable titles are in fact registered. In the fullness of time, therefore, unregistered conveyancing will all but disappear from the legal landscape and this process has accelerated since the entry into force of the **LRA 2002** on 13 October 2003. In fact, the **LRA 2002** operates on the fundamental assumption that registered land is intrinsically different from land of unregistered title. Moreover, and more importantly for students, examiners set problem questions that require students to explain how easements or mortgages, or whatever, operate in registered land and no amount of pre-1925 property law will solve these puzzles. There is, for example, no point in discussing the 'doctrine of notice' in registered land when it is entirely irrelevant and an answer that includes such a discussion might lead an examiner to conclude that the student fundamentally misunderstands the nature of modern land law.

If a plot of land is described as 'registered', this means that 'title' to it (that is, an estate of freehold, or leasehold of over seven years) is recorded and guaranteed by the Land Registry. In contrast, 'unregistered land' is land to which title is not registered but is established by the title deeds of the particular property. Whether title is registered or unregistered depends simply on whether there have been any dealings with the land such as to give rise to an obligation to register (compulsory registration), or whether the 'owner' has applied for voluntary first registration of title. As such, there is no magic about land being 'registered': it is simply a way of saying that the title is recorded and guaranteed and that dealings with the land fall within the procedures established by the **LRA 2002** and the **Land Registration Rules 2003** (as amended in 2008 and 2011). When answering problem questions in an examination, one of the first things to establish is whether the land is registered, and normally you will be told. For example, there may be references to the 'registered proprietor' or the land's 'title number'. If you are not told, it cannot be important for your answer as there is no way that you can deduce whether title is registered. After all, whether there has been registration of title does not depend on the quality of the land or the interests in it, but whether an event has occurred that has triggered registration of title.

Aim Higher

The system of registered land falls into four parts and a sound knowledge of these distinctions will enhance answers to examination questions.

Registered titles: these are the freehold or legal leasehold over seven years and they are substantively registered in their own right with a title number. Most questions in land law examinations require no more than a basic knowledge of the mechanics of registering or transferring titles and of the different qualities of title with which a person may be registered. A wider knowledge enhances the answer. Of more complexity are the rules relating to the transfer and creation of interests *in* the land such as easements, mortgages, covenants and shorter-term leases (that is, those that cannot be registered as titles, being currently leases for seven years or less).

Unregistered interests which override (also known as *overriding interests*): these are interests in the land that will have automatic priority over a registered proprietor (such as a new purchaser of the land). They do not have to be registered anywhere to take effect against the registered proprietor. They are defined in **Sched 1** to the **2002 Act** in relation to first registered proprietors and in **Sched 3** in relation to purchasers of an existing registered title (although the Schedules are broadly very similar). In substance, these unregistered interests which override are inherently proprietary (i.e. *capable* of binding third parties), although some are legal and some are equitable. No student should attempt a land law paper without a thorough understanding of overriding interests and an ability to use the statutory Schedules. Being aware of the small differences between the Schedules, and why they exist, will improve an essay question on the **2002 Act** in general and overriding interests in particular.

Registered protected interests: these are those interests enjoyed by third parties (i.e. not the registered proprietor) that are entered on the register of title against the burdened land and thus are protected in the event of a transfer of that registered title. If they are not registered, generally they do not have priority over a purchaser, unless the right falls (fortuitously) into the category of overriding interest. The 'doctrine of notice' is entirely irrelevant in this regard and talking about it in a registered land question will create a poor impression. In essence, under the **LRA 2002**, this class of interest is meant to comprise the great majority of third party rights in land, the point being that as much as possible about the registered title should be clear from the register of title itself. Examples include easements, covenants, options to purchase and shorter leases.

Registrable charges: these are essentially mortgages. They, too, must be registered to take effect as legal mortgages (otherwise they may be equitable) and are considered in more detail in the chapter on mortgages. Sometimes an examiner will leave doubt about whether the mortgage is legal or equitable as this may affect remedies and so understanding this distinction can add marks.

QUESTION 1

'The primary reasons for the introduction of a land registration system in England and Wales were realised by the **Land Registration Act 1925**. That system was not perfect, but it has been enhanced by the entry into force of the **Land Registration Act 2002**.'

▶ **Discuss.**

How to Read this Question

The examiner here is looking for you to go beyond basic description of the **LRA 2002**, but instead to analyse the Act's relationship with its aims and with the aims of the 1925 property legislation.

How to Answer this Question

❖ Pre-1925 problems – briefly.
❖ The mechanics and principles of land registration, including the priority rules (s 28 and s 29 LRA 2002).
❖ Titles and the mirror principle.
❖ Trusts and the curtain principle.
❖ The insurance principle.
❖ The role of unregistered interests which override.
❖ The role of registered protected interests.
❖ Some problems and solutions: undiscoverable but binding interests and the changes made by **LRA 2002**; protecting the purchaser or the occupier?; the nature of the guarantee of title embodied in s 58; and Scheds 4 and 8.

Up for Debate

The nature of the guarantee of title in s 58 is a matter of some debate. The decisions in *Parshall v Hackney* (2013), *Richall v Fitzwilliam* (2013), *Swift 1st Ltd v Chief Land Registrar* (2014) and the series of cases surrounding *Barclays Bank v Guy (No 1)* (2008) have been the subject of much academic commentary. The meaning of 'mistake' in **Sched 4** is critical to the determination of these issues. The approach to rectification in *Baxter v Mannion* (2011) and *Walker v Burton* (2013) should also be considered when analysing the extent to which the **LRA 2002** embodies the insurance principle. See Lees, 'Title by registration: rectification, indemnity and mistake and the Land Registration Act 2002' (2013) 76 MLR 62, Dixon, 'A not so conclusive title register?' (2013) 129 LQR 320 and Goymour, 'Mistaken registrations of land: exploding the myth of "title by registration"' (2013) 72 CLJ 617.

Applying the Law

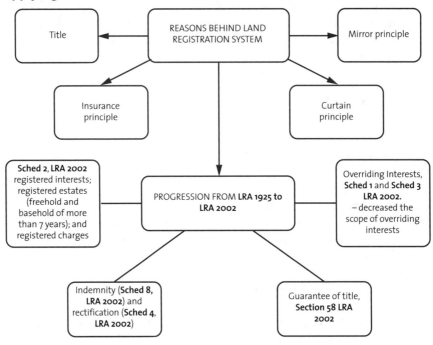

This diagram demonstrates the main principles of land registration and the progression from the **Land Registration Act 1925** *to the* **Land Registration Act 2002.**

ANSWER

The 1925 property legislation inaugurated a fundamental change in the structure of land law in England and Wales. Before then, the mechanics of conveyancing were hindered by formalism, beset with danger for all but the most conscientious purchaser. The operation of the doctrine of notice meant not only that holders of equitable rights could have their rights destroyed through chance or caprice, but also that purchasers of property might find their land burdened by legal rights of which they had no knowledge. Reliance on title deeds to prove ownership of land was cumbersome and expensive. The net result was a choking of the property market at a time when free movement of capital was essential. The **Land Registration Act 1925** sought to simplify and codify. It aimed to bring certainty where there was obscurity, and equity where there was often inequality. The **Land Registration Act 2002**, which has replaced the **Land Registration Act 1925** in its entirety, seeks to reinforce these goals and make the system fit for the twenty-first century.[1]

---

1   This essay is asking for an assessment of the progress towards meeting the principles of land registration from the position pre-1925 to the current day, and this introduction does a good job of setting this out clearly.

The basic principle of the **LRA 1925**, and now the **LRA 2002**, is that title to land should be recorded in a register and guaranteed by the state. On 1 December 1990 all of England and Wales became subject to compulsory registration of title. In addition to establishing a mechanism for registering ownership, the **Land Registration Act 1925** also established three other mechanisms for protecting other people's rights in that land. This has been continued under the **LRA 2002**.[2] If correctly used, these procedures will ensure that rights in land are not destroyed by a transfer of a registered title to a new owner. First, there are registrable charges (mortgages), which must be registered before they can be regarded as legal mortgages – **ss 25**, **27** of and **Sched 2** to the **LRA 2002**. Once registered, these bind subsequent transferees of the mortgaged land unless the mortgage is paid off (as most will be) by the proceeds of that sale. If not registered, such mortgages take effect as equitable interests only.

Second, there are unregistered interests which override ('overriding interests'). These are interests, found in **Scheds 1** and **3** to the **LRA 2002**, that take effect automatically against a first registered proprietor (**Sched 1** rights) or a transferee of an existing registered title (**Sched 3** rights). They require no registration and the old doctrine of notice is entirely irrelevant – **ss 11**, **12**, **29** and **30** of the **LRA 2002**. It is immaterial whether such interests are legal or equitable, so long as they fall within one of the classes defined in the appropriate Schedule to the **2002 Act**. The logic behind the automatic effect of such interests is that they comprise such rights as *should* be obvious to a purchaser on physical inspection of the property or are such that they benefit the community as a whole without seriously restricting a purchaser's enjoyment of the land.

Third, there are registered protected interests. This category essentially comprises all other interests that may subsist in or over land. In order to have priority over a first-registered proprietor or a purchaser of a registered title, such interests, whether legal or equitable, must be protected by entry on the register. Actual 'notice' of the right (or lack of it) is irrelevant – **ss 11**, **12**, **29**, **30** of the **LRA 2002**. Under the **LRA 2002**, this class is meant to comprise the vast majority of third party rights in land. Failure to make such an entry means that the right loses its priority over a purchaser of the registered title unless the right fortuitously falls within the category of overriding interests. Note, however, that such rights, whether registered or not, will have priority over a transferee of a registered title who is not a purchaser, such as when there has been a gift or an inheritance (**s 28** of the **LRA 2002**).

This classification obviously places much more emphasis on statutory definition than it does on the legal or equitable quality of a right. Such a radical shift in 1925 was designed to bring certainty and stability and this aim also prevails as the motivator for the **2002 Act**. Land registration is said to operate on three principles: the mirror principle, the curtain principle and the insurance principle. The mirror principle suggests that the register should be a mirror of all the proprietary rights that exist in any given piece of land. This has only been partially achieved by the **2002 Act**. The inclusion of overriding interests compromises the mirror principle. But, in itself, this is not a cause of serious

---

2 The examiner here will be looking not only for a description of the rules contained in the 1925 and 2002 legislation, but will also be looking for you to draw parallels between the provisions.

criticism.[3] Overriding interests remain crucial to the proper functioning of the system. They were deliberately created by the legislature and exist precisely because such rights should be obvious to any prospective purchaser or because their enforcement is too important to depend on registration. Social and judicial developments however have enlarged the opportunity for the existence of overriding interests. It is conceivable that a purchaser might not be able to determine whether such interests exist by inspection of the land. The most obvious example is the right of equitable co-ownership, originally stemming from *Pettitt v Pettitt* (1970), the effect of which under the old **s 70(1)(g)** of the **LRA 1925** on an unwary purchaser was first fully appreciated in *Williams and Glyn's Bank v Boland* (1981). Another example is *Ferrishurst Ltd v Wallcite Ltd* (1999), in which the plaintiff's overriding interest was undiscoverable because his 'actual occupation' (under the then **s 70(1)(g)** of the **LRA 1925**) extended only to part of that property. However, this difficulty has been largely overcome by **Sched 3** to the **LRA 2002**. Under **Sched 3**, actual occupation gives rise to an overriding interest *only* where the occupation is discoverable by a purchaser (or the purchaser already knows about the right) and then only achieves priority to the extent of the land actually occupied (thus reversing *Ferrishurst*). This should do much to alleviate the problem of undiscoverable adverse rights.

The curtain principle was, perhaps, the most ambitious goal of the original **1925 Act**. It remains a key principle under the **2002 Act**. The aim is to keep *certain* types of equitable interest off the register completely. Such equitable rights, being those taking effect behind a trust of land, will not bind a purchaser on sale of the land because of overreaching. In essence, a purchaser will not be concerned with such equitable rights – they are behind the curtain of a trust – so long as the purchase money is paid to two trustees of land: **s 2** of the **LPA 1925**.[4] The equitable interests then take effect in that purchase money. Such a system works well when the statutory requirement of two trustees exists. However, on some occasions there will be just one trustee of land and so overreaching will not be possible. In such circumstances, a purchaser must 'look behind the curtain'. As *Boland* shows, if the purchaser does not raise the curtain, the purchaser can easily be bound by such equitable interests. This problem involves striking a balance between protection of the purchaser and protection for the occupier of land and it arose largely due to social and judicial changes. Cases such as *Abbey National Building Society v Cann* (1991), *Mortgage Business plc v Cook* (2012), *Equity & Homes Loans v Prestridge* (1992) and *Birmingham Midshires Mortgage Services Ltd v Sabherwal (Sudesh)* (2000) illustrate the complexity of this balancing act.

Finally, there is the insurance principle. Once title is registered, the state guarantees the authenticity and effectiveness of that title: **s 58** of the **LRA 2002**. Obviously, such a system cannot be absolute and there are provisions for alteration of the register: **s 65** and **Sched 4** of the **LRA 2002**. The potential wide-ranging discretion to alter the register is clearly a cause for concern – contrast *Derbyshire County Council v Fallon* (2008), *Baxter v Mannion* (2010) and *Walker v Burton* (2013) – and the interaction of **s 58** and **s 65** still needs to be clarified. A

---

3   This section is good in that it goes beyond simply assessing whether the mirror principle is complied with and considers whether full compliance with this principle is in fact desirable.

4   It is important always to be as specific as possible in the use of statutory provisions – cite **s 2** here, rather than just the **1925 Act** etc.

second limb of the 'insurance principle' is to be found in **Sched 8** to the **LRA 2002**, which stipulates the circumstances in which a person suffering loss by reason of the operation of the registration system can receive an indemnity (money compensation). These provisions support strongly the effectiveness of the land registration system. Recent case law has however called the strength of the guarantee of title into question. *Fitzwilliam Holdings v Richall* (2013) suggests that **s58** guarantees only legal title, such that following a void conveyance, the new registered proprietor would hold on trust for the original proprietor. This decision, based on *Malory v Cheshire Homes* (2002), if subsequently followed, will render the guarantee of title largely worthless. The effects of this decision have however been lessened by the approach of the court in *Swift 1st v Chief Land Registrar* (2014).

On a general level then, the current land registration system now found in the **2002 Act** is a success. The success was built on the **1925 Act** and has been enhanced by the **2002 Act**. The introduction of a system of land registration brought certainty, fairness and relative simplicity. Of course, there are problems of detail. However, the overhaul of the law by the **LRA 2002** has been beneficial. Indeed, the **LRA 2002** goes further than a mere tinkering with the system and brings the system up to date, even without the coming into force of the e-conveyancing provisions. Currently, there is a tension between the purchaser of land and the occupier of it, but generally speaking the provisions on overreaching can deal with this if the statutory mechanisms are observed.

Common Pitfalls

The temptation with such a routine question is simply to repeat the sections of the **LRA 2002**. However, it is important to use case law to illustrate points and in essays you should also mention academic commentary. In addition, you should try to avoid discussing only the mirror, insurance and curtain principles: every student will know this basic information and you need to be more critical.

QUESTION 2

In 2012, Karen sold her large farm, title to which is registered to Bonny. At the time of the purchase, Bonny's solicitor made an official search of the register and obtained a clear result. Unfortunately, the search was carried out by an inexperienced clerk and failed to reveal a restrictive covenant correctly registered against the land for the benefit of the adjoining farm owned by Richard. The covenant stipulated that no trade or business other than farming may be carried out on the land. When walking over the farm on the day after she had been registered with title, Bonny discovered that Zeus, a new-age squatter, had established a home in a derelict farm cottage. Next door, Bonny found Lulu who claimed to have been paying rent to Karen for the last two years under an agreement that she could live in the cottage for six years. Lulu produced a written record of the agreement typed on a plain piece of white paper.

▶ Bonny comes to you for advice as she wants to build an out-of-town supermarket on part of the site and, in any event, wants possession of the cottages.

How to Read this Question

The examiner is looking for you to analyse the facts, to identify the relevant issues and to apply your legal knowledge to these facts. Credit will be given both for the detail and accuracy of your answer, but also for analysis of the law you are applying. Here, you should identify what Bonny wishes to achieve, and what is required for such an outcome.

How to Answer this Question

❖ The effect of registration as owner – **s 29** of the **LRA 2002** and the special priority rule.

❖ Whether there are any overriding interests under **Sched 3** to the **LRA 2002**.

❖ The role and effect of registered protected interests.

❖ The primacy of the register over search certificate.

❖ The possibility of alteration, rectification and indemnity.

Applying the Law

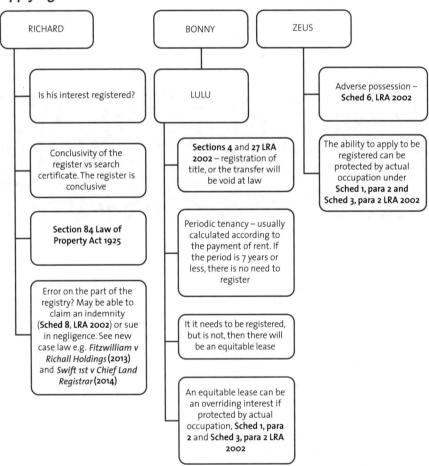

This diagram shows how to apply the rules of registered land to the situation involving Bonny.

ANSWER

When Bonny is registered as proprietor of the farm, the estate in the land is transferred to her statutorily and conclusively under **s 58** of the **LRA 2002** (although see *Fitzwilliam v Richall Holdings* (2013) for information as to the operation of this guarantee). However, under **s 29** of the **LRA 2002**, a new registered proprietor who gives value (i.e. a purchaser) takes the land subject to any interests appearing on the register and any unregistered interests which override under the provisions of **Sched 3** to the **LRA 2002**. It is necessary, therefore, to establish whether Bonny's registered title is subject to any third party interests that may prohibit her proposed development. Second, if Bonny's title is affected by a third party interest, the next question is whether she can ask for alteration of the register or claim an indemnity.

(a) The Restrictive Covenant[5]

Bonny will be unable to build the proposed supermarket if she is bound by the restrictive covenant because the person entitled to the benefit of it (i.e. to enforce it) may be able to obtain an injunction, although it is possible that damages be awarded instead. Assuming that all the conditions for its enforceability required by the law of freehold covenants are established (see – **s 78 LPA 1925** and *Tulk v Moxhay* (1848)), the issue turns on whether the restrictive covenant has been properly protected within the system of registered land – in other words, whether it has been protected by means of a unilateral or agreed notice: **ss 29** and **32** of the **LRA 2002**.

When Bonny requested a search from the Land Registry (through her solicitor), she received a clear search certificate. However, it is clear from **s 32** of the **LRA 2002** (and see the earlier case of *Parkash v Irani Finance Ltd* (1970)) that it is the register itself that is conclusive, irrespective of any statements made on an official certificate or by an officer of the Registry. In our case, therefore, Bonny is bound by the restrictive covenant because it has been properly registered by means of a notice, and this is so even though she is entirely blameless in failing to discover it. Of course, Bonny can make an application to the Lands Tribunal under **s 84** of the **Law of Property Act 1925** to have the restrictive covenant modified or discharged if she wishes to proceed with her proposed development, but as a matter of property law it is binding on her. It is possible that Bonny will be eligible for a statutory indemnity under **Sched 8** to the **2002 Act, para 1(1)(c)** if she can show that she has suffered loss by reason of a mistake in an official search (*Swift 1st v Chief Land Registrar* (2014)). Failing this, she should be advised to sue the Land Registry in negligence (*Minister of Housing and Local Government v Sharp* (1970)).

(b) The Squatter

Zeus appears to be in the process of trying to establish a right to the land under the law of adverse possession – see *Pye v Graham* (2002). Again, whether Bonny is bound depends on the application of the relevant provisions of the **LRA 2002**. In the case of adverse possessors,

---

5   The use of sub-headings here makes the answer easier for the examiner to follow and also assists in time management.

it is clear that they may have an overriding interest against a new proprietor under **Sched 3, para 2** to the **LRA 2002**. This is because even a person in the process of adverse possession has a property right in the land, albeit one that is weak and liable to be defeated. Thus, so long as Zeus was in the process of acquiring his rights on the day when Bonny was registered with the title to the farm (*Abbey National BS v Cann* (1991); *Mortgage Business plc v Cook*), and was in discoverable actual occupation (or Bonny knew of his right when he was in occupation), he has an overriding interest under **Sched 3, para 2** to the **LRA 2002** that has priority to the limited extent that any adverse possession is effective under the **LRA 2002**.[6] However, this overriding interest merely protects the period for which he has been in possession and he will not actually acquire title unless he applies for registration as proprietor under **Sched 6** to the Act. If he does so apply, assuming none of the exceptions are relevant (estoppel, boundary disputes, other entitlements – **Sched 6 LRA 2002** – and they appear not to be), Bonny will be able to object and she will have a further two years to evict him. If she fails to object, or after objecting does not evict within two years, Zeus will acquire title. However, given the circumstances of this problem, it is more likely that Bonny will proceed to evict if Zeus applies for title. If he does not even apply, she may evict him in the normal way.

(c) The Lease

Lulu is in occupation of the second farm cottage under some form of lease given to her by Karen. Is this lease binding on Bonny? Clearly, the lease claimed by Lulu is of less than seven years' duration (in fact, it is six), so it need not have been substantively registered in its own right – it is not currently within **ss 4** or **27** of the **LRA 2002**. So, the lease can only be binding on Bonny if it is a registered protected interest or an overriding interest.

If this is a legal lease, then it constitutes an overriding interest under **Sched 3, para 1** to the **LRA 2002**. However, the lease is not made by deed – it is *written*, but not in a deed – so the only circumstance in which it could be a legal lease is if it amounts to a legal periodic tenancy under which the period is three years or less – see **ss 52(1)** and **54(2)** of the **Law of Property Act 1925** (and Chapter 5). The question makes no reference to the period for which Lulu pays rent; we are told only that she has been in occupation for two years and expects to be free to occupy for another four. In such circumstances, the implication is against a legal periodic tenancy. It is worth noting, however, that, even if this were a legal periodic tenancy, binding as an overriding interest under **Sched 3**, there would be nothing to prevent Bonny from terminating it according to its own terms – that is, the giving of notice to quit of one period.

It is more likely that the lease is equitable. There is written evidence of it and it is probably capable of specific performance (see **s 2** of the **Law of Property (Miscellaneous Provisions) Act 1989** and *Walsh v Lonsdale* (1882)). Equitable leases can be protected by an entry on the register by way of a notice, but Lulu has not done this. However, this lease – assuming it is equitable – is still binding on Bonny for its intended duration (six years from grant by

---

6 Although this problem is concerned largely with the operation of the registration requirements, it is important to be aware of the strength of the rights thus protected and the consequences of that right for the purchaser.

Karen) because Lulu falls within **Sched 3, para 2** to the **LRA 2002**, being a person with a proprietary interest (the lease) in discoverable actual occupation at the time the property was transferred:[7] **s 29** of the **LRA 2002** and see *Thompson v Foy* (2009), *Link Lending v Bustard* (2010) and *Chaudhary v Yavuz* (2011) for the general principle.

To conclude, then, there is every possibility that Bonny must allow Lulu to occupy one cottage until her lease expires, assuming, of course, that, in the meantime, Lulu does not breach the terms of the lease and continues to pay rent to her new landlord. Although Zeus's rights as an adverse possessor are binding on Bonny, she can resist any application he may make for the title and can evict him. She is bound by the restrictive covenant even though it was not disclosed on the search certificate because it is registered. Bonny's real hope for substantive remedies because she has innocently purchased a property bound by an adverse right (the covenant) lies in negligence against her solicitor and possibly in contract against Lulu.[8]

Common Pitfalls

Avoid skipping over the substantive law behind this problem. For example, the examiner will not assume that you know the law concerning restrictive covenants if you do not make reference to it, even briefly. In the absence of information about how a property right comes into existence, do not assume that formalities exist. For example, do not assume that Lulu's lease is 'by deed' and note the difference between a lease by deed and a lease 'in writing'.

QUESTION 3

In 2012, Oswald owns a large detached house, divided into two self-contained flats, title to which is registered in his sole name. In anticipation of an overseas posting, Oswald had advertised for a tenant for the upper flat and entered into negotiations with Bluebell. Unfortunately, they could not agree terms but, on payment of a deposit, Bluebell was allowed to occupy the flat while their solicitors negotiated an acceptable lease. Meanwhile, Oswald agreed in writing to sell the bottom flat to his daughter Nigella should he be posted abroad. Hearing of Oswald's possible departure, Eric, his neighbour, asks whether he can use Oswald's drive for easier access to his large double garage. Oswald readily agrees, provided that Eric pays for resurfacing of the drive. Eric employs contractors and the drive is completely resurfaced. On hearing of his overseas posting, Oswald realises that he needs to raise some capital. Hera, his mistress, is willing to buy the property at much more than his daughter could ever afford. Realising that Nigella has not registered her interest, he sells the entire property to Hera by registered disposition. Hera wishes to re-convert the house and asks Bluebell to leave. She also erects a fence

---

7   A common mistake is to assume that actual occupation itself is a right which registration will protect. This is wrong. The right protected by the actual occupation must itself be a recognised property right – here, a lease.

8   This is a creative alternative solution to the problem and one worth mentioning like this in a conclusion.

preventing Eric from using her drive. Nigella hears of the sale and seeks to enforce her right to buy the bottom flat against Hera.

▶ **Advise the parties.**

How to Read this Problem Question

Problem questions test your legal knowledge and your ability to apply the law to the facts. You ought to divide up the issues and deal with Oswald's relationship with each of the parties. The examiner will be looking for a logical and clear structure.

How to Answer this Question

- ❖ The effect of registration as owner – ss 58 and 29 of the **LRA 2002**.
- ❖ The extent and effect of any overriding interests.
- ❖ The existence of any registered protected interests.
- ❖ The formality rules for the creation of leases.
- ❖ The conditions for proprietary estoppel and s 116 of the **LRA 2002**, *Midland Bank Trust Co v Green* (1981).

Applying the Law

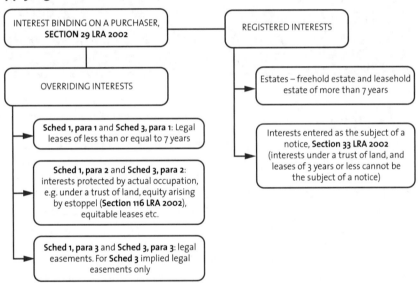

This diagram demonstrates which interests are binding on a purchaser under the **Land Registration Act 2002**.

ANSWER

As the new registered proprietor of the land, Hera will be bound only by those overriding interests subsisting at the date of registration of her new title (that is, those in **Sched 3** to the **LRA 2002**; *Abbey National BS v Cann* (1991), *Mortgage Business plc v Cook* (2012)), as well as any registered protected interests – see s 29 of the **LRA 2002**. In addition, there is the possibility that she could be bound by proprietary interests that are not protected in the proper fashion if there has been some fraud or bad faith associated with her purchase (see, for example, *Lyus v Prowsa Developments* (1982), but note *Lloyd v Dugdale* (2002) and *Chaudhary v Yavuz* (2012)).

(a) Bluebell

The question here is whether Bluebell has any estate or interest in the land and, if so, whether it has been protected against a third party purchaser under the appropriate mechanism of the **LRA 2002**. In order for a right to have priority over a purchaser, it must be *capable* of being binding – that is, it must be proprietary. In this case, there is the possibility that Bluebell has a lease and, of course, this is a proprietary interest. For example, Bluebell has paid some money and she appears to have gone into occupation in pursuance of it. Indeed, her lease in these circumstances could be a legal periodic tenancy of three years or less and having priority (until terminated by appropriate notice) as an overriding interest under **Sched 3, para 1** to the **LRA 2002**. (There is no possibility of an equitable tenancy because there is no written document within the formality requirements of **s 2** of the **Law of Property (Miscellaneous Provisions) Act 1989**.) However, there is also the possibility that Bluebell does not have a lease at all. She has, in fact, gone into occupation pending the negotiation of a lease in the knowledge that no agreement has been concluded with the landlord. Following *Javad v Aqil* (1991), there will be no lease if there was no intention to create legal relations, as seems likely while negotiations are still proceeding. Bluebell will, therefore, be a 'tenant at will', which (contrary to its name)[9] confers no estate or interest in the land, being a mere licence. If this is the case, there is no proprietary right capable of being a registered protected interest or an overriding interest and so Bluebell must vacate the flat (see *Ashburn Anstalt v Arnold* (1989) and *Lloyd v Dugdale*).

(b) Eric

In the case of Eric, the position is not so clear. From his point of view, he will be claiming, first, that the right to use the drive amounted to an easement (right of way), and, second, that this easement is binding on Hera. First, does the easement exist? It is axiomatic that a right of way can amount to an easement but, in this case, there is the question of whether it has been properly created. Clearly, there is no deed or even a written record of the agreement between Oswald and Eric: thus the easement is not legal and cannot be equitable within *Walsh v Lonsdale* (1882). However, it may be that Eric can claim the creation of an easement in his favour under the law of proprietary estoppel, as explained generally in *Taylor Fashions Ltd v Liverpool Victoria Trustees* (1982) and *Thorner Majors* (2009) and, in respect of easements in particular, in *Ives v High* (1967). In our case, there appears to have been an assurance – by Oswald to Eric that he could use the drive – which was relied upon by Eric to his detriment. How else is it possible to explain Eric's expenditure on the driveway: see *Greasely v Cooke* (1980)? This may well mean that Eric has the benefit of an easement, albeit an easement that must be equitable because of the informal manner in which it was created. If this is true, Eric has a right that is capable of binding Hera and will do so if it is registered by means of a notice against the title or can amount to an overriding interest (**s 29**

---

9   Short 'asides' such as this are a good way to introduce some analysis without detracting from main point being made.

of the **LRA 2002** and see the analysis in *Chaudhary v Yavuz* (2012)). Clearly, there is no registration in this case. Moreover, under the **LRA 2002**, equitable easements are not capable of amounting to overriding interests under **para 3** of **Sched 3**, for the Act deliberately reverses *Celsteel v Alton* (1985) and *Thatcher v Douglas* (1995). Likewise, use of the easement on the servient land does not amount to 'actual occupation' of it so as to generate an overriding interest under **para 2** of **Sched 3** (*Chaudhary v Yavuz* (2012)). Consequently, it looks as if the easement, if it exists, will not have priority over the purchaser of the registered title.

(c) Nigella

By his written agreement with his daughter, Oswald has granted Nigella some right in connection with the flat. What is the nature of that right?[10] At first sight, it appears that Nigella's right could be a 'right of pre-emption' – a right of first refusal to the land should the owner decide to sell. If this were the case, it would amount to a proprietary right (**s 115** of the **LRA 2002**; see also *Dear v Reeves* (2000)), but it would be effective against the purchaser *only* if Nigella were in discoverable actual occupation of the flat to which it relates (or the purchaser knew of the right and she was in occupation) under **Sched 3, para 2** to the **LRA 2002** (overriding interest) or if she has registered it by means of a notice.

However, the better view is that Oswald has granted Nigella an option to purchase the flat. The essence of an option is that the grantee (Nigella) has an enforceable right to purchase the property at a moment of their choosing, provided that any conditions in the option are fulfilled (see, for example, *Ferrishurst Ltd v Wallcite Ltd* (1999)). Here, the fact that the option is conditional upon the overseas posting does not alter its character because, if Oswald is posted, Nigella has an enforceable right to buy at her choosing. Oswald has no choice if the condition is fulfilled (if he is posted) and he has no control over whether the condition will be fulfilled (see *Haslemere Estates Ltd v Baker* (1982) in support of this view). Assuming this to be an option, it is clear that it is a proprietary right, capable of binding third parties. Yet, once again, in order to take priority over a new purchaser/owner, the proprietary right must be protected in the proper manner under the **LRA 2002**. There is no prospect of the option being an overriding interest as it does not fall within any of the statutory definitions of **Sched 3 LRA 2002** (e.g. Nigella is not in actual occupation under **para 2**). Moreover, in this case, the option has not been protected by entry on the register, and therefore has no priority against a purchaser. It cannot be enforced against Hera: **s 29** of the **LRA 2002**.

In such circumstances, the only slender hope – and it is very slender – is for Nigella to establish that her unregistered interest has been defeated by fraud and for this reason should remain valid. However, even if Hera knows that Oswald is selling the property partly to defeat his daughter's claim, the better view is that this is not fraud – see, for example, *Midland Bank Trust Co v Green* (1981) in a similar context in unregistered land. In this respect, *Peffer v Rigg* (1977), which seemed to require the purchaser to act 'in good faith' if they were to be free of unregistered interests (where 'good faith' is defined almost synonymously with notice), was probably bad law and in any event such a concept

---

10 It is always best to outline the precise right it is suggested that someone in a problem has, even if this ultimately does not affect the conclusion reached.

is irrelevant under the **LRA 2002** (see also *HSBC v Dyche* (2010) and *Chaudhary v Yavuz* (2012)). Only if Hera had promised Nigella and/or Oswald that she would honour the option despite the lack of registration (and had, thereby, obtained the property more cheaply) could the purchaser be said to have committed fraud – see *Lyus v Prowsa Developments* (1982), although this is very difficult to establish and *Chaudhary*[11] regards *Lyus* as a very special case. If that were the position – and there is no evidence to support it – Hera would be a constructive trustee of the option for Nigella and necessarily bound by it.

In conclusion, then, Hera is not bound by the easement as it does not qualify as an overriding interest and is not registered. She is not bound by the option to allow Nigella to purchase the ground-floor flat and may ask Bluebell to leave as she has no estate in the land capable of being binding on Hera.[12]

Common Pitfalls

❖ Do not assume that the purchaser *must* be bound by the claimant's rights. It may be that the purchaser takes the land free of the claim, even if this looks 'unfair' in some general sense. Land registration is about certainty.

❖ Avoid importing unregistered land concepts into land registration questions: it is not about what the purchaser 'knows' but about the rules of the **LRA 2002**.

QUESTION 4

The Law Commission proposed fundamental changes to the system of registered land and these have now taken shape in the form of the **LRA 2002**. The **LRA 2002** is a considerable improvement on the **1925 Act**, although some uncertainties in its operation have come to light.

▶ **Discuss.**

How to Read the Question

The examiner will be expecting you to assess the uncertainties in the **2002 Act** as well as to examine the relationship between the **1925 Act** and the **2002 Act**. It is a question of carefully balancing the structure to address both issues. This is a potentially complex question, but which therefore has scope for detailed analysis.

How to Answer this Question

❖ The general thrust of **Law Commission Report No 271**.

❖ The potential problems with overriding interests identified by the Law Commission – nature, extent and undiscoverability.

❖ Potential problems with other interests – simplifying the methods of protection.

---

11 *Chaudhary* is relied on a lot in this answer – this demonstrates good knowledge of recent case law and will be given much credit by the examiner.

12 It is always good to have a short conclusion like this in problem questions to summarise the application of the law to the facts.

- ❖ Adverse possession of registered land and its relation to the **2002 Act** system of registration.
- ❖ The future – formalities for the creation of interests in land, rectification of the register and electronic conveyancing.

Up for Debate

The Law Commission has in fact recently assessed whether changes to the **LRA 2002** itself are required. In particular, they are looking into the question of changes to the guarantee of title embodied by the register (**s 58**), but also into questions of adverse possession and e-conveyancing. The Land Registry has announced that e-conveyancing is now on hold, and it is up for debate whether this means that amendments to the **2002 Act** are required.

Applying the Law

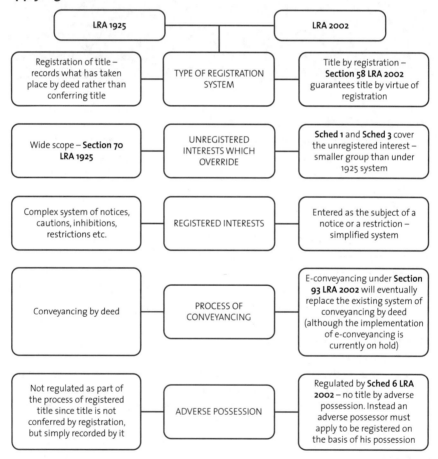

This diagram shows the key differences between the *Land Registration Act 1925* and the *Land Registration Act 2002*.

ANSWER

The land registration system inaugurated by the **LRA 1925** had been in operation for over 75 years before it was reformed by the **LRA 2002**. Throughout this period, the role of 'land' within the economy had changed, as had the methods by which legal transactions could be undertaken, and it was perfectly accurate for the Law Commission to conclude that the system of land registration needed modernising. We should not forget that the **LRA 1925** was itself an experiment in title registration and no one would argue that it was flawless. Time has revealed, however, that it was not fatally flawed.

The underlying rationale of the **LRA 1925** was relatively straightforward: title to land was to be recorded and guaranteed by the state through title registration and interests in land were either obvious on physical inspection of the land itself or noted in a clear and unambiguous fashion on the register of title. The advantages were also obvious: purchasers could buy in the certainty that they were purchasing land suitable for their requirements, and owners of interests in land had a relatively easy and inexpensive method of ensuring that their rights survived a conveyance of the land to a third party. These remain fundamental objectives of the land registration system. However, we now live in a different age, in which both technological advances and the need to iron out deficiencies in the original 1925 system required that title registration should be overhauled. The Law Commission had been working on this task for some time. The publication of **Law Commission Report No 271** including a draft Bill, brought the process to fruition. **The Land Registration Bill 2001** became the **LRA 2002** and this far-reaching statute came into force on 13 October 2002. The **LRA 2002** has then completely replaced the **LRA 1925**.

Much of the **2002 Act** is groundbreaking and truly significant, not least the claim that the **2002 Act** replaces 'registration of title' with 'title by registration'. No longer is it the case that a person acquires a title that is then registered; rather, under the **LRA 2002**, the act of registration itself, and only that act, comprises the grant of title. Registration as proprietor is conclusive: **s 58 LRA 2002** – see *Walker v Burton* (2013). This means that a person dealing with the registered proprietor should be able to deal with them in complete confidence (see **s 23 LRA 2002**) without fear that they are not really the owner, even if it should later emerge that there was some 'flaw' in the proprietor's title (e.g. even that they never should have owned it – *Walker v Burton* (2013)). The decision in *Fitzwilliam v Richall Holdings* (2013) and confirmed in *Swift 1st v Chief Land Registrar* (2014) does however call this into question – suggesting that only bare legal title is guaranteed by **s 58**.

Another major issue addressed by the Law Commission is that of overriding interests (now called 'unregistered interests which override'): being those rights that bind a purchaser of the land without entry on the register and irrespective of whether the purchaser has any knowledge or notice of them. Indeed, under the **LRA 1925**, they bound the purchaser even if they could never have discovered such rights (i.e. they were undiscoverable, as opposed to undiscovered, as in *Chhokar v Chhokar* (1984)).[13] Of course, the great

---

13 This essay is asking not only for an outline of the changes brought about by the **2002 Act**, but of an assessment of the seriousness of the problems that existed in the earlier legislation.

majority of overriding interests under the **LRA 1925** were in fact discoverable from a reasonable inspection. Nevertheless, it is true that the mere existence of a category of 'overriding interests' compromises the integrity of the register. Consequently, the 2002 legislation attempts to reduce the effect of overriding interests, both by eliminating certain categories of overriding interest and by inaugurating a change in the way that we think about these important rights. Thus, the rights that once fell within **s 70(1)** of the **LRA 1925** were reclassified. Under the **2002 Act**, there are some rights – the larger category – that override a first registration of title – that is, they override the estate of the person who first registers when the land ceases to be unregistered land (see **ss 11** and **12** of, and **Sched 1** to, the **LRA 2002**). These rights include the major categories of legal leases of seven years or less, interests of persons in actual occupation of the relevant part of the land, and legal easements and profits.

Second, there is a narrower category of rights that override a disposition of registered land. These include the above categories narrowed down to reflect the fact that some rights that override a first registration should have been entered on the register after first registration if they are to continue to be binding. Thus, any lease that is required to be registered as a title is excluded (at first, this will be those over seven years – reduced from 21 years under the old law); a right of a person in actual occupation is excluded if, either the occupation is not patent (that is, if it is not discoverable) or the right is not known of by the purchaser (**para 2**) and see *Thompson v Foy* (2009), *Link Lending v Bustard* (2010) and *Thomas v Clydesdale Bank* (2010);[14] expressly granted easements are excluded (because they will not exist at all unless entered on the register (**para 3**)), equitable easements and certain types of legal easement not falling within **para 3**. Obviously, there is a general emphasis on discoverable overriding interests (with undiscoverable ones generally not having priority over a purchaser) and there is a connection with the way in which rights in land are to be created.

A second area of reform was the way in which so-called 'minor interests' were to be protected. Under the **1925 Act**, the provisions concerning the various forms of protection for a minor interest (notice, caution, restriction, inhibition) were complicated and unsystematic and, as we know, from *Clarke v Chief Land Registrar* (1994), the caution offered only procedural protection. The **LRA 2002** has only two means of protecting 'minor interests' and, in fact, they are no longer even called minor interests! A new form of restriction performs the functions of the old restriction and inhibition, and a new form of the notice combines the functions of the old notice and the caution. Despite criticism of the rule concerning the priority between minor interests under the **LRA 1925** (that is that, *inter se*, the first in time prevails, irrespective of whether either are registered: *Barclays Bank v Taylor* (1973)), the **2002 Act** provides that the rule concerning priority of competing registered interests should remain essentially unchanged. Likewise, although there seems to be no definition of a 'purchaser' for the purposes of the **2002 Act**, there is equally no reference to 'good faith', so it seems that (fortunately) *Peffer v Rigg* (1977) will not be reappearing (although note its apparent use in *HSBC v Dyche* (2010)).

....

14 Listing cases in this way is a good technique for showing off knowledge without taking up too much time in the exam.

Third, the **2002 Act** envisages a new method of creating and transferring rights in land – electronic conveyancing. Currently, the project is 'on hold' pending resolution of technical difficulties and a more favourable economic climate.[15] The ultimate aim is to ensure that many (indeed most) property rights concerning registered land will not exist at all unless they are entered on the register of title. The act of creation will be the act of registration and this will be electronic. Eventually, this will apply to all registrable estates (freeholds and leases over seven years) and to many other rights such as mortgages and expressly created easements. Clearly, this will revolutionise the way we think about rights in land. Even more importantly, the fact that creation and registration will be achieved by the same act of electronic registration means that it is certain that the 'registration gap' will disappear.

The **2002 Act** also reforms completely the law of adverse possession as it relates to registered title. In effect, there is no longer a limitation period. Instead, an adverse possessor has the ability to apply for registration as owner after ten years of adverse possession. If this occurs, the Registrar will then notify the 'true owner' (the current registered proprietor) who, if he objects, will be given a further two years to evict the adverse possessor unless certain exceptional situations exist. Failure to evict within these two years will result in the adverse possessor being registered as owner. There is no obligation on the adverse possessor to apply for registration after ten years, so if he waits for 30 years before applying for title, the registered owner still has a further two years in which to take action. Obviously this will mean – and is intended to mean – the end of adverse possession in the great majority of cases in registered land. The paper owner will be notified and will usually object and evict within two years. Moreover, given that the 'old' law of adverse possession will remain for unregistered land, this new system provides a powerful incentive for owners to register their land voluntarily.

Of course, the general success of the **2002 Act** should not blind us to the fact that there have been some difficulties. The delay in introducing electronic conveyancing is a serious setback, as it was one of the main motivations for the reform. Likewise, uncertainty about the extent of the power to rectify the register (*Baxter v Mannion* and *Walker v Burton*) raises issues about the integrity of title guarantee under **s58** (see *Fitzwilliam v Richall Holdings* (2013), *Parshall v Hackney* (2013) and *Swift 1st v Chief Land Registrar* (2014)) and there may well be further difficulties in defining overriding interests within **Sched 3**, especially the meaning of 'actual occupation'. The consequences of the changes to the law on adverse possession are also still being worked out – see e.g. *IAM Group v Chowdrey* (2012). Nevertheless, taken as a whole, the **2002 Act** remains a remarkable achievement given that, relatively speaking, there has been so little difficulty in the application of its provisions since 2003.[16]

....

15 This shows awareness of the practical circumstances in which these rules must operate.

16 This balanced conclusion demonstrates that the writer is aware of the practical difficulties in implementing the entirety of the **2002 Act** and the consequences this must have for our assessment of the Act's success.

Common Pitfalls

❖ Do not frame the answer in terms of 'mirror', 'insurance' and 'curtain' principles. The question asks about the 2002 Act, not general theories about land registration.

❖ Avoid generalities, and consider specific provisions of the Act, especially ss 23, 28, 29 and 58.

❖ Do not forget case law. There are now a number of decisions on the 2002 Act and these will enhance an answer.

2

Unregistered Land

INTRODUCTION

On 1 December 1990, all land in England and Wales became subject to compulsory first registration of title. In effect, this means that on the first conveyance of a title to an estate in unregistered land (or one of various other dealings with it: s 4 of the **Land Registration Act (LRA) 2002**), the title must be registered and thereafter, ceases to be governed by unregistered land rules. It is most unlikely, therefore, that a question in an examination will turn entirely on the conveyance of an unregistered title unless it is made clear that all of the relevant transactions are completed before 1990. It is much more likely that a question will focus on the transfer of an unregistered estate that triggers compulsory first registration of title under the **2002 Act**. That does not mean, however, that the rules concerning unregistered land are no longer important. There are many situations in which questions concerning the enforceability of interests in unregistered land are relevant, especially as a vehicle for assessing a student's understanding of other areas of law, such as the creation and enforceability of freehold covenants or easements.

Aim Higher

When land is described as unregistered, this means that title is to be found in title deeds rather than on any register. The law of unregistered conveyancing is, therefore, related to the rules of property law as they stood prior to the 1925 property legislation. However, it would be a mistake to think that the law of unregistered land was unaffected by the 1925 reforms. The **Law of Property Act (LPA) 1925** applies in full to unregistered land in the same manner as registered land. What is different is that the enforceability of rights and interests in unregistered land – being those rights and interests capable of existing under the provisions of the **LPA 1925** – is governed by its own set of rules and procedures separate from the law of the **Land Registration Acts**.

Remember the four principal rules of unregistered conveyancing:

❖ Legal estates, both freehold and leasehold, are generally to be found in title deeds, not on a register.

❖ In unregistered conveyancing, it is still true that 'legal rights bind the whole world'. Once it is established that a right is 'legal' that estate or interest is binding on whomsoever comes into possession of the land. There is, by definition, no question of registration and no relevance for 'the doctrine of notice' in relation to legal estates and interests. The sole exception to this is the 'puisne mortgage', a legal mortgage for which the documents of title have not been deposited with the lender as security. Such a mortgage, despite being a legal interest, is registrable as a 'land charge' under the **Land Charges Act (LCA) 1972** as discussed immediately below.

❖ With certain well-defined and very limited exceptions, the 'doctrine of notice' plays no part in unregistered land. It is a common mistake to believe that it does. By statute, unregistered land has its own system of registration of equitable interests. This was the **LCA 1925**, and is now the **LCA 1972**. One of the most frequent errors is to forget that in unregistered land there is also a requirement of registration for certain – indeed most – equitable interests. These 'registrable' equitable interests (called 'land charges') are binding if registered correctly under the **LCA 1972** but void against a purchaser if not, irrespective of whether the purchaser has notice. This registration system has *nothing to do* with registered land.

❖ There are a small number of equitable rights that, either deliberately or by subsequent judicial development, are excluded from the operation of the **LCA 1972**. In other words, they are 'non-registrable' as *land charges*. For these rights, their enforceability against a purchaser still does depend on the doctrine of the 'bona fide purchaser of a legal estate for value without notice' (sometimes known as *equity's darling*). This is the *only* circumstance in which notice should form part of the answer to an examination question in land law today.

QUESTION 5

Analyse the way in which third party property rights are protected in unregistered conveyancing. Was the **Land Charges Act 1972** successful in protecting these interests in the event that the land over which they existed was transferred?

How to Read this Question

The examiner here is looking for you both to explain how third party rights are protected in unregistered land, and then to analyse whether this protection is 'successful'. This requires a description of the rules of course, but your answer should also look at any difficulties with these rules.

How to Answer this Question

❖ The crucial distinction between legal and equitable rights in unregistered land.
❖ Briefly, the problems prior to 1926, especially in protecting equitable interests.
❖ The general scheme of the **Land Charges Act 1972**.
❖ Identification of problems with a name-based system.
❖ Identification of problems with 'root of title' and compensation rules.
❖ There is no protection for occupiers per se.
❖ Analysis of rights that are not land charges and the continuing relevance of the doctrine of notice.

Up for Debate

The degree to which third party interests should be prioritised over the interests of a purchaser is a foundational debate in land law, and it is relevant here. In addition, the impact of the expansion of doctrines such as proprietary estoppel and common intention constructive trusts to meet current needs upon the principles of unregistered conveyancing is one which should be addressed.

Applying the Law

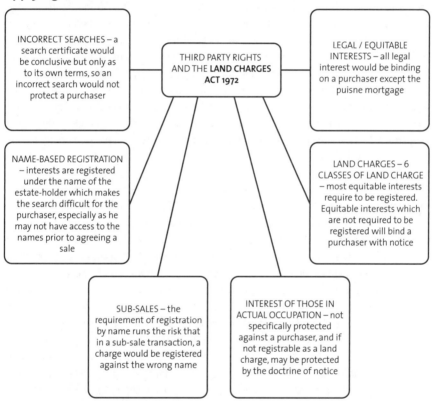

INCORRECT SEARCHES – a search certificate would be conclusive but only as to its own terms, so an incorrect search would not protect a purchaser

THIRD PARTY RIGHTS AND THE **LAND CHARGES ACT 1972**

LEGAL / EQUITABLE INTERESTS – all legal interest would be binding on a purchaser except the puisne mortgage

NAME-BASED REGISTRATION – interests are registered under the name of the estate-holder which makes the search difficult for the purchaser, especially as he may not have access to the names prior to agreeing a sale

LAND CHARGES – 6 CLASSES OF LAND CHARGE – most equitable interests require to be registered. Equitable interests which are not required to be registered will bind a purchaser with notice

SUB-SALES – the requirement of registration by name runs the risk that in a sub-sale transaction, a charge would be registered against the wrong name

INTEREST OF THOSE IN ACTUAL OCCUPATION – not specifically protected against a purchaser, and if not registrable as a land charge, may be protected by the doctrine of notice

*This diagram shows the position of third party rights in relation to the **Land Charges Act 1972**.*

ANSWER

Prior to 1 January 1926, the conveyancing system in England and Wales was under considerable strain. Purchasers of land were faced with many difficulties when trying to establish whether any other person had interests in that land. Owners of equitable interests in that land might find that the interest was destroyed by a simple sale to a purchaser who was unaware of its existence. To meet both of those problems, it was decided to move towards full title registration. It was recognised, however, that this mammoth task had to proceed in stages. The result was the **Land Charges Act 1925** (now the **Land Charges Act 1972**), which was intended to operate for only some 30 years. Although there is now a system of compulsory first registration, full title registration is still a little way off, meaning that a certain amount of unregistered conveyancing remains.[1]

The scheme of the **LCA 1972** is relatively straightforward. Equitable interests are divided into categories known as land charges. Bearing in mind that these equitable interests affect the title of land belonging to another person, s3 of the **LCA**[2] provides that a land charge should be registered against the name of the estate owner whose land is to be bound by the charge. Under **s4** if the owner of an equitable interest has not registered their interest, it will be void against a purchaser (*Petrou v Petrou* (1998); *Midland Bank Trust Co v Green* (1981)), provided that the transferee is a true purchaser who actually provides consideration (*Merer v Fisher* (2003)).[3] To be more precise, an equitable interest that should have been registered as a Class C(iv) or Class D land charge will be void against a purchaser of a legal estate in the land for money or money's worth, and an equitable interest that should have been registered in any one of the other classes will be void against a purchaser of any estate in the land for valuable consideration. If an equitable interest is correctly registered, it will be binding on any purchaser (**s198** of the **Law of Property Act (LPA) 1925**). Even an unregistered equitable interest is binding against someone who is *not* a purchaser.

This simple picture masks serious difficulties that have emerged in practice.[4] One of the most serious criticisms is the reliance on a name-based system of registration. An owner of an equitable interest has to register it as a land charge against the *name* of the estate owner. All depends on both the owner of the equitable interest and any prospective purchaser knowing the correct name of the current estate owner. This has caused problems in three respects. First,[5] there are some circumstances in which a prospective purchaser has no way of ascertaining the name of the estate owner. For example, under the rule in *Patman v Harland* (1881), an intending purchaser of a lease has no automatic way of obtaining the names of previous owners of the land against whom he should make a land charges search. He is, nevertheless, bound by land charges registered against former estate owners because **s198** of the **LPA 1925** takes priority over the purchaser's apparent protection found in **s44(5)** of the **LPA** (*White v Bijou Mansions* (1937)). Likewise, now that 'root of title' in unregistered land is only 15 years (**s23** of the **LPA 1969**), the purchaser may well have no way of ascertaining the names of persons who held the land previously. However, any charges registered against these names are binding on the purchaser irrespective of the fact that the purchaser could not have discovered those names.

....

1   The background and intended role of the **LCA** is an important aspect of this essay and the introduction helps to put the rest of the analysis into its context.
2   It is always better to give a precise statutory citation where possible.
3   Cases or statutes should be used to back up every principle stated – this is the best way to ensure really good marks in both essay and problem questions.
4   A difference between the theory behind the rules and their operation in practice is always a useful angle of analysis.
5   The use of the list of problems here is a good way to make the structure easy to follow.

Second, there is the problem of incorrect searches. A name-based system will work only if all parties both register and search under the correct names. This is by no means a foregone conclusion. In *Diligent Finance Co Ltd v Alleyene* (1972), for example, a wife had registered a Class F land charge against her husband, but not against his full name as shown on the title deeds. When the purchaser then searched against the correct name, they received a clear search certificate (which is conclusive: **s10** of the **LCA**) and the wife's rights lost their priority. An even more complicated set of circumstances arises when there is both a defective search and a defective registration. Thus, in *Oak Cooperative Building Society v Blackburn* (1968), both the registration and the search were made in different, but incorrect, versions of the estate owner's name. In the event, the registration was deemed less defective than the search, but this was simply a pragmatic solution made necessary by the deficiencies of the system. It is also true that registration of a land charge against the *correct* name will be effective, even if the land to which it relates is incorrectly described, provided that the description is a reasonable version of the land described in the conveyance (*Horrill v Cooper* (2000)).

Third, there is a problem with sub-sales. The **LCA** requires interests – such as a contract to buy the land – to be registered against the actual estate owner at the time the charge is created: **s3**. If, therefore, a person is buying land at the end of a chain and their seller has not yet completed his own purchase, the sub-sale should be registered against the head vendor – that is, the estate owner at the time the sub-sale was agreed. Obviously, this can happen only if the end-purchaser is aware of the existence of the chain.

Apart from problems arising out of the use of a name-based registration system, there are other difficulties too. Thus, when a purchaser has exchanged contracts with the vendor, only then will he be in a position to search the Land Charges Register. Of course, by that time he is bound to complete the contract and also bound by any registered land charges. It is only because of later statutory amendment (**s24** of the **LPA 1969**) that a remedy has been found that enables a purchaser to pull out of the contract if he had no actual knowledge of the charge that he subsequently finds. Further, in unregistered land there is no equivalent of **para 2** of Scheds 1 and 3 to the **LRA 2002**. So, even those owners of equitable interests who are in actual occupation of property at the time of a sale to a purchaser are not protected. As *Hollington Brothers v Rhodes* (1951) shows, these interests must be positively protected through land charge registration (or the doctrine of notice if that is applicable). Whether or not this was deliberate, clearly it is a significant weakness in the system. Finally, there is one problem which has emerged due to legal, social and economic changes in the use of land. It is essential to the success of this legislation that virtually all equitable interests fall within its ambit. Unfortunately, that is not the case. There are a number of equitable interests that are not registrable as land charges. These unregistrable interests are still capable of binding a purchaser, but their effect depends entirely on the capricious doctrine of notice. The equitable rights included in this residual category are diverse. On the one hand, there are estoppel easements (*Ives v High* (1967)) and, on the other, such matters as the right of re-entry in an equitable lease (*Shiloh Spinners v Harding* (1973)) and the right of a tenant to recover fixtures at the end of an equitable lease (*Poster v Slough Estates* (1968)). However, the most important is the right of equitable ownership behind a trust of land. Such rights are specifically excluded from the category of land charges by **s2(4)** of the **LCA 1972**, mainly because they are overreachable. As we now know, however, not all cases of a trust of land will have two trustees (*Pettitt v Pettitt* (1970); *Stack v Dowden* (2007); *Geary v Rankine* (2012)) and, in such cases, the doctrine of notice plays a vital part in assessing whether the purchaser of the co-owned land is bound (*Kingsnorth Finance v Tizard* (1986)).

The simple fact that there is an entire class of equitable rights that cannot be 'land charges' and the viability of which still depends on the doctrine of notice is a serious criticism of the **LCA 1972**. This criticism would have been tolerable had the **LCA 1972** really been the temporary measure that it was intended to be. That, however, is not the case, although we may at least be seeing the demise of unregistered conveyancing. Of course, if one has registered an equitable interest properly and against the correct name, the system of land charge registration is much more reliable than the doctrine of notice. That, however, is not saying a great deal and it will be something of a relief to conveyancers, purchasers and owners of equitable interests when the system of unregistered conveyancing is fully replaced by that of the **LRA 2002**.

Don't be Tempted To

This is not a question about the **LRA 2002** and it is easy to misread the question; it cannot be answered simply by reciting the provisions of the **Land Charges Act**. You need to be clear that the cases you rely on – and you must use them – are actually cases about unregistered land. Many land law courses no longer study this topic precisely because unregistered conveyancing is being replaced by registered conveyancing.

Do not confuse land charges, which fall within the **LCA 1972**, with 'charges by way of mortgage'. A *land charge* is a third party equitable right in unregistered conveyancing and is a generic term that could mean any type of third party right (e.g. option, certain leases, equitable mortgages, covenant, equitable easement). A 'charge by way of mortgage' is a legal mortgage and specifically security for a debt.

QUESTION 6

In 1970, when he retired, Alfonso sold his large farm to Benedict and produced a conveyance from his (Alfonso's) father dated 1935 as proof of title. Benedict, through his solicitors, made an official search of the Land Charges Register against the name of Alfonso and Alfonso's father. The certificate revealed a restrictive covenant, registered against Alfonso's father in 1934, preventing the building of more than one domestic residence on the farm. In 1970, Alfonso wished to live in peace and quiet (in the house he had built on the edge of the farm on land that he now retained), and so a restrictive covenant was inserted in the sale to Benedict preventing any trade or business on the farm except agricultural works. This was correctly registered against Benedict. In 1982, Benedict granted his daughter (Vanessa), for £100, 'the right to buy my farm when I retire from farming at half its current market value'. By 1984, Benedict had fallen in love with a younger woman and wished to start a new life in Australia. Realising that his farm had quadrupled in value since 1982, he decided to sell the land to Desmond, his friend, who was also a property developer. Desmond thought he might turn the farm into an industrial estate. Desmond paid three-quarters of the market value in order to get a quick sale. The farm was not then in an area of compulsory first regis-tration of title. Desmond searched against the name of 'Benny' (always having known his friend by this name) and Alfonso. He received a clear certificate.

Vanessa has just heard of the sale and wishes to buy the farm at the cheaper price. Desmond has just received a letter telling him that he cannot build the industrial estate. Desmond wonders whether this is true and asks whether, in any event, he can build a housing estate instead.

▶ **Advise the parties.**

How to Read this Question

The examiner has set this problem question to test your knowledge of the unregistered conveyancing rules, but also of the substantive law against the background of which the conveyancing rules must operate.

How to Answer this Question

❖ The period necessary to obtain good root of title.
❖ The possibility of registered, but hidden, land charges.
❖ Whether compensation for hidden land charges may be obtained under the **LPA 1969**.
❖ The various classes of land charge under the **LCA 1972**.
❖ The effect of land charge registration under the **LCA 1972**.
❖ The possibility of fraud and its effect.

Answer Structure

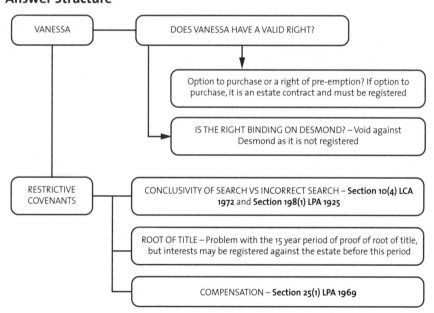

This diagram shows how to apply the rules relating to purchasers of unregistered land to Vanessa.

ANSWER

As indicated in the facts of this problem, all the relevant transactions and events are completed *before* registration of title became compulsory in England and Wales and there is nothing to suggest that the land is of registered title or that it needed to be registered. Thus, this problem falls to be decided under the rules of unregistered conveyancing. These rules, it might be noted, are a mixture of common law and statute, the most important being the **Land Charges Act (LCA) 1972** (a replacement for the **LCA 1925**).[6]

(a) Vanessa's Claim to Purchase the Property

Whether Vanessa can claim a right against Desmond to purchase the property depends on whether her father, Benedict, granted her a proprietary right over the land and, second, whether this right is enforceable against Desmond. First, there may well be some dispute about the nature of the right granted to Vanessa, for it may be that it cannot be regarded as proprietary in nature. On the one hand, the right may be a right of pre-emption – that is, a right of first refusal in the event that the grantor (Benedict) wishes to sell the property. If this is the case, despite the wording of **s 2** of the **LCA 1972**, *Pritchard v Briggs* (1980) and *University of East London v LB Barking & Dagenham* (2004) suggest that a right of pre-emption cannot be regarded as proprietary until it is exercised (thus, registration would be effective from this later date only). (Note, however, if the title had been registered, the right of pre-emption would be proprietary from the moment of its creation: **s 115(1)** of the **LRA 2002**.)[7] Nevertheless, in any event, the better view is that the right in this case is an option to purchase. An option to purchase is clearly an interest in land from the moment of its creation, whether conditional or not (*London and South Western Railway v Gomm* (1882); *Ferrishurst Ltd v Wallcite Ltd* (1999)).[8] Moreover, it is clear that an option to purchase is an 'estate contract' within **s 2** of the **LCA 1972** (*Armstrong v Jones* (1869)) and, therefore, it must be registered against the name of the estate owner who created it (that is, Benedict) if it is to bind a subsequent purchaser of a legal estate for money or money's worth: **ss 3** and **4(6)** of the **LCA 1972**. In our case, there is no evidence to suggest that Vanessa has registered her option as a land charge and, presumptively, it is void against Desmond – clearly, he is a purchaser of a legal estate for money's worth.

There is, however, one small hope for Vanessa. She may be able to claim that she was fraudulently deprived of her right because of dishonest collusion between Benedict – the creator of the right – and Desmond, the purchaser who obviously benefits from the fact that it is not binding on him. As the problem tells us, Benedict wished to sell to Desmond in order to obtain a higher price and he must have known that he would thereby defeat his daughter's claim. However, there is no suggestion that the sale was solely in order to defeat the daughter's claim or that Desmond ever knew that she had an option to

---

6 The dates of a problem are always crucial.

7 This aside shows awareness and understanding of the rules of registered conveyancing without suggesting they are applicable here and this is a good technique to show off extra knowledge.

8 Where possible, two cases will be better than one!

purchase. Indeed, even if this was the case, the House of Lords'[9] decision in *Midland Bank Trust Co v Green* (1981) makes it clear that mere knowledge by the purchaser of the existence of a third party's right in or over the land would not be enough to enable the right to be enforced. To recognise the validity of the sale to Desmond, even though it destroys Vanessa's right, is to uphold the policy of the LCA, not to subvert it.

(b) The Restrictive Covenants

(i) The Covenant Against Industry

If Desmond wishes to build an industrial estate, he must establish that the covenant against non-agricultural trade is not binding on him. This will be difficult. Desmond has obtained a clear search certificate and we know that under s 10(4) of the LCA 1972, an official search is conclusive. However, it is conclusive only 'according to its tenor' and, therefore, is conclusive only in respect of the names actually searched. Here, Desmond searched against 'Benny'. 'Benny' is not the estate owner and so the clear certificate is of no avail. In fact, Desmond will be bound by the correctly entered covenant under s 198(1) of the LPA 1925. In consequence, he cannot use the land for industrial purposes unless he can persuade the person entitled to enforce the covenant (Alfonso) to waive it, possibly in return for a sum of money.

(ii) The Restriction on Building Dwelling Houses

In the original conveyance from Alfonso's father to Alfonso in 1935, there was a restrictive covenant against building more than one dwelling house. This had been registered against Alfonso's father and clearly was binding on Alfonso. The question arises whether it is also binding on Desmond, the successor in title to the burdened land.

Assuming that there was originally some land that could benefit from this covenant and that the benefit of it has passed in orthodox fashion to the person now seeking to enforce the covenant (that is, the rules in *Tulk v Moxhay* (1848) and s 78 LPA 1925), the question here involves consideration of the particular problems caused by the Land Charges Register being a name-based register. When Desmond buys the land, he must investigate root of title. Under s 23 of the LPA 1969, root of title is 15 years, and so Desmond can rely for good title on the conveyance by Alfonso to Benedict (his vendor) in 1970. This was the first conveyance, which was at least 15 years old. Seeing this document, Desmond will realise that he must search against Benedict and Alfonso – both are revealed in the root of title. Of course, he would not have discovered the restrictive covenant because it was registered against Alfonso's father, of whom Desmond knew nothing and, indeed, about whom he could not have known. The covenant is hidden behind the root of title and was in effect 'undiscoverable'. However, because of s 198(1) of the LPA 1925, Desmond is deemed to have notice of all covenants correctly registered 'for all purposes' and it is binding on him. It may be enforced by the person entitled to the benefit of the covenant.

---

9   Not only does this show that the writer knew that the case was decided in the House of Lords, it also demonstrates the strength of the authority being relied on.

However, even though Desmond is bound by a registered, but essentially undiscoverable,[10] land charge, he may be entitled to compensation under s 25(1) of the **LPA 1969** if he can fulfil the three conditions stipulated therein. First, it is clear that the transaction that caused him loss has occurred after the commencement of the Act (that is, after 1 January 1970). Second, we can infer that Desmond has no actual (that is, real) knowledge of the charge, as he would not otherwise have purchased the property and, third, the name of the estate owner against whom the charge was registered (Alfonso's father) was not comprised in any title document that Desmond would have seen when purchasing the property. He would be aware of Alfonso and Benedict only. Although, then, he cannot build if the person entitled decides to enforce the covenant, he can claim compensation.

Don't be Tempted To

Do not ignore entirely matters of substantive law. For example, restrictive covenants are only enforceable if the relevant conditions of *Tulk v Moxhay* (1848) have been met and covenants may be discharged by application to the Lands Tribunal under s 84 **LPA 1925**. These may be discussed briefly *but* the main thrust of the question is about the mechanics of unregistered conveyancing.

Do not confuse a purchaser with a person who receives the unregistered title 'not for value'. Examples of non-purchasers include people who inherit under a will and who receive a gift. Non-purchasers and purchasers are treated differently in unregistered conveyancing.

Do not use the 'doctrine of notice' when talking about a land charge. The issue is one of registration, not whether the purchaser 'knows' of the right. Talk of 'equity's darling', even in unregistered conveyancing can be confusing.

QUESTION 7

The protection of equitable interests in unregistered land is far weaker than the protection given to equitable interests in registered title.

▶ **Do you agree?**

How to Read this Question

The examiner here is looking for a comparison between the principles of registered and unregistered conveyancing, and specifically the protection given to equitable interests in these systems. It is important that you focus your answer on the comparative 'strength' of the protection given to such rights.

How to Answer this Question

- ❖ A brief outline of the systems of the **LCA 1972** and the **LRA 2002** for the protection of equitable interests.
- ❖ The differences in the registration procedures between the systems.
- ❖ The role of the search certificate and different priority periods.

---

10 In problem questions as well as in essays you want to analyse the law, and where the rule causes significant difficulties in practice, comment on this can be woven into the answer.

❖ The protection for the rights of persons in actual occupation under the **LRA 2002** in contrast with the **LCA 1972**.

❖ Loopholes in unregistered land – the continuing relevance of the doctrine of notice and questions of 'knowledge' in registered title.

Up for Debate

Behind the specific question set here is the deeper question as to how much protection should be given to equitable interests in relation to purchasers and what the right balance here is. When analysing the strength of the protection, therefore, it is important to consider whether very strong protection is the goal, or whether the goal is a balance between purchaser and interest-holder.

Applying the Law

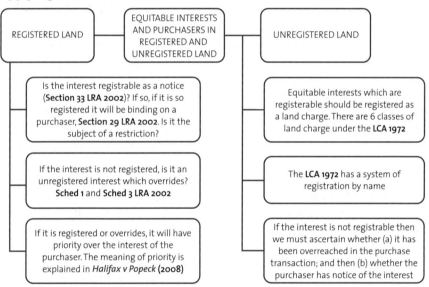

This diagram shows the rules that apply to equitable interests and their effect on purchasers in registered and unregistered land.

ANSWER

The machinery instituted by the **LCA 1972** and the **LRA 2002** was intended to achieve the same objective.[11] In essence, both of these systems are intended to bring stability to the system of conveyancing in England and Wales by protecting purchasers of land and owners of rights over that land.

....

11 Acknowledging from the outset that the aim of the two systems is largely the same is an interesting perspective from which to begin comparing them.

The **LRA 2002** achieves this objective by ensuring that title to land and many interests over land are recorded or otherwise protected. In respect of equitable interests, the protection is twofold. First, equitable interests can be protected by substantive registration or, second, they may qualify in limited circumstances as unregistered interests which override (**Sched 1** and **Sched 3**). Indeed, it is the ability of an equitable interest to qualify as an 'overriding interest' that gives registered land its advantages over unregistered land. Thus, under **para 2** of each of the Schedules an owner of such a right is protected so long as they are in occupation of the land to which the right relates (and are 'discoverable' in that occupation or the right is known about if **Sched 3** applies) whether or not the claimant knew they had a right or whether they knew that it should be registered. This is particularly useful if the equitable rights are acquired informally, as with estoppel or common intention constructive trusts (*Stack v Dowden* (2007); *Geary v Rankine* (2012)).[12]

Of course, problems with registered land do exist. The fact that an owner of certain equitable rights need not actually register their right in order to achieve priority poses something of a problem to a prospective purchaser. However, the range of binding, but unregistered, rights has been reduced by the **LRA 2002** and we must remember that the Schedules seek to ensure that interests override only when they are (or should be) obvious to a purchaser conducting a reasonable inspection of the land.

Of course, the **LRA 2002** makes it clear that an equitable interest that does not qualify as an overriding interest or is not protected by an entry on the register loses its priority against a correctly registered purchaser of the title (**s 29** of the **LRA 2002**). It is not yet clear what 'loss of priority' means. It is not clear whether the unprotected equitable interest is rendered unenforceable against only the particular purchaser or is 'void' for all purposes – see *Halifax v Popeck* (2009).[13] Be that as it may, it is clear that the purpose of the **LRA 2002** is to ensure that as many interests as possible are registered, and, as a corollary, that failure to protect through registration will cause loss of the right unless the limited provisions concerning overriding interests come into play.

Furthermore, these are but small issues compared to those found when considering the protection of equitable interests in unregistered conveyancing. Unregistered land also has a system of registration of equitable interests that is intended to give those interests the same degree of protection as would be available in registered land, but it is obvious that the **LCA 1972** falls considerably short of this goal. In unregistered land, equitable interests can be divided into three broad categories. First, there are those equitable interests that are registrable as land charges. These registrable land charges must be protected by entry on the Land Charges Register in order to bind a purchaser of the land they burden: **s 4** of the **LCA 1972**. In the case of Classes A, B, C (except C(iv)) and F, an

....

12 There is an enormous range of cases that could be used here, but *Geary* in particular is a good choice because it shows an awareness of recent case law.

13 The meaning of loss of priority is a highly complex question and there would not be time to go into it in detail in the exam in this question, but it is worth showing that you aware of the difficulty nonetheless even if there is no scope within the answer for resolving the difficulty.

unregistered charge will be void against the purchaser for valuable consideration of any interest in the land, while Classes C(iv) and D will be void against the purchaser of a legal estate for money or money's worth. In short, as with registered land, registration means validity and non-registration means invalidity (*Midland Bank v Green* (1981)).

However, the system of land charges does suffer from one considerable defect: its lack of protection for persons with equitable interests who occupy land. There is no equivalent of **para 2** of **Scheds 1** and **3** to the **LRA 2002** as amply illustrated by *Hollington Brothers v Rhodes* (1951). It is regrettable that equitable interests in unregistered land are not protected in this way (see *Harpum* (1990) for further discussion).[14]

The second category of equitable interests in unregistered land is the 'family' interests which are overreachable as existing behind a trust of land. As with registered land, if there are two trustees of land or a trust corporation, there is nothing the equitable owners can do to prevent sale or to remain in occupation of the property against a purchaser (*City of London BS v Flegg* (1988); *Birmingham Midshires BS v Sabherwal* (2000)). However, if there is only one trustee, in registered land, the equitable interest may be overriding (*Boland* (1981)), whereas, in unregistered land, these equitable interests are not registrable (protectable) as land charges (**s 2** of the **LCA 1972**) but can bind a purchaser only under the old doctrine of notice (*Kingsnorth v Tizard* (1986)). Although it will be rare that a purchaser does not have notice, it is undesirable that the inherently uncertain concept of notice should play a part in such a vital area as co-ownership of domestic property.

Indeed, it is not only with these equitable interests that notice is still relevant, for there is a third category of equitable interest within the scheme of unregistered land. These are equitable interests that are outside the operation of **LCA 1972**. These are unregistrable equitable interests the validity of which against a purchaser rests on the doctrine of notice. They have no equivalent in registered land as the categories of overriding and registered protected interests are all-embracing. Of course, some rights, such as leasehold covenants, cause few problems (although see *Dartstone v Cleveland* (1969)) and this is why they were deliberately omitted from the scheme of the **LCA 1972**. Indeed, equitable co-ownership would not have been a problem had the 'two-trustee' trust of land been the norm. However, such matters as estoppel easements (*Ives v High* (1967)), equitable rights of re-entry (*Shiloh Spinners v Harding* (1973)) and a tenant's right to remove fixtures at the end of an equitable lease (*Poster v Slough Estates* (1968)), which have emerged as unregistrable interests since 1925, can cause difficulties. The existence of these rights means that a purchaser cannot rely with total security on a search of the Land Charges Register. There is always the possibility that an unregistrable but potentially binding equitable interest will exist that will affect the purchaser's title through the medium of notice. Such matters would not have been so important in practice had the **LCA** been replaced swiftly by full title registration, but only now is that coming to fruition.

---

14 Credit will always be given where an answer shows awareness of academic commentary.

Finally, there are some other differences in the application of the **LRA 2002** and the **LCA 1972** that can cause practical difficulties. An obvious one is the fact that the **LCA 1972** depends on a system of name registration. The problems that this gives rise to are well known, as in *Barrett v Hilton* (1975) (sub-sales), *Oak v Blackburn* (1968) (defective registration and defective searches) and *White v Bijou Mansions* (1937) (hidden charges). These are difficulties that do not arise under the **LRA 2002**. Likewise, it should be noted that the priority periods conferred on a person are different under the **Land Charges Acts** and the **Land Registration Acts** (15 business days and 30 business days, respectively) and that, in unregistered land, it is the official search that is conclusive – **s10(4)** of the **LCA** (even if a charge is actually registered) – whereas, in registered land, it is the register that is conclusive – *Parkash v Irani Finance* (1970) (even if the official search is clear).

The **LCA** and the **LRA 2002** have both done much to introduce certainty into the whole area of the purchaser and the third party's equitable interest. There is no doubt, however, that, as far as protecting equitable interests is concerned, the **LRA 2002** offers considerably more comfort than the **LCA**. Above all, the safety net provided by the concept of actual occupation under **Scheds 1** and **3** to the **LRA 2002** provides a considerable advantage over the unregistered land system. For the purchaser too the registered land system has its attractions. Although the existence of overriding interests may compromise a title, most of these interests are reasonably ascertainable on inspection of the property. In any event, by introducing the concept of 'discoverable' actual occupation in **Sched 3**, the chances of a purchaser being bound by an interest of which they were not aware, or of which they should have been aware, are reduced considerably. Moreover, the purchaser in unregistered land must always fear the existence of an unregistrable equitable interest that will be binding on him through the mechanism of constructive notice. These problems and the name-based registration system made the introduction of countrywide compulsory registration of title on 1 December 1990 very welcome.

Don't be Tempted To

This is a question which requires you to contrast registered and unregistered conveyancing. Do not describe one in detail and add a few sentences about the other. You need some detail about each.

Do not think that everything in registered land is wonderful! There are difficulties, but the issue is whether registered title is an improvement on unregistered title.

Do not merely describe how the legislation works. You must reach a conclusion about its effectiveness in the light of the question actually asked.

3

INTRODUCTION

The law relating to concurrent interests in property (co-ownership) has changed considerably in recent years. This is a result both of changes in the legislative framework surrounding co-ownership (that is, the **Trusts of Land and Appointment of Trustees Act (TOLATA) 1996**) and because the increased incidence of co-ownership has revealed many practical problems for which the 1925 legislation did not clearly provide. Many difficulties have been caused by social and economic changes in the pattern of property ownership, particularly of residential or domestic houses. The emergence of the *Pettitt v Pettitt* (1970), *Lloyds Bank v Rosset* (1989) and *Stack v Dowden* (2007) line of authority, whereby a partner or spouse can acquire an interest in a house that formally belongs to someone else, has done much to channel the law of co-ownership in new directions. Co-ownership is no longer confined to commercial or business situations but is virtually an expected attribute of domestic life. The **Law of Property Act (LPA) 1925**, which established the original scheme of co-ownership, was ill-equipped to deal with this shift of emphasis and the changes made by the **TOLATA** (which came into force on 1 January 1997) have done much to remedy deficiencies in the law, although many would argue that much remedial work had been done already by sensible judicial application of existing statute. As we shall see, where land (for example, a house) is deliberately co-owned, in the sense of having been conveyed originally to two or more people (for example, husband and wife, or an unmarried couple), few serious problems exist about who owns it, although there may be issues about the size of each owner's share. However, where co-ownership arises informally – usually in respect of land that was conveyed originally to only one person (for example, the man alone) – considerable practical problems can arise, and not even the new legislation has dealt with all of these. Importantly, the issues remain the same even if the co-owners are not in an intimate relationship. Thus, a number of recent cases concern parents and children and some arise in non-family relationships, such as the infirm and their live-in carers.

Checklist

In this chapter, the various issues relating to co-ownership will be considered in turn and the student needs to have an understanding of the following issues. First, there is the question of the statutory machinery and the reasons for the 1925 reforms. This must be addressed in the light of the legislative changes made by the TOLATA 1996 and the reasons for them. Without this background understanding, much of the law of co-ownership will make no sense. Second, there is the question of the actual share that each co-owner really has in co-owned land: problems of severance and the like. Third, there are important issues as to how implied co-ownership can arise or, in other words, when does single ownership turn into co-ownership without any formal documentation? This is the law of resulting and constructive trusts based on House of Lords' decisions in *Pettitt v Pettitt* (1970), *Lloyds Bank v Rosset* (1989) and, most importantly, *Stack v Dowden* (2007) and *Jones v Kernott* (2011). Fourth, there are issues about the consequences for purchasers when buying land subject to co-ownership, especially if that co-ownership has been informally created. In this context, 'purchasers' means mortgagees (banks, building societies, etc.) who lend money and so 'purchase' an interest in the co-owned land as security. In an examination, it is quite common for at least two questions on co-ownership to appear on the examination paper and it is quite possible for one question (usually a problem question) to raise all four matters.

QUESTION 8

Analyse the reforms introduced by the **Trusts of Land and Appointment of Trustees Act 1996**. Does the 'trust of land' differ significantly from the 'trust for sale of land'?

How to Read this Question

The examiner is looking for you to compare the position under **TOLATA 1996** with the previous law. You should aim to focus on the comparison for your analysis and not simply describe the provisions of the **1996 Act**.

How to Answer this Question

❖ Definition of 'co-owned land' and brief discussion of the types of co-ownership: joint tenancies and tenancies in common.

❖ Legal and equitable ownership distinguished.

❖ Analyse the statutory scheme prior to the **TOLATA 1996**: the trust for sale of land.

❖ Note the judicial application of the pre-**TOLATA** scheme and mitigation of some of its problems.

❖ Analyse the effect of the **TOLATA 1996**: the trust of land.

Up for Debate

The extent to which the **1996 Act** has changed the law in practice is a complex question. Judicial creativity with the **1925 Act** provisions, and some resistance to change with regards to the likelihood of sale in cases of dispute mean that the position in practice is perhaps closer than it appears on paper. See for example the contrast between *Mortgage Corp v Shaire* (2001) and *Bank of Ireland v Bell* (2001).

Applying the Law

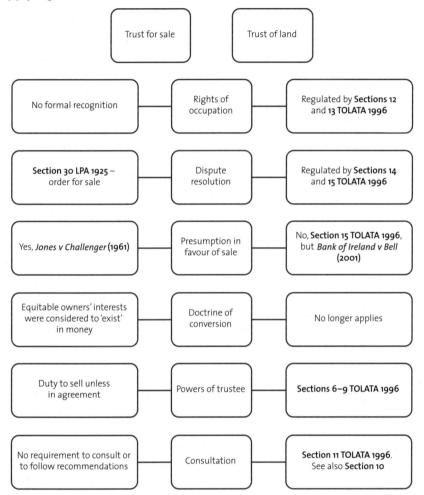

Trust for sale		Trust of land
No formal recognition	Rights of occupation	Regulated by **Sections 12** and **13 TOLATA 1996**
Section 30 LPA 1925 – order for sale	Dispute resolution	Regulated by **Sections 14** and **15 TOLATA 1996**
Yes, *Jones v Challenger* (**1961**)	Presumption in favour of sale	No, **Section 15 TOLATA 1996**, but *Bank of Ireland v Bell* (**2001**)
Equitable owners' interests were considered to 'exist' in money	Doctrine of conversion	No longer applies
Duty to sell unless in agreement	Powers of trustee	**Sections 6–9 TOLATA 1996**
No requirement to consult or to follow recommendations	Consultation	**Section 11 TOLATA 1996.** See also **Section 10**

This diagram shows the main differences between the trust for sale and the trust of land.

ANSWER

Prior to 1925, there were several forms of co-ownership: the legal relationship between the individual co-owners could take various forms. However, this caused numerous problems and one of the most important reforms of the **Law of Property Act 1925** was to limit the types of co-ownership that could be created thereafter. From 1926, land may be co-owned only under a joint tenancy or, alternatively, under a tenancy in common. In a joint tenancy, as far as the rest of the world is concerned, the individual persons are as one owner. There is but one title to the land and the individuals own that title jointly. Under a tenancy in common, each tenant in common, although in physical possession of the whole of the property in common with the others, is regarded as having a distinct share in the land.

Under the **1925 Act**, a legal tenancy in common cannot exist – **s1(6)**. So, after 1925, all legal titles to co-owned land must take the form of a joint tenancy. Whenever land is conveyed to two or more persons for concurrent ownership, it is statutorily deemed to be conveyed to them as joint tenants of the legal title (**ss34** and **36** of the **LPA**) and a mandatory trust is imposed. In equity, the co-ownership can take the form of either a joint tenancy or tenancy in common according to the circumstances existing when the land was conveyed. The mandatory imposition of a trust is, therefore, a device to ensure that all legal title to co-owned land is held as a joint tenancy whilst also ensuring that in equity (where, after all, the real interest lies) the co-owners can be either joint tenants or tenants in common.

The overriding aim of the use of the trust was to make co-owned land more saleable while at the same time giving some degree of protection to the rights of all the co-owners. To this end, the original statutory trust was a trust for sale, meaning that the trustees were under a duty to sell the property unless they all agreed to postpone sale.[1] Of course, in the normal course of events, at least with residential property, the two trustees (for example, husband and wife) would agree to postpone sale because they had purchased the property to live in it. Yet, if such agreement to postpone sale could not be maintained, an application could be made to the court under what was then **s30** of the **LPA 1925** for an order for sale. Such an order would be granted unless there were pressing contrary reasons relating to the purpose for which the land was originally acquired (*Jones v Challenger* (1961); *Banker's Trust v Namdar* (1997)). Moreover, when a sale did take place, the statutory mechanism revealed its considerable advantages. First, because the legal title must be held by way of joint tenancy, the purchaser need investigate only one title. Second, **s34(2)** of the **LPA 1925** limited the number of potential legal co-owners (that is, trustees) to four. Third, because there must be a joint tenancy of the legal title, the right of survivorship applies. So, if one legal owner dies, no formal documents are needed to transfer title to the remaining legal owners. Fourth, if there are two or more legal owners (trustees), any purchaser automatically will receive the land free of the rights of all the equitable owners, because, by statute, a payment to two or more trustees overreaches the equitable interests existing behind the trust (**ss2** and **27** of the **LPA 1925**; *City of London BS v Flegg* (1988); *State Bank of India v Sood* (1997)). Of course, the equitable owners' rights are not destroyed; rather, they take effect in the purchase money paid, which is then held on trust by the trustees.

It should be apparent from this that the **1925 Act** greatly assisted the easy transfer of co-owned land, both by simplifying the conveyancing machinery and by protecting the purchaser through the device of overreaching. However, this original scheme was not without its problems. First, the equitable owners may have their rights transformed from rights over land to rights in money by action of the legal owners conducting an overreaching transaction. Second, the duty to sell meant that disputes between trustees (that is,

---

1   Tying the shape of the provisions to their original purpose is a good starting-off point for analysis.

legal owners) very often resulted in a court-ordered sale, even if one party wished to remain in the property. Third, in theory, the equitable owners' rights were regarded as interests in money, not land, and this could affect the rights of the equitable owners to require the legal owners to allow them into possession.

To meet these difficulties, and generally to re-cast the scheme of co-ownership for the modern era, the **Trusts of Land and Appointment of Trustees Act (TOLATA) 1996** was enacted. This came into force on 1 January 1997 and applies to virtually all co-ownership trusts. Its effect is, broadly, to ensure that the legal scheme of co-ownership accords with how co-owned land is owned in practice.

First, and most importantly, trusts for sale of land become simple *trusts of land* and all future co-ownership trusts must operate under the trust of land scheme found in the **TOLATA**. The land remains held by trustees (still a maximum of four) on trust for the equitable owners, but the nature of the trust has changed. There is no longer a duty to sell the land so, in cases of dispute, it may well prove to be the case that courts do not feel such a compulsion to order a sale (see *Mortgage Corp v Shaire* (2001) but note the contrary in *Bank of Ireland Home Mortgages v Bell* (2001)).[2] This was undoubtedly a sensible reform. Second, the doctrine of conversion is abolished, effective for all new and nearly all existing trusts of land (**s 3** of the **TOLATA**). So, no longer are the interests of the equitable owners regarded as interests in money rather than land. Third, as under the original scheme, the trustees have all the powers of an absolute owner, but their ability to delegate such powers to an equitable owner is made explicit (**ss 6–9** of the **TOLATA**). This may be useful in cases in which the equitable owner is not also a trustee but where the trustees are content to leave the everyday management of the land to the person in possession of it – the equitable owner. Fourth, the trustees of land must consult with the equitable owners, and give effect to their wishes in so far as is consistent with the purposes of the trust of land (**s 11** of the **TOLATA**) but, as under the old system, failure to consult (or to agree after consultation) does not appear to invalidate any dealings with the land by the trustees (see *Birmingham Midshires BS v Sabherwal* (2000)). More significantly, under the **TOLATA 1996**, the ability to make any of the trustees' powers subject to the consent of the beneficiaries is explicit. Fifth, the **TOLATA** now formally recognises that the equitable owners have a right to occupy the property (**s 12**), which can be modified subject to safeguards, including being made subject to an obligation to pay compensation to a non-possessing co-owner (**s 13**). Again, this is formal confirmation of judicial developments prior to the **TOLATA**. Finally, again in similar fashion to the position under the original scheme, any person with an interest in the land can make an application to the court under **s 14** of the **TOLATA** for a variety or orders (replacing **s 30** of the **LPA 1925**). As before, there are special criteria specified for cases of bankruptcy (**s 15** of the **TOLATA**; **s 335A** of the **Insolvency Act 1986**) and these largely mirror the position under the old scheme.

---

2 This quick reference to arguably conflicting case law shows that you are aware of the potential for the shift in attitude from trust for sale to trust of land to be less significant than the language of the statutes might suggest.

Clearly, then, the fundamentals of the statutory co-ownership scheme under the **TOLATA 1996** are the same or similar as under the original **LPA** scheme.[3] There may be only joint tenancies of the legal estate, the legal owners are trustees and overreaching applies. In matters of detail, however, changes have been made. Some of these introduce new law (for example, no longer a duty to sell, no doctrine of conversion), while others give statutory recognition to principles previously validated by judicial decision alone (for example, a right to possession). All in all, the **TOLATA 1996** is a success.

Common Pitfalls

This is not an essay asking you to repeat the provisions of **TOLATA 1996** – which, after all, is likely to be part of the material available to you in the examination. You must contrast the old law with the new, and so do not attempt such a question unless you are aware of the nature of the now defunct 'trust for sale' of land. Case law is vital as it illustrates both the problems pre-**TOLATA** and how judges interpreted away some of those difficulties.

QUESTION 9

In 2008, Tim and Tina decided to live together as an experiment before getting married. They purchased a semi-detached house, of registered land, in the centre of town with the aid of a 90 per cent mortgage from the Steady Building Society. The rest of the purchase price was provided by Tim out of his savings. The house was conveyed to Tim alone, as Tina does not have a full-time job. Tim had an excellent job in the construction industry and Tina had no need to work. She stayed at home from where she did occasional work as a dressmaker, the money from which she used to pay for holidays. In 2009, with the construction industry in decline, Tina's income was useful to help pay the mortgage and Tim often said that he did not know how they would meet their commitments if Tina gave up dressmaking. Later that year, however, Tim inherited enough money from his uncle to pay off the mortgage and the couple decided to get married, as Tina was now pregnant. They had a tropical wedding costing several thousand pounds but, on their return, they found that Tim's employer had gone into liquidation and he was unemployed. Despite the birth of their child, Tina took on more dressmaking to meet the mounting bills. Unfortunately, Tim's attempt to start his own business has failed and he owes the bank several thousand pounds. He is now bankrupt and his trustee in bankruptcy is pressing for the house to be sold.

▶ Advise Tina.

How to Read this Question

The examiner is looking for you to apply your knowledge both of implied trusts and the statutory mechanisms regulating disputes between co-owners of rights in land. It is therefore testing your ability to apply different sets of rules in a logical and structured manner to a single set of facts.

---

3   The provisions may be the same, but the philosophy behind them is different. Has this difference been overplayed, underplayed etc., in the case law?

How to Answer this Question

❖ A résumé of the statutory machinery of co-ownership; in particular the trust of land under **TOLATA 1996** – ss 34 and 36 of the **Law of Property Act 1925**, as amended, and ss 4 and 5 of the **TOLATA 1996**.

❖ Analysis of the acquisition of beneficial ownership – *Stack v Dowden* (2007); *Abbott v Abbott* (2007); *Fowler v Barron* (2008); *Jones v Kernott* (2011).

❖ The sale of co-owned property – s 14 of the **TOLATA**.

❖ **Insolvency Act 1986**, as amended by the **TOLATA**.

Applying the Law

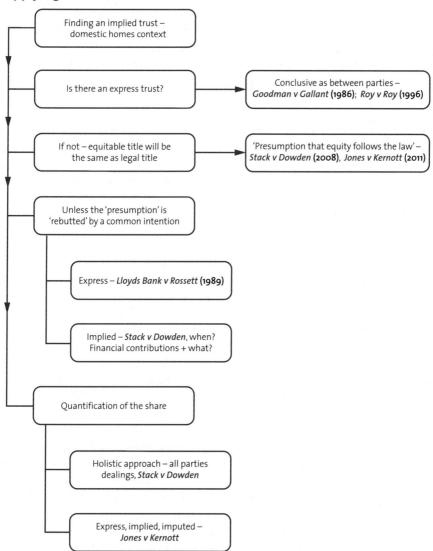

This diagram demonstrates how to find an implied trust in a domestic homes context.

ANSWER

Much depends in this case on whether Tina owns a share of the house or, in other words, whether she has any equitable interest in it. If Tina can establish that she has an 'ownership interest' in the property, she may be able to resist the application of her husband's trustee in bankruptcy for sale of the property.

When the property is purchased, it is conveyed into the sole name of Tim. The purchase is by mortgage and by cash deposit. Tim pays the entire cash deposit and, because he is to be the sole legal owner of the property, the mortgage is made with him. Title is registered in his name alone and there is no express declaration of trust in writing in favour of Tina.[4] Clearly, therefore, at the time of purchase, Tim is owner of the property both at law and in equity. There is no co-ownership – express or implied – and there is no trust of land. In such circumstances, if Tina is to establish any interest at all, she must fall back on a line of authority stemming from the House of Lords' landmark decision in *Pettitt v Pettitt* (1970) and now remodelled by *Stack v Dowden* (2007) and the recent decision in the Supreme Court in *Jones v Kernott* (2011).

This line of cases has established that it is possible for a non-legal owner of property to claim an equitable ownership interest in someone else's property. The basic principle flowing from *Pettitt* and a similar House of Lords' decision in *Gissing v Gissing* (1971) is that a person may claim an equitable interest in property belonging to another if they can establish a common intention that this was to be the case. This may either be by way of resulting trust – as in *Curley v Parkes* (2004) and *Laskar v Laskar* (2008) – or by constructive trust – as in *Grant v Edwards* (1986) and *Abbott v Abbott*.

The ability of a non-legal owner to claim of another person's land has always been controversial. The House of Lords' decision in *Lloyds Bank v Rosset* placed the law on a firm, but relatively narrow, footing whereby a person could establish an interest in the property by one of two routes. This has now been supplemented by a third route, expounded in *Stack v Dowden* and confirmed in *Kernott*.[5] First, the claimant could show that the legal owner had made an express promise to her that she should have an interest and that she has relied on that promise to her detriment, as in *Eves* (1975), *Grant v Edwards* and *Babic v Thompson* (1998).[6] Such an interest arises under a constructive trust, but it seems that, on the facts, Tina cannot establish such a claim. It is doubtful whether Tim's words of gratitude about the value of her dressmaking count for this purpose. Second, the claimant may establish an interest if she contributes directly to the purchase price of the house. If Tina contributed at the time of purchase, the size of her interest will be in proportion to her payments (probably a resulting trust see *Curley v Parkes*, but note that *Kernott* suggests that resulting trusts are inappropriate in the domestic homes context) or, if contributions were later, the share can be equivalent to the share she agreed with Tim that she

---

4   If there were such a trust, there would be no room for an implied trust, *Goodman v Gallant* and *Roy v Roy*.

5   Highlighting the history of a set of case law principles helps to put them into context.

6   In this context, it is tempting to rely on the main cases but putting in some of the less well-known or older cases will show a breadth of knowledge.

should get as a result of making the payments, or even that which is fair in the circumstances (*Crossley v Crossley* (2005); *Oxley v Hiscock* (2004)). Does she have an interest by this 'payment' route?

Lord Bridge[7] in *Rosset* accepts that such an interest can arise through mortgage repayments and we are told that Tina does make these payments. As noted, the court now appears to be able to quantify this 'payment interest' by either the traditional route of awarding a proportional share in the property (*Drake v Whipp* (1995)) or, on the basis that the parties had a shared intention as to the size of the claimant's interest (or what is fair absent that intention – *Kernott*), the payments being the trigger for it (*Cooke* (1980); *Oxley*). In order to quantify Tina's share we would need to know whether she and Tim had ever discussed the question of share of ownership. If they have not, the court will follow *Jones v Kernott* and take a holistic (and therefore unpredictable, *Aspden v Elvy* (2012)) approach to quantification which takes account of all the dealings with the property and which can rely on an imputed, as well as an implied, intention.

However, even if Tina is unsuccessful by either of these two 'traditional' routes, she may well be able to rely on *Stack v Dowden* and *Jones v Kernott*. According to the Supreme Court in *Jones v Kernott*, a person may establish a common intention, on the basis of the parties' entire course of dealings with each other, in relation to the property. Even if there is no express promise (route 1), and no payment towards the purchase price (route 2),[8] a constructive trust can arise if the parties' entire relationship to each other and the way they regard the property indicates a common intention as to ownership. It is important to remember however that although imputation is permitted at the quantification stage of the process, it is not permitted at this, the 'acquisition' stage. The parties must show a genuine, if implied, intention that their equitable interests would not be the same as the legal interest. This, clearly, is a more flexible approach. Of course, there must still be detrimental reliance, but this too can be raised from the facts of the parties' relationship. Once again, the size of the share can then be quantified by taking the holistic approach, relying on an imputed intention if necessary.

If Tina can establish her interest in the above fashion, Tim, the legal owner, will hold the property on trust for himself and Tina as tenants in common in the shares determined. There is, of course, only one trustee of land and, therefore, no possibility of overreaching (*Williams and Glyn's Bank v Boland* (1981)). Any purchaser may well be bound by Tina's interest under the normal rules of registered conveyancing – **s 29** of the **LRA 2002**. If Tina is in discoverable actual occupation of the property at the time of any sale to the purchaser (*Abbey National BS v Cann* (1991)), or being in occupation the purchaser knows of her interest, she will have an overriding interest under **para 2** of **Sched 3** to the **LRA 2002** in similar fashion to *Williams and Glyn's Bank v Boland*.

---

7   Mentioning the name of the judge gives a good impression.
8   Labelling the routes in this way avoids spending too much time explaining the same factual situation multiple times.

However, that is not the end of Tina's difficulties. When Tim becomes bankrupt, the trustee in bankruptcy becomes vested with all his property, including the legal title to the house. As we have just established, the trustee cannot sell the property immediately. In such circumstances, the trustee will apply to the court for an order for sale under **s14** of the **TOLATA 1996**. If such an application is made, the court will have to balance the claims of the creditors against the claims of Tina (assuming she resists the sale) and **s335A** of the **Insolvency Act 1986** (inserted in that Act by **Sched 3** to the **TOLATA**) provides a list of the criteria that the court should consider (as required by **s15(4)** of the **TOLATA**). These include her interests and any children, but, in any event, the court will permit a postponement of sale for only one year unless there are 'exceptional circumstances' (**s335A(3)** of the **Insolvency Act 1986** and see *Nicholls v Lan* (2006)). If postponement is ordered – perhaps to give Tina a chance to find another home irrespective of the size of her share – one year is the maximum she can hope for. There are no exceptional circumstances here (see, for example, a refusal to postpone in *Re Harrington* (2001) and note *Barca v Mears* (2004) on how the court is to approach exceptional circumstances in a way that is compatible with human rights). In short, then, Tina will have an interest, but a court is likely to order sale in due course. Of course, Tina's interest will not be subject to that of Tim's creditors and will be satisfied out of the proceeds of sale before those proceeds are distributed. As above, the precise amount will depend on how the court quantifies her share.

QUESTION 10

Carrie, a rich widow, is the registered proprietor of a large house in London. Recently, at a friend's party, she met Simon, an 18-year-old student, and, after a passionate affair of a few weeks, she invited him to live with her. Simon accepted. Being a proud man, Simon insisted that he share the expenses of running the house and, over the next few months, he paid the occasional bill and even paid for the cost of having the house redecorated both inside and out. Simon was a little concerned that, because of the difference in age, Carrie would soon tire of his charms and he repeatedly asked her about the future. Last year, after one particularly splendid dinner together, Carrie told Simon: 'What's mine is yours!' Next day, thinking that his future was secure, Simon spent his life savings on a sports car. Unfortunately, unknown to Simon, Carrie was paying school fees for her five children and, two months ago, she had to take out a mortgage with the Harrow Building Society to cover next year's fees. The building society visited the property when Simon was on a field trip abroad and Carrie executed the mortgage that day. The building society registered its charge at the Land Registry the day after he returned.

Carrie has now met someone more her own age and has emigrated to Australia. The building society is seeking possession of the property in order to realise its security.
▶ Advise Simon.

How to Read this Question

This question is testing your knowledge of the interaction betweeen implied trusts and third parties, a complex and difficult area.

How to Answer this Question

❖ Acquisition of beneficial interests under resulting and constructive trusts.

❖ The implied trust of land: *Bull v Bull* (1955).

❖ Analysis of the overreaching machinery: **ss 2** and **27** of the **Law of Property Act 1925**.

❖ Registered land: one trustee; overriding interests; meaning of discoverable actual occupation; time of occupation.

Up for Debate

The nature of discoverable actual occupation has been discussed at length in *Thompson v Foy* (2009) and *Link Lending v Bustard* (2010) and is the first consideration of the **2002 Act**. The very best answers would deal in more detail with this and also an issue raised in *Thompson* – the time at which a person must be in actual occupation. Contrary to the prevailing view, Lewison J in *Thompson* suggests (*obiter*) that a person might have to be in actual occupation at the time of registration of the purchaser's title as well as the earlier time when the sale was completed. This issue will, however, disappear under e-conveyancing.

Applying the Law

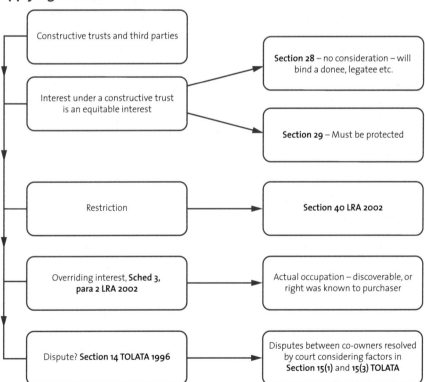

This diagram shows how the rules relating to implied trusts operate in relation to third parties.

ANSWER

This question concerns the acquisition of beneficial interests in property belonging to another and the effects of such ownership, if any, on a third party – here, a mortgagee. In concrete terms, this problem revolves around a contest between the building society, who has an interest in the property and a power of sale under **s 101** of the **LPA 1925** by virtue of its duly registered mortgage, and Simon who must claim an equitable right of ownership to it. The crucial questions are, therefore, whether Simon has such an interest and, if so, whether the building society is bound by that interest. If the building society is bound, there is no prospect of a sale of the property with vacant possession unless an application is made to the court under **s 14** of the **TOLATA 1996** (see *Bank of Baroda v Dhillon* (1998); *Bank of Ireland v Bell* (2001)) and, in any event, Simon would be entitled to the monetary equivalent of his interest before the building society could be paid.

If Simon is to have an interest in the property, it is clear that this must be established under the principles elaborated in *Pettitt v Pettitt* (1970) and codified by the House of Lords in *Stack v Dowden* (2007) and by the Supreme Court in *Jones v Kernott* (2011). There is no express conveyance to Simon as owner and no express written declaration of trust by Carrie in his favour.[9] His only hope is the law of constructive or resulting trusts. In this respect, *Stack* and *Kernott* make it clear that a person claiming an equitable interest in property must be able to show either some contribution to the purchase price of the property – so as to raise a resulting trust in their favour (see *Laskar v Laskar* (2008) – although *Stack* and *Kernott* cast doubt on the appropriateness of using resulting trusts in the domestic homes context)[10] – or must prove some express oral assurance that they were to have an interest in the property, or a common intention implied from later contributions to the cost of acquisition, or a common intention derived from the parties' whole course of dealings with each other, provided in each case that there is detrimental reliance. On the facts as stated, it seems clear that when Simon met Carrie, Carrie was sole legal owner of the property. It follows that Simon cannot pursue the resulting trust path to an equitable interest.

It would seem, then, that Simon should rely on the doctrine of constructive trusts: he must plead an express promise plus detrimental reliance or rely on the parties' whole course of dealings with each other. Are the costs of decorating the house relevant here? If Simon can show that he spent his money on improvements because there was a promise or agreement that he should part-own the property, then a case is clearly made out. There is, however, no evidence to support this, and such statements that Carrie does make are made *after* Simon spends money. Such expenditure could not have been made as a result of those particular statements. There is no reliance.

Eventually, Carrie does make a promise of sorts to Simon and it is a matter of construction whether this is sufficient for the *Stack* and *Kernott* principles. First, a problem exists with intention: does Carrie, after a romantic dinner, intend by her words 'what's mine is yours'

9 Where time permits, explain why the existence of an express trust means that there is 'no room' for an implied trust – *Goodman v Gallant* (1986).
10 Why might the resulting trust not be appropriate here?

that Simon should have an interest in the property? On the other hand, no case has denied that, if a reasonable person would have believed that the property owner was making a statement about ownership of the property, the particular promisee is entitled to rely on it even if this was not the actual intention of the property owner (see, for example, *Eves v Eves* (1975)). In our case, we do not know what Carrie actually meant, but a reasonable person in Simon's position might well conclude that this was an assurance about the ownership of the shared home. This would also fit in with the underlying reasoning in *Stack* approved in *Kernott*, which suggests that a court should not be too formulaic in seeking to find a common intention. On this ground, Simon has a case that the relevant promise was made and it seems clear from the facts that he relied on that promise.

There is here, however, a further problem. Certain cases, such as *Gissing* and *Christian v Christian* (1981) suggest that the detriment suffered as a result of the promise must be related to the property in question. However, another view is that, so long as the detriment was referable to the promise – that is, was caused by it – it does not matter that the actual detriment suffered was not property related. If the reason why an interest arises under a constructive trust is that a promise has been made and relied on (not that the property has been paid for), it should make no difference what form that detriment takes: whether it is property related or not, the promisee has still spent money that they would not otherwise have done – a view again supported by *Stack*. The size of any interest which thus arises lies in the discretion of the court (*Oxley v Hiscock* (2004)) unless there is express agreement as to share (*Crossley v Crossley* (2005)). Indeed, as the Supreme Court has made clear in *Kernott* the court is entitled to impute an intention (where it is not possible to imply one) with regard to quantification of the relevant share, and this may well take account of Carrie leaving the property (as was relevant in *Kernott* itself).

Assuming that Simon does have an interest, what is his position vis-à-vis the purchaser-mortgagee? Clearly, when Harrow advanced the money, it did not pay it to two trustees of land: Carrie is the single trustee and, therefore, there can be no overreaching.[11] This makes the building society potentially subject to Simon's interest under **s 29** of the **LRA 2002** if he can establish an interest which overrides under **Sched 3, para 2** to that Act.[12] First, Simon must have an interest in land and this we have just established. Second, he must be in discoverable actual occupation or his interest must be known to the purchaser. On the facts, given that the house is his regular home, we might expect there to be some evidence of his existence that would mean his occupation would have been discoverable to a reasonably prudent purchaser making the usual enquiries. However, we cannot be sure, and if his occupation is deemed undiscoverable, he would not qualify for an overriding interest under **Sched 3** to the **2002 Act**. Third, Simon must be in actual occupation at the relevant time and, following *Abbey National BS v Cann* (1991), it is likely that the crucial time under the **LRA 2002** is the moment of creation of the mortgage (confirmed in *Barclays Bank v Zaroovabli*

11 Remember in problem questions like this your answer should not end with establishing that Simon has an interest in the house – you must demonstrate the consequences of this conclusion for the parties.

12 A lot of students struggle with the interaction between overreaching and overriding but it is a fundamental issue and you will want to demonstrate that you have clearly understood it.

(1997) although see the comments of Lewison J in *Thompson v Foy* (2009)).[13] Thus, we must determine whether Simon was in discoverable actual occupation at the time the charge was created. On the above facts, this seems to be established.

To conclude, then, Simon has an interest under a constructive trust and he was in discoverable actual occupation of the property at the time the mortgage was made. Thus, under **Sched 3, para 2** to the **LRA 2002**, he has an overriding interest against the building society and takes priority over it: **s 29** of the **LRA 2002**. It cannot obtain vacant possession under its normal powers as mortgagee and must apply to the court under **s 14** of the **TOLATA** for an order for sale. Even if this is granted, it is unlikely to recover its money in full as Simon's interest takes priority and he must first be paid out of any proceeds of sale. The building society might pursue Carrie personally for the mortgage debt and make her bankrupt (*Alliance & Leicester v Slayford* (2001)).

QUESTION 11

'The decisions in *Stack v Dowden* (2007) and *Jones v Kernott* (2011) produced much uncertainty, but subsequent case law means that we can now be relatively sure when a constructive trust will arise. What remains unclear however is the explanation for the trust – not when does it arise, but why.'

▶ Discuss.

How to Read this Question

The primary focus of this question is the state of the law after the landmark cases of *Stack v Dowden* and *Jones v Kernott*, but it is also looking for you to consider the reasoning behind these cases.

How to Answer this Question

- ❖ The background to the decisions in *Stack* and *Kernott*.
- ❖ Sole names and joint names cases.
- ❖ Role of imputation.
- ❖ Quantification and variation over time.
- ❖ Later cases – *Chapman v Jaume, Geary v Rankine, Thompson v Hurst, Laskar v Laskar, Agarwala v Agarwala*.

Up for Debate

The normative justification for the jurisdiction in *Stack* and *Kernott* is unclear. There is much academic debate as to the policies at work in this area, and also as to whether the judicial forum is the correct one in which to address what is essentially a problem arising through social change. See for example Gardner, 'Family property today' (2008) 124 LQR 422; Gardner and Davidson, 'The future of Stack v Dowden' (2011) 127 LQR 13; Gardner and Davidson, 'The Supreme Court on family homes' (2012) 128 LQR 178.

---

13 The timing of actual occupation has been the subject of much discussion, both judicial and academic, and so you can bring in much analysis when discussing this issue.

Applying the Law

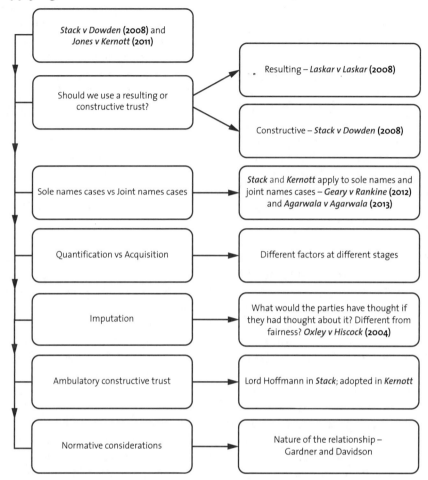

This diagram demonstrates many of the main issues arising from the decisions in Stack v Dowden *and* Jones v Kernott.

ANSWER

The House of Lords and then the Supreme Court have recently taken two opportunities to analyse the law relating to co-ownership in the context of co-habiting but unmarried couples. The decisions have proved controversial. In order to look at the levels of uncertainty that persist after *Kernott*, it is necessary to look a certain key areas of the decisions – the importance of joint versus sole names distinction, the role of imputation, and the correct approach to be taken at the acquisition stage and the quantification stage. Each of these issues has now received some attention in the Court of Appeal. The cases, without doubt, do provide some certainty with regard to the preferred approach, but there is much that remains uncertain, not least the justification for the trust arising.

In *Stack v Dowden* (2007), legal title to the property was registered in joint names, but there was no express declaration of trust. Ms Dowden argued that on sale of the property she was entitled to a greater share of the proceeds of that sale. To achieve this the court held she would need to establish that a constructive trust has arisen in response to a common intention. The first step in so-doing, in the language of the court, is to rebut that the 'presumption that equity follows the law' by establishing that there was a common intention that the equitable interest would be held otherwise than as joint tenants. This common intention could be express or implied. In this case the separate finances of the parties was sufficient evidence to demonstrate the existence of such a common intention. Once the intention is established, at the so-called 'acquisition stage', the next step was to quantify the parties' shares. Lady Hale suggested that a court should take a holistic approach when quantifying the share and should take account of all the parties' dealings with the property, as well as the nature of their relationship. In *Stack* this calculation resulting in Ms Dowden being awarded an equitable share of 65 per cent.

Jones v Kernott was also a joint names case. Ms Jones sought a declaration as to the size of her share under s14 **TOLATA 1996**. Ms Jones, like Ms Dowden, was claiming that she was entitled to more than the 50 per cent of the proceeds of sale. Mr Kernott had left the house some 12 years earlier and in that time Ms Jones had paid for the mortgage, bills and general upkeep of the house. The court was thus grappling with the question as to whether this change in the parties' circumstances from the time of purchase should be taken into consideration when assessing the parties' shares, and in what way. They were also asked to clarify the ruling in *Stack v Dowden* in the face of much criticism of their earlier decision. The court, far from moving away from their earlier decision, expressly supported *Stack*. The court held that the conduct of the parties after the split was sufficient to 'rebut the presumption' such that Ms Jones could acquire a share larger than 50 per cent in the property. This was based on an implied common intention. From here the court would quantify the parties' shares, taking a holistic approach bearing in mind all their dealings with the property. This process led them to conclude that Ms Jones was entitled to a 90 per cent share of the proceeds of sale.

These decisions left open some questions, which have now been addressed by the Court of Appeal.[14] First, it was clear that although the resulting trust was no longer to be relied on in domestic situations, the position of 'mixed' or borderline cases was less certain. In *Laskar v Laskar* (2008), Neuberger MR confirmed that the resulting trust can still be used where there is an investment-type relationship with the property, even where the property itself is a dwelling house and where the relationship between the parties is a familial one. This has been recently confirmed in *Chaudhary v Chaudhary* (2013) where a resulting trust was again used to reflect initial purchase price contributions. Thus, we know that the resulting trust can still be used in appropriate cases, even if there is still some vestige of uncertainty as to what exactly will constitute an appropriate case.

----

14 This question is asking you to discuss both the decisions in *Stack* and *Kernott* and later decisions of the Court of Appeal. You need to have good knowledge of these later decisions in order to do this properly.

Second, a very much open question following *Stack* and *Kernott* was the difference of approach (if any) that ought to be taken in sole names versus joint names cases. Again, subsequent decisions of the Court of Appeal have gone some way to resolving this uncertainty and only the most trenchant 'anti-*Stack*' approach can justify relying on *Lloyds Bank v Rossett* (1990) in sole name cases. The stongest authority in this respect is *Agarwala v Agarwala* (2013), a very recent decision of the Court of Appeal where *Rossett* is not even mentioned, and the principles outlined in *Stack* are applied in such a way as to give rise to an implied trust. *Geary v Rankine* (2012) too provides very strong evidence that *Stack* and *Kernott* apply equally to sole names as to joint names cases, albeit that the different starting points mean inevitably that the principles will apply differently in practice. The difficultly however is that the starting point is not just different, it is quite radically different. It is still not clear whether, for example, a more stringent test will be applied in terms of 'exceptionality' or whether the holistic approach will be carried out in the same way.

Furthermore, the role of imputation after *Stack* was in considerable doubt, and due to the disagreements between the judges[15] in *Kernott* we cannot say that we are necessarily much further on in terms of the fine line to be drawn between implying an intention and imputing one. More guidance will be required from the higher courts before we are confident where this boundary lies and subsequent decisions have not assisted in this to date.

Finally, there is uncertainty in the notion of the ambulatory constructive trust. The general idea is that the parties' shares in the property can vary over time in accordance with the different circumstances and intentions of the parties at the relevant time. We do not know what will transform a normal constructive trust into an ambulatory constructive trust and when this will happen. In addition to this, it is important to note that the interaction between an ambulatory constructive trust and third parties may also prove to be a highly complex one, especially where there is a charge over one party's share.

There are therefore still areas of remaining uncertainty, despite the emergence of useful guidance from the Court of Appeal. Crucially, however, what this uncertainty demonstrates is that we have not clearly articulated the normative basis for this jurisdiction. It is far from clear what factors will trigger the imputation of an intention to share. More than this there is an inherent and unavoidable uncertainty in the holistic approach to quantifying the share and imputation generally which lies in the unpredictability of the ensuing result. We may well be certain that the court will impute an intention where there is no express or implied intention as to share, but we cannot know beyond that what the court is likely to feel is an appropriate allocation of the equitable title.

And so there is much we now know following *Kernott*. We know that *Stack* is here to stay; we know that the approaches at the acquisition and quantification stages are different; and we know that imputation is permitted at the latter stage only. We know too following

---

15 Not only does highlighting the disagreement in the court bolster the argument as to certainty here, it also demonstrates that you have read the case and are aware of the judgments themselves, rather than simply a summary of the main points.

decisions in the Court of Appeal how the court will treat sole names cases. What we are less clear on is the precise role of imputation, the nature of the ambulatory constructive trust and the practical results that will emerge from an application of the principles in these cases. The uncertainty that comes from the open-texture of the discretion in these cases cannot be solved by more cases – instead we need to work out why the courts have quantified a share in a particular way.[16] This will require detailed and thoughtful consideration as to why some relationships and actions justify a court-imposed trust, and others do not.

QUESTION 12

Alfonso, Bertie, Clive, Denny and Ernie are all trainee solicitors in London and they decide to buy a house together. All contribute equally to the purchase price and the house is conveyed to 'Alfonso and Bertie as joint tenants in law and in equity'. Several months later, Bertie is made redundant and forges Alfonso's signature to a mortgage made with the Easy Loan Bank. At the same time, Alfonso agrees in writing to sell his interest in the property to Ernie and the agreement is executed. Meanwhile, Clive has plans to marry and asks Denny whether he will buy his share in the house. Denny is very keen but disputes the price. Before they can come to an agreement, Clive is killed in a road accident, leaving all his property to his fiancée, Wilma. Very soon after, Ernie becomes entangled in a City deal that goes badly wrong and, owing many millions, is made bankrupt. Before Ernie is formally adjudged bankrupt, Denny commits suicide, leaving all his property to the Battersea Dogs' Home.

Ernie's trustee in bankruptcy, Wilma, the Dogs' Home, Bertie and Denny's next of kin all claim an interest in the property.

▶ **What is your advice?**

How to Read this Question

This question is testing your ability to apply the relatively straightforward rules relating to severance to a complex fact scenario. It is therefore important to approach the question in a structured manner.

How to Answer this Question

❖   Construction of the conveyance and the nature of the parties' interests.
❖   The purpose of the law of severance.
❖   *Williams v Hensman* (1861):
    o   an act operating on one's own share
    o   mutual agreement
    o   possible course of dealing.
❖   The nature and effect of the right of survivorship.
❖   The effect of bankruptcy of co-owner.
❖   **Section 36(2)** of the **Law of Property Act 1925**: *Kinch v Bullard* (1999).

---

16   Recognising that 'uncertainty' can mean more than one sort of problem gives your engagement with the specific question more depth.

Applying the Law

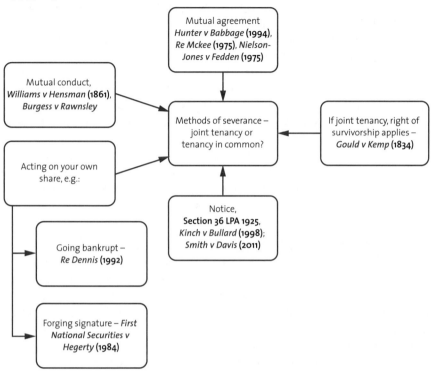

This diagram shows the different methods of severance.

ANSWER

This question concerns the law of severance. Severance is the process by which an equitable joint tenancy can be converted into an equitable tenancy in common. Under the **LPA 1925**, the only form of co-ownership that can exist at law is the joint tenancy. This legal joint tenancy is unseverable. In other words, when we talk of severing the joint tenancy, we are talking about severing the joint tenancy in equity.

The law relating to severance is to be found both in statute and at common law. Under **s 36(2)** of the **LPA 1925**, any equitable joint tenant may give notice in writing to the other joint tenants of their intention to sever (unless it seems they have promised not to: *White v White* (2000)) and this actually results in a severance in equity – see, for example, *Burgess v Rawnsley* (1975) and *Kinch v Bullard* (1999). Similarly, at common law, *Williams v Hensman* (1861) establishes that severance may occur by three methods: first, where one joint tenant does 'an act operating on their own share' (such as a sale of his interest); second, where joint tenants agree to sever by 'mutual agreement' (this acts to sever the shares of all those agreeing, even if the agreement is never carried out or is actually unenforceable – *Burgess*); third, by 'mutual conduct' (where the party's conduct is of a kind sufficient to evince an intention no longer to be part of a joint tenancy).

Alfonso and Bertie are the legal owners and are, by statute (**s 35** of the **LPA**), the joint tenant trustees of the legal estate holding for the equitable owners on a trust of land under the **TOLATA 1996**. Who are the equitable owners, and are they joint tenants or tenants in common? Although the conveyance expressly declares that Alfonso and Bertie are joint tenants, this conveyance can be conclusive only between the parties to it: *Goodman v Gallant* (1986). Therefore, the doctrine of resulting and constructive trusts is not excluded for Clive, Denny and Ernie. Following *Dyer v Dyer* (1788), *Pettitt v Pettitt* (1970) and *Curley v Parkes* (2004), there is no doubt that Clive, Denny and Ernie will be able to claim a share of the equitable ownership by virtue of their contribution to the purchase price of the property at the time of acquisition. In fact, because all five people contributed to the purchase price equally, they are, in equity, joint tenants. So, the picture of the ownership of the house is as follows: Alfonso and Bertie hold the property as trustees of land for Alfonso, Bertie, Clive, Denny, and Ernie as joint tenants in equity.

(a) Bertie's Attempted Mortgage to the Easy Loan Bank

Bertie is a trustee of the legal title, but jointly with Alfonso. Thus, no action on his part alone can deal with the legal title and, without Alfonso's agreement, there can be no mortgage to the bank. Both legal owners must genuinely agree to any conveyance of the legal title. Forging the signature of the other legal owner is not sufficient to create a mortgage of the legal title – *First National Securities v Heggarty* (1984). However, following *Ahmed v Kendrick* (1987), *Banker's Trust v Namdar* (1997), *First National Bank v Achampong* (2003) and **s 63** of the **LPA 1925**, the attempted mortgage by Bertie will be sufficient to mortgage to the bank such interest as Bertie does control – in other words, his equitable interest. Without doubt, this mortgage of his equitable interest is 'an act operating on his own share' within *Hensman* and means that Bertie severs his share of the equitable interest. He is now a tenant in common of one-fifth, albeit mortgaged to the bank. The other owners are still within a joint tenancy of the remaining four-fifths. Legal title remains in Alfonso and Bertie as before.[17]

(b) The Transfer by Alfonso

When Alfonso agrees in writing to sell his interest in the property to Ernie, this is an enforceable agreement to sell his equitable interest (see **s 2** of the **Law of Property (Miscellaneous Provisions) Act 1989**). This is not an agreement to sell the legal title as Bertie would have had to concur. As above, this is an act operating on his own share within *Hensman* and will sever Alfonso's interest from the joint tenancy. Thus, when the agreement is executed, Alfonso's equitable share passes to Ernie. The overall position is now that Alfonso and Bertie hold on trust for Ernie as tenant in common of one-fifth, Bertie as tenant in common of one-fifth (but mortgaged) and Clive, Denny and Ernie as joint tenants of the remainder.[18]

---

17 Severance questions are often factually complex, and it is useful to summarise where you have got to at the end of each section like this.

18 Remember that it is possible to have a 'mix and match' of joint tenancy and tenancy in common.

(c) Mutual Agreement or Mutual Conduct

It is unclear whether Clive's discussions with Denny lead to any severance of the joint tenancy between them. It seems that there is no 'mutual agreement' within *Hensman* as, although Denny is keen to buy, no price has been agreed. This probably prevents severance by mutual agreement. Assuming that mutual agreement is inapplicable here, can the discussions between Clive and Denny amount to severance by 'mutual conduct', being a course of dealing between the parties that show an intention to hold as tenants in common? This is unclear, because, as a matter of principle, it is difficult to see why a failed attempt to agree (as here) should be treated as effective to sever even though there is no agreement to sever. If that were possible, the difference between mutual agreement and mutual conduct would become virtually non-existent. However, if one reads Lord Denning's judgment in *Burgess*, it is clear that he does suggest that negotiations between joint tenants can give rise to severance. Essentially, the answer will depend on the facts of each case. In our case, the tentative conclusion is that severance has not occurred because of the potential overlap with mutual agreement. Thus, the position remains as at (b) above.

(d) The Right of Survivorship

When Clive dies, he dies as a joint tenant of three-fifths of the property with Denny and Ernie. He has not severed his interest and, thus, it accrues to Denny and Ernie under the right of survivorship. The fact that he left his property by will to Wilma is irrelevant as survivorship takes precedence over testamentary dispositions (*Gould v Kemp* (1834)). Thus, Alfonso and Bertie hold on trust for Ernie as tenant in common of one-fifth, Bertie as tenant in common of one-fifth (but mortgaged) and Denny and Ernie as joint tenants of the remainder.

(e) Ernie's Bankruptcy and the Suicide

Under the **Insolvency Act** (as applied in very similar circumstances to these in *Re Dennis* (1992)), it is clear that a bankrupt's property does not become vested in the trustee in bankruptcy until he or she is formally adjudicated bankrupt. At that moment, of course, there is alienation (that is, transfer) of the bankrupt's property such as to cause a severance of any joint tenancy of which he may be part – it is really an act operating on his own share, albeit an involuntary one. In our case, however, when Denny dies and leaves his property to the Dogs' Home, Ernie has not been adjudicated bankrupt and so there has been no severance between the remaining two joint tenants. Unfortunately, therefore, Denny's interest passes to Ernie under the right of survivorship. In other words, when Ernie is adjudicated bankrupt, he is, in fact, the sole surviving joint tenant and all the property subject to that joint tenancy accrued to him and will fall to the trustee in bankruptcy to pay the creditors.

The final position is, therefore, that Alfonso and Bertie are legal owners of the property holding as joint tenant trustees in equity in the following way:

❖ for Ernie as tenant in common of one-fifth, which will pass to the trustee in bankruptcy;

❖   for Bertie as tenant in common of one-fifth, but as mortgaged to the bank;

❖   for Ernie as owner of the remainder, having succeeded to the shares of Clive and Denny under the right of survivorship. This also passes to the trustee in bankruptcy for distribution among his creditors.

Common Pitfalls

Many students make two common mistakes with this type of problem. First, as it is about the law of severance, at the outset of the problem, the parties *must* be joint tenants. If they are not, they would already be tenants in common and severance would be irrelevant. Do not assume this – make it explicit and be clear that they are not tenants in common. In this case, the joint tenancy is expressly created by the words of the conveyance. Second, make sure you 'sum up' the position after each act of severance. This provides focus for you and for the examiner.

4 Successive Interests in Land

INTRODUCTION

Although it is now less frequent, it was once quite common for property to be left to one person for their life, then to another, then to another and so on. These are *successive* interests in land and they arise when one person is entitled to the possession of land in succession to another, a typical example being where land is left to A for life, with remainder to B for life, remainder to C in fee simple. In such a case, A has a life interest in possession (and is known somewhat confusingly as the 'life tenant'), B has a life interest in remainder (and will be the life tenant when A dies) and C has a fee simple in remainder (and will become the absolute owner on the death of A and B).

The reasons for creating successive interests can, of course, be many and varied, although one very common reason was so that land could be 'kept in the family' by limiting its ownership to successive heirs. Nowadays, this is less of a motivating factor, although successive interests may still be created in family or commercial relationships where the settlor (the person who makes the settlement in the first place) desires to make provision for several persons out of his land. Today, the law concerning successive interests is to be found in two distinct sets of statutory provisions. First, for 'settlements' in existence prior to 1 January 1997, the operating statute is the **Settled Land Act (SLA) 1925**. This is a complicated piece of legislation and the machinery it establishes is rightly regarded as unwieldy. Land subject to this statute (that is, land subject to successive interests created before 1 January 1997, even if 'resettled' after this date) is known as 'settled land'. Second, life interests created on or after 1 January 1997 are subject to the provisions of the **Trusts of Land and Appointment of Trustees Act (TOLATA) 1996**. Such interests are held under a 'trust of land' and are excluded from the operation of the **Settled Land Act**. To put it another way, on 1 January 1997, it became impossible to create any new 'settlements' under the **Settled Land Act** and any attempt to create a successive interest in land after this date will, by statute, create a trust of land under s2 of the **TOLATA 1996**. This move to abolish the strict settlement for all future successive interests reflects both the changing social uses to which land subject to successive interests is put and the fact that the **Settled Land Act 1925** had become outdated, cumbersome and expensive to operate.

There is no doubt that the law of successive interests is complicated, especially when there is an 'old-style' settlement and the **Settled Land Act** is in play. Unfortunately, we cannot yet abandon the strict settlement to the legal graveyard as many existing settlements have time to run and, indeed, because any resettlement of existing settled land will be governed by the **Settled Land Act**, even if such resettlement takes place on or after 1 January 1997 (**s 2** of the **TOLATA 1996**). An old-style settlement will cease to exist only when there is no land or heirlooms subject to the settlement (**s 2(5)** of the **TOLATA 1996**). The relatively new-style trust for successive interests – the trust of land under the **TOLATA** – is simpler and, therefore, less expensive to establish. The mandatory use of the trust of land for all new successive interests has already simplified this area of land law. One side effect is that the law of concurrent co-ownership (Chapter 3) and successive co-ownership are now governed by the same statutory provisions of the **TOLATA 1996**.

Checklist

It is important to have a working knowledge of the Settled Land Act 1925, of the scope of the powers of the 'tenant for life' under it, of the controls placed on the tenant for life and of the differences between the settlement and the trust of land as a means of regulating successive ownership. An awareness of the history of settled land is also helpful. In addition, for new successive interest trusts, it is imperative to have a clear understanding of the provisions of the TOLATA 1996 and much of what has been said in the previous chapter (concurrent co-ownership) is also relevant here. Particular attention should be given to the ability of the trustees under a trust of land to delegate powers to any beneficiary – such as the holder of a life interest. This will preserve the advantage enjoyed under strict settlements that the person most interested in the land has power to deal with it in specified circumstances.

QUESTION 13

Compare the mechanisms of the **Settled Land Act 1925** and the **Trusts of Land and Appointment of Trustees Act 1996** as a means of regulating successive co-ownership of land.

How to Read this Question

The examiner here has explicitly asked for a comparison between the **1996 Act** and the **1925 Act**, but they have not specified what aspects of the regulation you should compare. It is important therefore to bring a logical structure to the comparison and to cover a broad range of issues.

How to Answer this Question

- ❖ Identify the nature of successive interests in land.
- ❖ Analyse the effect of the **TOLATA 1996** on successive interests in general.
- ❖ Discuss the salient features of the **SLA 1925** and its defects.
- ❖ Identify and assess the reasons for reform.
- ❖ Draw a comparison between the **SLA 1925** and the **TOLATA 1996**.

Up for Debate

It would be easy to expand this answer, time permitting. More consideration could be given to the case law on **TOLATA**, particularly discussion of whether the trustees are limited in any way – see for example *HSBC v Dyche* (2009). The impact of informally created interests is particularly interesting given that these are (relatively) easily protected under a trust of land, but very difficult to protect under a strict settlement.

Applying the Law

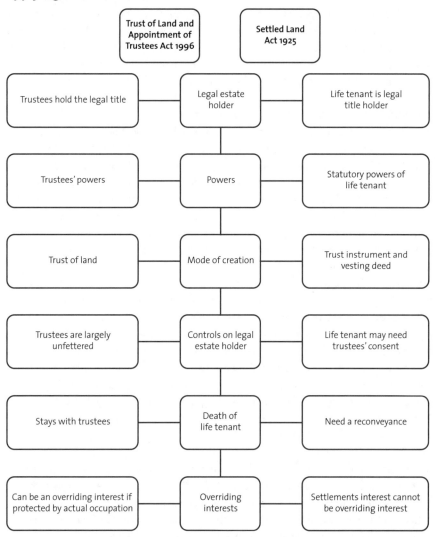

This diagram shows the difference between the operation of the **Settled Land Act 1925** and the **Trusts of Land and Appointment of Trustees Act 1996** to successive interests in land.

ANSWER

Land can be said to be held in successive ownership when two or more persons are entitled to enjoyment of that land (or the income from it) in succession to each other. An example of successive co-ownership is where land is left to A for life, then to B for life, then to C absolutely. After 1925, two mutually exclusive statutory regimes are in operation. First, for land subject to a 'settlement' (sometimes called a 'strict settlement') that was created before 1 January 1997, the **Settled Land Act (SLA) 1925** is the governing statute. This is 'settled land': see **ss1** and **2** of the **SLA 1925** and *Re Austen* (1929). Second, however, all attempts to create successive interests in land on or after 1 January 1997 (save for a 'resettlement' of existing settled land) must take effect as a *trust of land* under the **Trusts of Land and Appointment of Trustees Act 1996** (s2 of the **TOLATA**, which came into force on 1 January 1997). Clearly, this is a major reshaping of the law of successive interests, designed to lead to the eventual disappearance of settled land governed by the **SLA**. For the present, however, the two statutes operate in parallel, each defined by reference to the time of creation of the successive interest.

Settled land is land held on trust. Consequently, there will be 'trustees of the settlement' and beneficiaries under the settlement. These beneficiaries will be the person having a life interest and those persons entitled in remainder – that is, after the life tenant has died. The settlement will have been created by the 'settlor', by deeds, and these deeds will usually identify the trustees and deal with the detail of the settlement. Under the **SLA**, various persons are given statutory powers to deal with settled land. The major purpose behind the grant of these powers is to ensure that the land itself can be freely dealt with. As with concurrent co-ownership, if the land is sold, the rights and interests of the beneficiaries will be transferred to the purchase money via the mechanism of overreaching.

The first point of particular interest in respect of settled land is that, under the **SLA**, the tenant for life has significant powers to deal with the land. The tenant for life is the holder of the legal estate in the land and they hold that legal estate on trust for the beneficiaries under the settlement: **ss4** and **107** of the **SLA**. Further, as just noted, in the great majority of cases, this tenant for life is also the person entitled to the equitable life interest in the property and so they will have two roles: holder of the legal estate in the land and owner of an equitable, but limited ownership. It is no accident that the person in possession of the land should also have the legal title and powers to deal with the land because, being the person in immediate possession, they are likely to be the best judge of how to deal with it.

Second, the tenant for life also exercises most of the important statutory powers to deal with the settled land. These are found in **Pt II** of the **SLA 1925** and effectively place the tenant for life in control of the land. They have the power to manage it for the best interests of all the beneficiaries. Consequently, the role of the 'trustees of the settlement' is limited. In general, they exercise supervisory functions in respect of the settlement: *Wheelwright v Walker* (1883). It is their responsibility to ensure that the rights and interests of *all* the beneficiaries under the settlement are protected.

Third, under the **SLA**, if the person with the statutory powers chooses to sell the settled land, the interests of the beneficiaries are overreached *if* the purchase money is paid to the trustees of the settlement or into court. If overreaching occurs, the purchaser need not concern themselves with the equitable interests because these take effect in the purchase money. If overreaching does not occur, the tenant for life cannot grant a good title to the purchaser and the purchaser may be bound by the equitable interests as specified under the provisions of the **SLA**.

Finally, brief mention also should be made of the process by which such settlements were once created (that is, before 1 January 1997). Under the **SLA**, all strict settlements had to be created by two deeds – a 'trust instrument' and a 'principal vesting deed': **ss 4** and **5** of the **SLA**. The trust instrument declared the details of the settlement, appointed the trustees of it and set out any powers conferred by the settlement that were in addition to those provided automatically by the Act. The principal vesting deed described the settled land itself, named the trustees, stated the nature of any additional powers and, most importantly of all, declared that the settled land was vested in the person to whom the land was conveyed (the tenant for life) on the trusts of the settlement. The principal vesting deed was, in one sense, the indicia of ownership of the settled land.

By way of contrast, 'new-style' successive interest trusts of land operating under the **TOLATA** follow a different statutory regime. This new regime represents a revamping of the old 'trust for sale' (which, prior to 1 January 1997, was the alternative to 'settled land') and is designed principally to avoid the complicated machinery of the **SLA**. As noted above, it is compulsory for all new successive interests in land.

A 'trust of land' is of course a trust, having trustees and beneficiaries. The trustees will be named in the instrument and the beneficiaries will be those entitled to a life interest and interests in remainder. Most importantly, however, the trustees have legal title and have all the powers in respect of the land of an absolute owner (**s 6** of the **TOLATA**). The exception is where the trustees' powers are limited by the **TOLATA** itself, or for a trust that is expressly created, by any provision in the instrument creating the trust (**s 8** of the **TOLATA 1996**). Primarily, therefore, it is the trustees of land who control it or its capital value. This is very different from the location of power and control under a settlement in which all lies with the tenant for life.[1]

Second, while the tenant for life under a settlement is subject to some controls on the exercise of their powers (*Wheelwright v Walker*) under a trust of land, the trustees are largely unfettered. They are subject to the provisions of the **TOLATA** and a person with an interest in a trust of land may make an application to the court under **s 14**. Yet, these are not powerful fetters. It is true that, under **s 10** of the **TOLATA**, the powers of the trustees of land can be made subject to the consent of another person. It is possible – perhaps probable – that settlors who deliberately create a successive interest trust of land will use **s 10** to limit the role of the trustees, but this will need careful drafting. In registered land, such a consent requirement will be entered on the register of title by means of a restriction. In unregistered land, a

---

1   It is good to highlight the comparison you are drawing throughout.

purchaser may deal with the trustees of land safely, even in violation of a consent require-ment, unless the purchaser had actual notice of it (**s16** of the **TOLATA 1996**). Finally, like all trustees, the trustees of land under the **TOLATA** and the trustees of the settlement under the **SLA 1925** are subject to the normal rules controlling persons in a fiduciary position.

Third, because of the complicated workings of the **SLA**, on the death of the tenant for life, the legal estate can be transferred to a new tenant for life only by 'vesting deeds', a relatively expensive process. However, in a trust of land under the **TOLATA**, the trustees must have the legal title and must be joint tenants of it (**ss34** and **36** of the **Law of Property Act (LPA) 1925**), irrespective of the complicated nature of the beneficiaries' interests or the circumstances surrounding the establishment of the trust. Thus, on the death of a trustee of land, legal title accrues automatically to the remaining trustees under the right of survivorship.[2]

Finally, while, under the **SLA**, the tenant for life has the statutory powers to deal with the land, we have seen that, under the **TOLATA**, the trustees have the powers of an absolute owner. However, the trustees of land under the **TOLATA** may delegate to a beneficiary 'any of their functions' that relate to the land (**s9** of the **TOLATA 1996**).

To sum up then, after 31 December 1996, all new successive interests will be trusts of land governed by the **TOLATA 1996**. Earlier trusts created under the **SLA 1925** are governed by the complicated provisions of that Act.[3] Under a settlement, the legal title and powers to deal with the land are vested in the tenant for life. Under a trust of land, title and power are in the hands of the trustees, although they may delegate to a beneficiary. Again, in settled land, the tenant for life is subject to control by the trustees of the settlement; in a trust of land, the trustees are not subject to such control unless express provision is made in the trust instrument or after an application to the court. Finally, transfer of title on the death of a tenant for life under the **SLA** is expensive and complicated, but no such prob-lems arise should a trustee of land die.

QUESTION 14

'The **Settled Land Act 1925** makes it clear that the tenant for life is in effective control of land subject to a strict settlement. This works well when he is a prudent manager of the estate, with a care for the interests of the other beneficiaries. However, if the tenant for life is uninterested, unskilled or downright selfish, there is little that can be done to control him in the exercise of his powers.'

▶ Do you agree?

How to Read this Question

The examiner here is looking for you to assess both the powers given to the tenant for life under the **SLA 1925**, and to analyse the controls on the use of those powers. Both aspects must be considered.

2   The expense of the conveyancing requirements of the **SLA 1925** is worth highlighting. The changes under the new law are not just legal, but also very practical.

3   This summarises the key difference between the regimes and allows the conclusion to draw the threads of the discussion together.

How to Answer this Question
❖ Briefly, the nature of a strict settlement under the **SLA 1925**.
❖ Analyse the position of the tenant for life in relation to the trustees and other beneficiaries under the settlement.
❖ Describe the powers of the tenant for life.
❖ Analyse the controls available to the trustees and the court.

Up for Debate

The very best candidates will consider the complicated arguments about how *Weston v Henshaw* (1950) and *Re Morgan's Lease* (1972) can be reconciled. There is considerable uncertainty as to whether (or when) a purchaser is protected if a tenant for life should carry out a transaction not authorised by the Act, even if in purported exercise of his wide powers.

Applying the Law

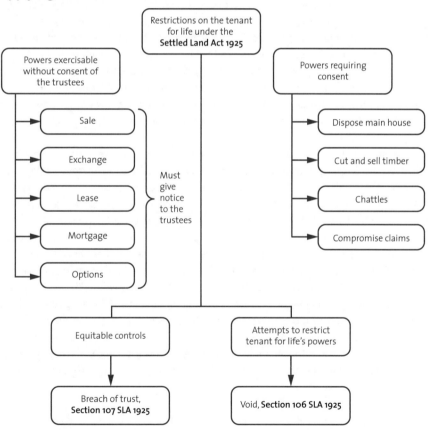

*This diagram shows the restrictions on the powers of the life tenant under the **Settled Land Act 1925**.*

ANSWER

It is in the nature of a settlement under the **SLA 1925** that there may be many occasions for conflict among the persons intended to be benefited by the settlor. A settlement necessarily gives one person a life interest in the property (the tenant for life) and another (or others) interests in the land after that life estate has ended. In this sense, therefore, two often contradictory interests need to be reconciled. Prior to 1926, it was the persons entitled in remainder who held the upper hand as it was relatively easy to restrict the life tenant's ability to deal with the land and their ability to diminish its value. Unfortunately, this meant that much settled land stagnated because the tenant for life had no means of raising the money necessary to use the land profitably. Indeed, given that the tenant for life's rights over the land were so limited, there was little incentive for them to manage the land effectively. Under the **SLA 1925**, the position changed, as it is a fundamental feature of the Act that the tenant for life shall have both the legal estate in the land and extensive powers to deal with it, even to the point of selling it and converting all the beneficiaries' interests into money.

In the normal course of events, when a settlement is created, the settlor will appoint trustees of the settlement and, in some exceptional circumstances, they will have legal title and the powers conferred by the Act. In the normal case, however, these powers and the title will rest with the tenant for life. Of course, being trustees, the persons appointed as such will have fiduciary responsibilities to all the beneficiaries, especially those entitled in remainder and, as *Wheelwright v Walker* (1883) illustrates, the trustees have a general supervisory function in relation to the settlement. However, the **SLA** makes it clear in no uncertain terms that the policy behind the Act will be best served by giving considerable control to the tenant for life via the legal title and statutory powers.[4]

Thus, a life tenant has a power of sale over the land (which will overreach the beneficial interests), although he is obliged to obtain the best price that can reasonably be made (*Wheelwright v Walker (No 2)* (1883)). There is also the power to exchange the land, to grant and accept leases, to mortgage the land in order to raise funds for its benefit and to grant options over the land. All of these powers may be exercised without the consent of the trustees, provided that the tenant gives written notice to the trustees and their solicitor, although it is clear from *Wheelwright* that, if there are no trustees, these powers cannot be exercised. However, even if the trustees have been given notice in the appropriate manner, they are under no obligation to interfere (*England v Public Trustee* (1968)) and they may accept less than the required one month's notice or waive it in writing altogether. Indeed, except for the power of mortgaging, the tenant for life may give general notice that he intends to exercise his powers at some point and this will suffice.[5] In any event, under **s 110** of the **SLA**, a purchaser from the tenant for life is protected against non-compliance by the life tenant. These are, then, fairly limited and relaxed controls. In respect of other powers – such

---

4   The tension between the formal content of rules and their hoped-for application is always a source of fruitful analysis.

5   It is good to highlight exceptions to general statements like this because it gives the examiner confidence that you have detailed knowledge of the relevant rules.

as the power to dispose of the main house, to cut and sell timber, to sell chattels and to compromise claims – there is more control and the exercise of these depend variously on obtaining the consent of the trustees or of the court. As such, this is not surprising, as these powers relate to those matters of a more personal nature (that is, as opposed to the land itself) in which the other beneficiaries may well have a legitimate interest. Even so, the fact that the tenant for life can sell the land with only minimal intervention by the trustees speaks volumes for the policy operating behind this statute.

Indeed, the matter is even clearer when we realise that it is virtually impossible to restrict the tenant for life in the exercise of their powers. Thus, under **s106** of the **SLA**, any provision in the settlement itself that attempts or purports to forbid the exercise of a statutory power by the tenant for life or which attempts, tends or is intended to induce the tenant for life not to exercise a power is void (e.g. *Re Patten* (1929) and *Re Orelebar* (1936)). Some limitation on this very wide protection for the life tenant was provided by *Re Aberconway* (1953), which decided that, if what might be lost to the life tenant by virtue of an exercise of a power was not a benefit or ancillary to their enjoyment of the land, **s106** would not operate to invalidate that stipulation. In a similar vein, the tenant for life cannot give up their powers, even if parting with all their interest (*Re Mundy* (1899)), although a surrender to the person next entitled (**s105** of the **SLA**), order of the court (**s24** of the **SLA**) and cases of lunacy can lead to those powers being exercised by other persons.

Perhaps, indeed, the only real control over the tenant for life arises under the general equitable jurisdiction to restrain breach of trust and supervise the actions of persons in a fiduciary position. By virtue of **s107** of the **SLA**, the tenant for life is deemed to be trustee for the beneficiaries of both the legal estate and the statutory powers. On sale, therefore, the life tenant must sell as fairly as any trustee would sell, for the best price and recognising the interest of those entitled after his death: *Wheelwright v Walker* (1883). Likewise, the tenant cannot accept payment in order to exercise his powers (*Chandler v Bradley* (1897); *Bray v Ford* (1896)) as he is under a trustee's duty not to profit from his trust. The tenant of course must not commit a fraud in exercising his powers (*Middlemas v Stevens* (1901)), but the transaction effected by the tenant for life will not be invalidated simply because he had an uncharitable motive (*Cardigan v Curzon-Howe* (1885)).

All in all then, the tenant for life has a very wide measure of control over settled land and the trustees of the settlement can do little to restrain them save in clear cases of abuse. This is entirely consistent with the purposes behind the **SLA**:[6] that use of land takes precedence over the motives of the settlor in trying to tie up land for their family. Such a strong position can work to the benefit of all persons interested in the settlement – e.g. by selling the land for a profit and successfully reinvesting the proceeds – but clearly there is room for an unscrupulous or incompetent tenant to exercise his powers largely without control and to the overall detriment of all the beneficiaries.

....

6 A good technique in the conclusion is to draw a clear argument as to the relationship between the rules and their aims as it helps summarise from an analytical rather than a descriptive perspective.

5

INTRODUCTION

Leasehold interests are one of the two estates (along with freeholds) that are capable of existing at law or in equity (**s1** of the **Law of Property Act 1925**). In fact, the leasehold estate, whether it be equitable or legal, is one of the most versatile concepts found in the whole of the law of real property. Even the terminology of leases reflects the many purposes to which they may be put. The 'term of years', 'tenancies', 'sub-leases' and 'leasehold estate' are all synonymous and in terms of the legal rules governing their creation and operation the principles are the same, although one particular description may be more appropriate than another depending on the situation. So, for example, the term 'lease' is most often used for commercial or long-term lettings whereas the term 'tenancy' is used for 'domestic' or shorter-term lettings.

One of the most important features of leaseholds is that they allow two or more estate owners to enjoy the benefits of the same piece of land at the same time: for example, the freeholder will receive the rent and profits and the leaseholder will enjoy physical possession and occupation of the property. Indeed, if a 'sub-tenancy' is involved, one lease will be carved out of another as where a freeholder, L, grants land to A for 30 years, who sublets to B for 25 years, who sub-lets to C for ten years, and so on. It is this ability of the leasehold estate to facilitate multiple enjoyment of land that gives it its special character. In addition, it is inherent in a lease that the rights and obligations undertaken by the original landlord and tenant concerning the land can be transmitted to persons who later step into the shoes of the original parties, as where a landlord assigns (transfers) the reversion or the tenant assigns the lease. The ability to make rights and obligations 'run' with the land is a special feature of the landlord and tenant relationship and legislation (**Landlord and Tenant (Covenants) Act 1995**) has enhanced this feature of the leasehold estate, at least for leases granted on or after 1 January 1996, the date on which the **1995 Act** came into force.

Aim Higher

❖ Be clear about the methods of creation of leasehold interests and the differences between creating equitable and legal leases.

❖ Use case law to explain the difference between a 'lease' and a 'licence'; just repeating the textbook will not earn many marks.

❖ Understand how leases fit into the system of registered land: some are registrable titles, some are overriding interests and some might require protection through the use of a notice against the superior title.

❖ Always check whether the lease was created before 1 January 1996 as this will determine which principles apply to the enforcement of leasehold covenants: the pre-1996 rules or the **Landlord and Tenant (Covenants) Act (LTCA) 1995**.

❖ Forfeiture is a very popular topic with examiners.

QUESTION 15

'There cannot be a tenancy if the grantor has no power to create a tenancy. Further, in order to have a leasehold estate there must be an intention to create legal relations, exclusive possession and a term. Identifying when these features exist will not always be straightforward. There are also some situations in which these 'indicia' or 'hallmarks' of a tenancy do exist and yet there is still no tenancy.'

(Bright, *Landlord and Tenant Law in Context* (2007) Oxford:
Hart Publishing, p. 68)

▶ Discuss.

How to Read this Question

The aim of this question is to test your knowledge of the case law and your ability to analyse it in what is a straightfoward topic. It is therefore asking you to be creative and thoughtful in your use of that case law.

How to Answer this Question

❖ Essentially, this question is asking, what is a lease?

❖ Definition of a lease – *Street v Mountford* (1985); *Bruton v London and Quadrant Housing Trust* (2000); *Clear Channel UK v Manchester City Council* (2005).

❖ Time certain – *Lace v Chandler* (1944); *Prudential Assurance v London Residuary Body* (1992); *Berrisford v Mexfield Housing Association* (2011).

❖ Exclusive possession.

❖ Rent.

❖ Formalities: **ss 52** and **54** of the **Law of Property Act 1925**; **s 2** of the **Law of Property (Miscellaneous Provisions) Act 1989**; periodic tenancies; *Walsh v Lonsdale* (1882).

Up for Debate

Certain controversial cases such as *Bruton v London & Quadrant Housing Trust* and *Berrisford v Mexfield Housing Association* have been the subject of extensive academic commentary. It is important to think carefully about the overall implications of these decisions for the nature of the lease as an estate in land.

Applying the Law

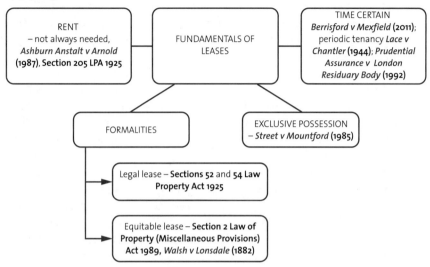

This diagram shows the fundamental features of leases.

ANSWER

By virtue of s1 of the **Law of Property Act 1925**, a term of years absolute in possession (or lease) is one of the two estates in land that may exist either at law or in equity. It is a concept of considerable versatility that can provide both occupation in a domestic context and premises for a commercial enterprise, as well as income for the freeholder and even the leaseholder if the premises are sub-let. It is a peculiar feature of the leasehold estate that it can give several different estate owners the use or enjoyment of the land or its profits at the same time.

According to *Street v Mountford* (1985), a lease can be defined as exclusive possession of property, for a term, at a rent. These three conditions are commonly regarded as the indicia of a leasehold. It is clear, however, from *Ashburn Anstalt v Arnold* (1989) (relying on s205 of the **LPA 1925**), that rent is not essential to the existence of a lease, although it will be a rare situation indeed in which the parties to a transaction have intended to be legally bound by the relationship of landlord and tenant but have not specified the payment of rent.

In addition to the principles established by *Street*, which are, in fact, conditions required by the common law, the nature of leases is also governed by various statutory provisions. These provisions are largely to be found in the **LPA 1925** and determine whether any particular lease is legal or equitable. Any lease for a period of more than three years must be by deed if it is to take effect as a legal estate (s52 of the **LPA**). Leases for three years or less that give the tenant an immediate right to occupy without the payment of an initial premium may also be legal (s54 of the **LPA**). Equitable leases, on the other hand, usually result from a binding contract between landlord and tenant that has not been put into effect by deed. If this contract is in writing (s2 of the **Law of Property (Miscellaneous**

Provisions) Act 1989) and is specifically enforceable, equity will regard the relationship between the parties as one governed by an equitable lease (*Walsh v Lonsdale* (1882)). The exception to this is an equitable lease arising out of proprietary estoppel. These can be completely oral and arise out of the inequitable conduct of the landlord (see *Taylor Fashions v Liverpool Victoria Trustees* (1982); *Thorner v Major* (2009)).

Turning, then, to the position at common law. The *Street* requirements define the inherent nature of a lease and set the parameters outside of which a lease simply cannot exist. The first is the requirement of 'time certain'. This means not only that the lease must start at a clearly defined moment, but also that the term granted must be certain. The lease must be of certain maximum duration at the commencement of the lease. In *Lace v Chandler* (1994), for example, a lease for the duration of the Second World War was held void as being of uncertain maximum duration. In recent years, the principle of time certain has been under attack and an important development occurred in *Berrisford v Mexfield Housing Association* (2012). In that case, the Supreme Court[1] confirmed that leases had to be of a certain duration (i.e. upholding *Prudential*). However, the Court went on to point out that, potentially uncertain leases given to *individuals* (but not companies) could be rendered certain by operation of law. This was because, first, a lease to an individual for an uncertain period could be interpreted at common law as a lease for their life (*Doe on the demise of Crake v Brown 172 E.R. 992*) and then, second, that leases for life are, by statute (**s149(6)** of the **LPA 1925**), converted to leases for 90 years, terminable by death. So, by a double step of reasoning, these uncertain leases to individuals are converted to maximum 90-year terms – they are 'certain' within the *Prudential* rule. Clearly, this will now 'save' many previously uncertain arrangements, but significantly not where the potential tenant is a company (as indeed many are). Note also, that provided that the overall duration of the term is certain, it need not be a single continuous term (e.g. *Cottage Holiday Associates Ltd v Customs and Excise Commissioners* (1983)). It often happens that a tenant may occupy premises and pay a regular sum to the landlord in respect of that occupation. There may well be no written record of this arrangement. In these circumstances, a tenancy of a certain duration will be presumed from the facts. Thus, if money is paid weekly in respect of a week's occupation, a periodic tenancy of one week will be presumed and, likewise, if payment is made monthly or quarterly. Although such a situation appears to be a lease for an uncertain period, in fact, it is a succession of periodic tenancies. These relatively short-term periodic tenancies are common in residential lettings and should not be thought to contradict the principle of time certain.

The other common law conditions for the existence of a lease are not as controversial. The concept of exclusive possession is notoriously elusive, as can be seen in the confused and confusing debate over the distinction between a lease and a licence. In essence, the existence of exclusive possession is a matter for the construction of the agreement between the parties in the light of their conduct in relation to the property (*Antoniades v Villiers* (1990); *AG Securities v Vaughan* (1990)). Thus, if the occupier has been granted the exclusive right to use the property then there is a strong presumption that the agreement amounts to a lease.

---

1   It is always good, where possible, to include information as to which court the case you are describing was decided in since it shows the strength of the authority on which you are relying.

The only exceptions to this are those cases identified by Lord Templeman in *Street*, in which, because of some special circumstances, exclusive possession may exist but a tenancy does not. An example is the service occupancy of *Norris v Checksfield* (1991), and cases in which the occupation is given as an act of generosity, friendship or charity, as in *Gray v Taylor* (1998).

Finally, we come to rent, the receipt of which is usually the main reason why the landlord has granted the tenancy in the first place. As noted above, under **s 205** of the **LPA**, it is clear that rent is not an essential requirement of a lease. In fact, the existence of rent as an adjunct to a lease is so likely that, in the absence of an express promise by the tenant, a covenant to pay rent can easily be implied from the words of a deed. Likewise, the absence of a rent obligation may mean that the parties have not intended to create any type of obligation at all (see *Javad v Aqil* (1991)). It is, however, a common misconception that rent has to be in monetary form. It can be in goods, services or payable in kind.[2] The only clear requirement is that the amount of rent must be capable of being rendered certain (e.g. *Bostock v Bryant* (1990)).

The defining features of the leasehold estate have been described above and reference to its versatility has been made. That relationship has many advantages, both for the landlord and the tenant and that is why it has survived the many statutory reforms of the law of real property in the twentieth century. Finally, mention must be made of the House of Lords' decision in *Bruton v London and Quadrant Housing Trust* (2000). In that case, it was suggested that 'a lease' could exist in favour of an occupier even though the 'landlord' did not actually have an estate in the land himself out of which to grant a lease (the landlord had a licence). This controversial view requires acceptance of the idea that not all 'leases' are really estates in the land after all, but may be personal to the original parties (a so-called 'non-proprietary lease'). Suffice it to say that this view has not been universally welcomed and remains suspect.

Common Pitfalls

Do not rely simply on *Street v Mountford* and textbook knowledge. Case law is everything in this area. Most students can write a basic answer to this question and if you want to stand out, case law can help you do this.

QUESTION 16

Are there any significant differences between the creation and the operation of legal, as opposed to equitable, leases and what are the effects of any such differences?

How to Read this Question

This question is asking you not just to compare legal and equitable leases, but to consider the significance of any similarities or differences that emerge.

2   This answer provides a nuanced account of the relevance and nature of rent in this area.

How to Answer this Question

- ❖ Sections 52 and 54 of the **Law of Property Act 1925** and periodic tenancies.
- ❖ Formalities for equitable leases: **s 2** of the **Law of Property (Miscellaneous Provisions) Act 1989** and *Walsh v Lonsdale* (1882).
- ❖ Legal and equitable leases in registered and unregistered land – different approaches.
- ❖ Leasehold covenants in pre-1996 leases – different rules for equitable leases.
- ❖ Creating easements – **s 62** of the **LPA 1925**.

Up for Debate

Following the signficant reforms introduced by the **Land Registration Act 2002**, there is a strong argument that what matters is not the legal or equitable status of a right, but whether it is registered or not. Consider whether the answer to this question supports or detracts from that idea, and what that tells us about the shape of modern property law.

Applying the Law

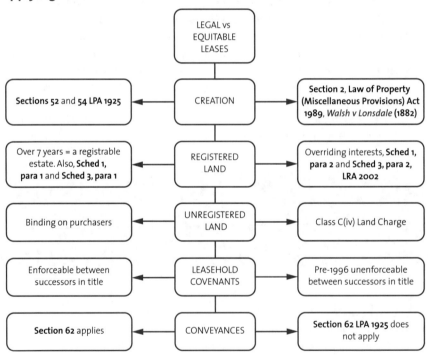

This diagram shows the difference between legal and equitable leases.

ANSWER

All legal leases except those that are exempt under **s 52(2) Law of Property Act 1925** must be created by deed. The exception granted by statute is for leases for three years or less, which entitle the tenant to go into immediate possession and which require only the payment of rent and not an initial lump sum. Thus, the periodic tenancy, whereby an occupier goes into occupation and pays a defined sum for a period usually of one week, one month or one quarter, will amount to a legal tenancy. It matters not that, in fact, the periodic tenant may occupy for many years because, in theory, this is just a succession of periodic tenancies. In fact, the provisions of ss 52 and 54 are relatively simple, but they tell us only how legal leases can be created. What of leases that take effect in equity only?

The practical reality is that many leases are created in the absence of a deed, but the majority of these are for three years or less and qualify as legal interests. It is unusual for a lease of over three years' duration to be created without the use of a deed. However, circumstances do arise where the parties do not proceed by deed. In such cases – that is, a lease of over three years not executed by deed – if there is a written contract the parties may be taken to have created an equitable lease. There are a number of distinct steps in this process. First, the contract between prospective landlord and tenant must be enforceable: namely, the contract must be in writing containing all the terms and signed by both parties: s 2 of the **Law of Property (Miscellaneous Provisions) Act 1989**. In this connection, 'written contract' means either a written document clearly expressed to be a contract or a written record of agreement that the law is prepared to treat as contract.

Second, this properly created contract must be specifically enforceable. If the contract is specifically enforceable, this means that it would be executed by order of a court and, because equity regards as done what ought to be done, the unexecuted but enforceable contract will be regarded as an equitable lease (*Walsh v Lonsdale* (1882)). A contract will be specifically enforceable if valuable consideration has been paid by the tenant, if damages for breach of contract would be an inadequate remedy and if the person seeking to enforce the contract has not behaved inequitably. Usually these three conditions are easily satisfied. Furthermore, *Walsh* makes it clear that, if in the circumstances there is a choice between a legal periodic tenancy and an equitable tenancy on the same terms as the proposed but defunct lease by deed, the equitable tenancy will take priority. So, for example, any intended covenants in the failed legal lease will take effect in the equitable lease.

It is plain to see, then, that the requirements for an equitable lease have changed somewhat since 1989, primarily because of the requirement of writing. There is, however, one small exception to this. It may still be possible to create a lease longer than three years entirely out of oral agreements provided that those oral agreements amount to a proprietary estoppel within the rules of *Taylor Fashions v Liverpool Victoria Trustees* (1982). So, if a landlord assures an occupier that they have a tenancy and the occupier relies on that to their detriment, an estoppel tenancy may well result (cf. *Orgee v Orgee* (1997)).[3] This will be equitable and, even if over three years without writing, will be enforceable against the landlord.

....

3   It is important when discussing estoppel to acknowledge that the remedy given by the court in response to the estoppel may not amount to what was promised since they will only do the minimum necessary to satisfy the equity in the instant case.

Despite the apparent ease with which an equitable lease can be created, it is clear that the parties to a legal lease do enjoy significant advantages. For example, in registered land, currently a legal lease for a period of seven years or more will be registered with its own title number. Even if it is not (say because someone has forgotten to register, as in *Barclays Bank v Zaroovabli* (1997)), the otherwise legal lease will (with only limited special exceptions) be an interest which overrides under **Scheds 1** and **3** to the **Land Registration Act (LRA) 2002** because the tenant is likely to be a person in 'actual occupation' of the land. Likewise, even in the absence of such occupation, short-term legal leases – that is, those for seven years or less – will similarly be protected under **para 1** of both Schedules. This means that a purchaser of registered land is going to be bound by the legal lease in all but the strangest circumstances.

Equitable leases can sometimes be difficult for a purchaser of the reversion to discover. Moreover, like all equitable interests, equitable leases are prima facie vulnerable to purchasers – that is, to purchasers of the freehold land over which the lease exists. In unregistered land, for example, the equitable tenant is required to register their interest as a Class C(iv) land charge under the **Land Charges Act 1972**. Should they fail to do so, the equitable tenancy is not binding on any purchaser of the reversion of a legal estate for money or money's worth (**s 4** of the **Land Charges Act**), (see *Hollington Brothers v Rhodes* (1951)). Moreover, if the equitable lease has resulted from proprietary estoppel, it is probably unregistrable as a land charge (cf. *Ives v High* (1967)). In that case, the old doctrine of notice comes into play and this is unsatisfactory for both the purchaser and the equitable tenant. In registered land, however, the position is more satisfactory, at least for the tenant. Whereas the equitable tenant may protect their interest by way of notice, they may rely on the alternative on **Scheds 1** and **3** to the **LRA 2002** to gain an interest which overrides as a person in actual occupation of the premises. It may be however that the purchaser is unaware of the equitable lease. In many situations, the fact of occupation (and, hence, the equitable lease) may well be obvious and the purchaser will be warned of the overriding interest. This situation is certainly aided by the two Schedules to the **LRA 2002** which remove the risk of apparently innocuous occupation of a small area protecting the entire plot and thus reverse the decision in *Ferrishurst Ltd v Wallcite Ltd* (1999), but this is not always going to be true especially with estoppel leases that can still be entirely oral (for example, see *Malory Enterprises Ltd v Cheshire Homes (UK) Ltd* (2002)).

Further difficulties with equitable leases also arise in the context of leasehold covenants, although these have been eliminated for leases granted on or after 1 January 1996 by the **Landlord and Tenant (Covenants) Act (LTCA) 1995**. So, for pre-1996 equitable leases, the general position is that although covenants in the lease will be enforceable between the original landlord and the original equitable tenant (because of privity of contract), they may well be unenforceable between successors in title to those persons. The traditional view is that there is no 'privity of estate' between a successor to the landlord and an assignee of the tenant. In fact, it is the landlord that suffers most in this situation because the burden of covenants entered into by the original tenant (that is, the obligation to perform them) may well not be passed to an assignee of an equitable lease, unless they can be enforced as restrictive covenants under *Tulk v Moxhay* (1848). Indeed, it is worse than this because the new equitable reversioner (the new landlord) is under the burdens of the equitable lease as these are statutorily transmitted on a sale of the reversion by **s142** of the **LPA**. Thus, the new landlord can be sued on the original covenants of an equitable lease, but unless *Tulk* applies, they cannot sue the new tenant. Fortunately, for equitable leases granted on or after 1 January 1996, the **LTCA 1995** ensures that both the benefits and burdens of leasehold covenants pass to both an assignee of the landlord and an assignee of the tenant.[4]

Ultimately, then, it is better for all parties if a legal lease is established. Not only is the very existence of the equitable lease dependent on the availability of specific performance, but its informal nature also poses problems for purchaser and tenant alike.

Common Pitfalls

There is more to this question that simply describing statutory formalities for the creation of legal or equitable leases, although that is a good place to start. Do not ignore the land registration issues as this is an important reason why legal and equitable leases have become almost identical effect in registered land.

QUESTION 17

'*Street v Mountford* creates a rule that the acid test for the existence of a tenancy is the presence of a grant of exclusive possession for a definite period of time, possibly but not necessarily involving rent.'

(Sparkes, *A New Landlord and Tenant* (2nd edn, 2001) Oxford: Hart Publishing, p. 150)

▶ Discuss.

How to Read this Question

The examiner here, in a similar way to the first question in this chapter, is asking you to consider the case law relating to a relatively straightfoward topic. This time however you must focus in on the impact of a specific case, *Street v Mountford*, without neglecting to show an overall knowledge of the issues raised.

How to Answer this Question

❖ The existence of rights versus the contractual intention of the parties.

❖ Lodgers and tenants.

❖ Cases where exclusive possession can exist without a tenancy: *Facchini v Bryson* (1952).

❖ Refining *Street v Mountford*: *Antoniades v Villiers* (1990); *Westminster CC v Clarke* (1992); *Bruton v London and Quadrant Housing Trust* (2000); *Kay v London Borough of Lambeth* (2004).

---

4 It is good to show that you are aware of the pre-1996 position in relation to leasehold covenants.

Up for Debate

There has been much case law attempting to determine the precise requirements of exclusive possession and time certain for the purposes of leases. It is worth considering whether the difficulty in pinning down these central concepts produces unsatisfactory uncertainty.

Applying the Law

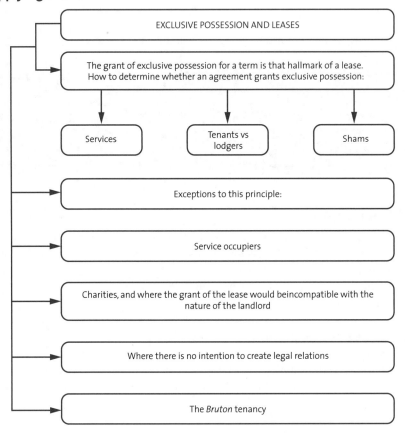

EXCLUSIVE POSSESSION AND LEASES

The grant of exclusive possession for a term is that hallmark of a lease. How to determine whether an agreement grants exclusive possession:

Services

Tenants vs lodgers

Shams

Exceptions to this principle:

Service occupiers

Charities, and where the grant of the lease would beincompatible with the nature of the landlord

Where there is no intention to create legal relations

The *Bruton* tenancy

This diagram demonstrates the importance of exclusive possession to leases.

ANSWER

A lease is properly regarded as a proprietary right, an interest in land capable of binding third parties (despite the unorthodox decision in *Bruton v London and Quadrant Housing Trust* (2000)). A licence is a personal right, usually arising out of contract, which as a matter of principle is not capable of binding third parties under property law principles (*Ashburn Anstalt v Arnold* (1989), confirmed in *Lloyd v Dugdale* (2002)). It is from this basic distinction that so many practical consequences flow. Indeed, the great majority of cases rests on the lease/licence distinction. The distinction between a lease and a licence forms the boundary between property and contract and will always be contentious.[5]

Lord Templeman's judgment in *Street v Mountford* (1985) (overruling the intention-based approach of *Somma v Hazlehurst* (1978)) caused something of a stir. Not only did he propound an abstract test for distinguishing between a lease and a licence ('exclusive possession for a term at a rent'), but he told us how to apply it. First, there are certain exceptional situations in which the occupier may (or may not) have exclusive possession of the property but, for special reasons, no tenancy will result. One example is where a mortgagee goes into possession under the terms of their mortgage and another where the occupation is based on charity or friendship, as in *Gray v Taylor* (1998), or where there is no intention to create legal relations between the owner and the occupier (cf. *Javad v Aqil* (1991)). These exempted categories were explained at length in *Facchini v Bryson* (1952) and that they are alive and well is demonstrated by *Norris v Checksfield* (1991).

Second, apart from the exceptional situations, according to Lord Templeman, an occupier must either be a lodger (a licensee) or a tenant. This practical distinction between a lodger and a tenant is crucial. A lodger is someone who receives attendance and services from the landlord. Such a person will be a licensee. However, if it is true that an occupier is either a lodger or a tenant, this means that no other kind of 'occupation licence' can exist. If someone is not a lodger, they are a tenant. There is no intermediate category of licensee. Obviously, this has far-reaching consequences, for it restricts the options open to a landlord when seeking to make use of their property. It is the triumph of property law over freedom of contract and it is precisely this that subsequent cases have found difficult to accept. Indeed, many of the apparently inconsistent decisions of the Court of Appeal have resulted from attempts to identify some middle way. *Hadjiloucas v Crean* (1998) and *Brooker Estates v Ayer* (1987), both decisions of the Court of Appeal quite soon after *Street*, are of this type.

Nevertheless, under the influence of Lord Templeman in the House of Lords (for example, *Antoniades v Villiers* (1990); *Westminster CC v Clarke* (1992)) and Lord Donaldson in the Court of Appeal (for example, *Aslan v Murphy* (1990)), a degree of certainty has emerged. First, cases of multiple occupancy may give rise to licences in favour of the occupiers because of the absence of the four unities necessary to support a joint tenancy of the whole premises. This is the result of *AG Securities v Vaughan* (1990). So, if four people occupy a four-bedroom house, but each signs different agreements, on different days and for a different rent, there can be no exclusive possession/joint tenancy because there is no unity of interest, title or time. The house, as a whole, cannot be held on a tenancy.

Second, there are certain types of public sector landlord who may be able to grant licences in circumstances in which a private landlord could not. Examples are *Westminster CC v Basson*

5 The introduction of this answer already shows the different approach that this essay will take when compared with question 17 which on its face is concerned with similar issues. There is cross-over, but the emphasis in the two answers is different.

(1991), *Ogwr BC v Dykes* (1989) and the House of Lords' decision in *Westminster CC v Clarke* (1992). In these cases, the licence is allowed not because of the intention of the landlord but because of a policy decision: namely, that public sector landlords must not be hindered in the exercise of their statutory housing duties.

Third, Lord Oliver in *Antoniades* suggests that there may be circumstances in which landlords can genuinely reserve to themselves the right to make use of the premises and, if such use is made, no exclusive possession is given. In effect, this is no more than a restatement of the distinction between exclusive possession and exclusive occupation. An example might be where an academic lets his house to students but reserves the right to enter the house and use his library. This is, of course, open to abuse and, in the light of his speech in *Antoniades*, it is doubtful whether Lord Templeman would agree that it is even a possibility.[6] However, the door has been left open by Lord Oliver for future development in genuine cases.

Fourth, in *Bruton v London and Quadrant Housing Trust*, a quasi-public sector manager of land (the Trust) was held by the House of Lords to have granted the plaintiff a valid lease to occupy, even though the Trust had no estate in the land. This is unusual as normally the absence of an estate in the landlord means, by definition, that the occupier cannot have an estate (a lease) but must have a licence. As noted, the Trust itself held only a licence to manage the land (granted to it by the local authority landowner) and argued that because it held no proprietary right, it could never have granted the plaintiff a tenancy. In rejecting this argument, the House of Lords said that a 'lease' was not always an estate in the land, but could be a merely personal arrangement between 'landlord' and 'tenant'. This decision and its reasoning have attracted some sharp criticism and it is not clear why this 'non-proprietary lease' is not properly identified as a licence! It means, however, that leases can exist even if the grantor has no estate in the land. Moreover, in the case of such a 'tenancy' although as between the original 'landlord' and 'tenant' it is binding, it will not be so on the original owner of the land (*Kay v London Borough of Lambeth* (2004); *London Borough of Islington v Green* (2005)).[7]

Finally, all of the above is subject to the doctrine of pretences. Any clause, in any agreement, will not be given legal effect if it is not intended to be relied on by either party to the agreement, but is merely inserted in it to avoid the grant of the tenancy that would otherwise arise. It should be noted in this regard, that the doctrine of 'pretences' has replaced that of shams: a 'sham' transaction is one in which only one party does not intend a clause in a lease to have legal effect and, of course, a landlord always intends in these cases to deny, by means of a clause like that used as in *Antoniades*, the creation of a lease.[8]

....

6 Discussing a potential conflict in the approach of different judges in the same case is a very good way of showing, first, that you have good knowledge of the case in question and, second, of highlighting an area of controversy.

7 The discussion of *Bruton* shows why this is such a divisive decision whilst still focusing on the question set rather than discussing the merits or otherwise of *Bruton* itself.

8 The clarification of the language used here is useful as it shows that the writer is aware of the way this issue has previously been discussed.

To conclude then, the case law after *Street* has finally taken a decidedly practical path[9] whereby the emphasis is on identifying those factual situations that can give rise to a licence and those that can give rise to a tenancy. This may not be the most intellectually satisfying approach – after all, we have not defined 'exclusive possession' – but it is the most realistic. The most serious reservation is the uncertainty caused by the House of Lords' decision in *Bruton v London and Quadrant*.

Common Pitfalls

Do not answer this question unless you have a reservoir of case law. It – or something like it – is a very common question on land law examinations and the best answers use a range of case law.

QUESTION 18

Rackman is the registered proprietor of freehold land comprising a large Victorian property in the centre of town. The house has four storeys, including a basement. Rackman has just inherited a small bungalow in the country and has decided to move out. He wishes to let the property, but is determined not to have long-term tenants just in case he wants to return to the city. He divides the house into two self-contained, one-bedroomed apartments on the first and second floors, and one self-contained two-bedroomed flat on the ground floor/basement. He agrees in writing with Harold and Matilda, a young unmarried couple, that they can occupy the two-bedroomed flat and produces two documents that state in each that 'this agreement does not intend to create a term of years'; he gets them to sign separately and on different days for a 'fee' of £90 per week each. He lets the first-floor flat to William, an apprentice carpenter, who is to carry out repairs to the premises. William pays no money, but each week £60 is deducted from his wages. Rackman keeps a key to William's flat, primarily to inspect the building works at the weekend when William is away. The top-floor flat is given to Rackman's daughter, Margaret, a university drop-out with nowhere else to go. Margaret is not the most reliable individual, so William is asked to keep an eye on her and to make sure that she gets regular meals.

Rackman has now decided to move to the country permanently and sells the entire premises to Edward, a property developer. Edward wishes to evict all the occupants and redevelop the site. Advise him.

How to Read this Question

The examiner is testing your ability to apply the law on the lease/licence distinction to a set of complex facts, and is therefore looking for you to show not only detailed knowledge of the rules, but also the ability to structure a response in a coherent way.

---

9 This conclusion in describing the route after *Street* as 'practical' not only summarises the law described, but also analyses it, assessing its merits.

How to Answer this Question
The question involves the application of the lease/licence distinction and the effect on a purchaser of the reversion.

❖ *Antoniades v Villiers* (1990).
❖ *Street v Mountford* (1985).
❖ *Mikeover v Brady* (1989) or *Aslan v Murphy* (1990).
❖ **Scheds 1** and **3** to the **Land Registration Act 2002**.

Answer Structure

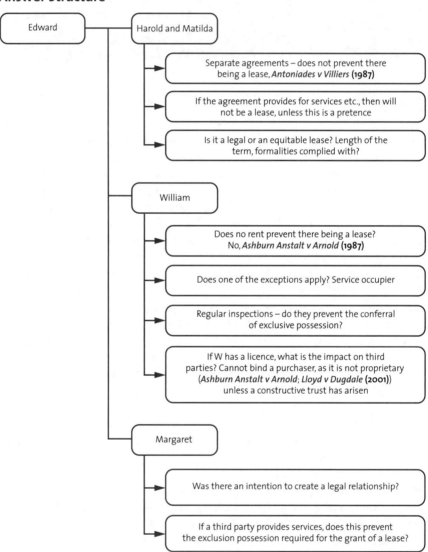

This diagram shows how to apply the lease/licence distinction to the situation involving Edward.

ANSWER

This problem concerns the distinction between a lease and a licence. If the arrangements entered into by Rackman with his respective occupiers amount to leases, then they have the ability to bind Edward the purchaser when he acquires the freehold title. If, however, the arrangements are properly to be regarded as licences, then, in principle, they cannot bind Edward and the occupiers will have to vacate the premises.

In general terms, the distinction between a lease and a licence was summarised by Lord Templeman in *Street v Mountford* (1985). A lease exists where an occupier has been granted exclusive possession of the property, for a term, at a rent. The answer is not to be found in the label attached to the agreement by the parties but in the nature of the agreement created by the parties. The main practical distinction resulting from Lord Templeman's formula is that an occupier must be either a tenant or a lodger, the latter being someone in receipt of attendance and services from the landlord and so without exclusive possession (*Markou v Da Silvaesa* (1986)). Finally, we must also be aware of the doctrine of pretences (see, for example, *Antoniades v Villiers* (1990)), whereby the court will examine an agreement between the parties to discover whether its terms genuinely reflect the actual relationship between the parties. Only if the agreement is 'genuine' in this sense will any clauses in the agreement affecting 'exclusive possession' be given legal effect.[10]

(a) Harold and Matilda[11]

Clearly, the agreement between Rackman, on the one hand, and Harold and Matilda, on the other, is designed to allow them to occupy the premises and, from Rackman's point of view, to prevent the grant of a tenancy. After *Street*, it is clear that it is the nature of the relationship that is important, not what the parties decide to call that relationship. Thus, if this agreement amounts to a lease under the Street formula, it will be a lease irrespective of the label attached to it.

Rackman has made every attempt to prevent the couple enjoying exclusive possession. He has, in fact, attempted to deny them a tenancy by seeking to grant each of them a separate licence whereby neither of them has exclusive possession of the whole (*Mikeover v Brady* (1989)). The only way that Harold and Matilda can refute this is to establish that they have been granted exclusive possession jointly. As was made clear in *AG Securities v Vaughan* (1990), for a joint tenancy of a leasehold estate to exist, the 'four unities' must be present: there must be unity of interest, title, possession and time. In this case, as in *Vaughan* itself, the landlord has persuaded the parties to sign different documents on different days. It looks as if there is no unity of time or of title. In *Vaughan*, these facts, plus the different rents paid by the occupiers, clearly meant that no leasehold joint tenancy of the whole property could exist. The parties were occupying separately, not jointly. Moreover, even if *Vaughan* is not quite in point, because, in that case, the property was always intended to be for independent, ever-changing, occupants, Rackman can clearly rely on the decision in *Mikeover v Brady*.

---

10 It is useful in a question like this to give an outline of the structure of the rules you are applying in the introduction.

11 Sub-headings are good in a problem question to help give clarity to an answer. It also helps to keep the answer on track in the exam.

Perhaps, however, there is one further possibility. In *Antoniades v Villiers*, the appellants were a young couple, living together as if married in a joint home. This fact was known to the landlord. In the House of Lords, this arrangement was held to create a joint tenancy of the leasehold estate, despite the fact of separate 'licence' agreements similar to those signed by Harold and Matilda. According to Lord Templeman, the landlord's attempt to deny the couple exclusive possession jointly was a pretence. As such, it would be ignored. If we follow *Antoniades*, then, and assuming Rackman knew that Harold and Matilda wished to live together, this agreement may still amount to a lease.

If the couple do have a lease, then it would appear to be equitable. The agreement is in writing (not by deed and not legal) and probably amounts to a specifically enforceable contract. Assuming this, equity will regard this as an equitable lease under *Walsh v Lonsdale* (1882). When the property is sold to Edward, presumably the couple are in actual occupation and would, therefore, have an overriding interest under **Scheds 1** or **3, para 2** to the **Land Registration Act 2002**. If the lease is not equitable, the arrangement may well amount to a legal periodic tenancy because of rent paid and accepted for the weekly term. If that were true, it would be overriding under **para 1** of the same two Schedules to the **LRA 2002** (*Barclays Bank v Zaroovabli* (1997), and contrast *Mortgage Business plc v Cook* (2012)). Of course, the lease is binding on Edward only according to its terms.

(b) William

William is in occupation of the first-floor flat and, again, the nature of his occupancy is crucial. Whether or not William has a tenancy may well depend on whether William's occupancy falls within one of the exceptional categories identified by Lord Templeman in *Street*. As a preliminary point, it might be thought that the apparent lack of rent destroys any chance of a tenancy. However, as confirmed in *Ashburn*, relying on **s 205** of the **Law of Property Act 1925**, the payment of rent is not essential for the existence of a tenancy. In any event, we can argue forcefully that the weekly deduction from William's wages does amount to rent. There is no rule that 'rent' must be described as such.

William's problem is, however, that his occupation seems to be a 'service occupancy'. He appears to be in occupation of the premises for 'the better performance of his duties' as Rackman's employee/builder. A bona fide service occupancy clearly creates a licence and was one of the original *Facchini* exceptions. That it still can occur has been confirmed in *Norris v Checksfield* (1991). Subject to the warning in that case that the court must be astute to detect 'pretences', as where the occupant is given minimal employment duties to make it appear as if there is a service occupancy, our case seems to fall into this category. If anything, William is more like a caretaker than a tenant. Assuming, then, that William has a licence by way of service occupancy Edward cannot be bound by the agreement (*Ashburn Anstalt v Arnold*; *Lloyd v Dugdale* (2002)).[12]

---

12 It is important to follow through the consequences of your conclusion – it is not enough here to establish that there is a licence and leave the matter there.

(c) Margaret

As far as Rackman's daughter, Margaret, is concerned, the circumstances also seem to give rise to a licence. There is every indication that Margaret's occupation of the top-floor flat can be put down to normal family considerations rather than the creation of a tenancy. As in *Heslop v Burns* (1974), this is not a situation in which the parties had an intention to enter into legal relations at all. This is within one of the *Facchini*-excepted categories: namely, occupation based on friendship, generosity or family arrangement (see also *Gray v Taylor* (1998)). Moreover, if this were not enough, Rackman could even argue that Margaret was a lodger and by definition not a tenant (*Street*). The facts suggest that Margaret is in receipt of attendance and services as provided by William, who may be regarded as Rackman's agent for these purposes. On this interpretation of the facts, Margaret could be within *Markou v Da Silvaesa* and a licensee by virtue of a genuine lodger relationship. Once again, as this is a licence there is no possibility of Edward being bound.

So, to conclude, with the possible exception of the arrangement agreed with Harold and Matilda, Rackman has successfully avoided granting any leases over his property. Edward can obtain vacant possession. Finally, we can note that Rackman would have been well advised to have granted short-term assured tenancies under the **Housing Act 1996**. These fall outside the Rent Acts and possession can be recovered easily. This would have avoided all the difficulties Rackman experienced.

Common Pitfalls

❖ As with the previous question, this is all about case law.
❖ In problem questions like this, it is important to allocate enough time to deal with all of the parties. Notice how the problem can be broken down into segments rather than being one long answer. This helps explanation and the examiner!

QUESTION 19

'The [**Landlord and Tenant (Covenants) Act 1995**] introduced a new code relating to the enforceability of covenants by landlords and tenants.'

(*Oceanic Village Ltd v United Attractions Ltd* (2000) per Neuberger J)

Were the defects in the law relating to the enforceability of leasehold covenants so serious as to justify the scheme introduced by the Act for leases granted after 31 December 1995?

How to Read this Question

This is a complex question as it contains both a quotation and a question. Nevertheless, the focus of your answer should be the question set, and the quotation is there to provide you with some material to work with.

How to Answer this Question

Consider the law before and after the **1995 Act** and assess whether the Act was needed and how successful it has been.

- ❖ Outline of rules applicable to pre-1996 leases and defects.
- ❖ Purpose of the **LTCA 1995**.
- ❖ Provisions of the **LTCA 1995** carrying these purposes into effect.
- ❖ Overall effect and assessment of the **LTCA 1995**.

Applying the Law

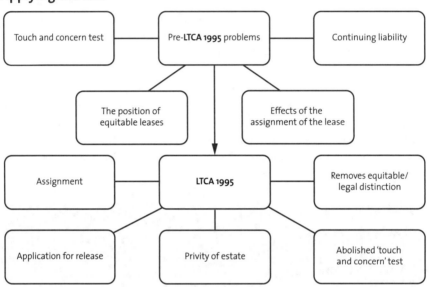

This diagram shows the problems of the pre-**Landlord and Tenant (Covenants) Act 1995** law and the solutions provided by that Act.

ANSWER

The **Landlord and Tenant (Covenants) Act 1995** governs the enforceability of leasehold covenants in leases granted after 31 December 1995. For leases granted prior to this, the 'old' rules apply. Consequently, there are currently two sets of distinct legal principles governing the enforceability of leasehold covenants and, by comparing them, we can discover whether the radical reforms of the **LTCA 1995** were really necessary.

For leases granted before 1 January 1996 (non-**LTCA** leases), the enforceability of leasehold covenants revolves around privity of contract, privity of estate and statutory magic. The original parties to a lease will be bound throughout the entirety of the term to perform the covenants they have agreed to. Thus, both the original landlord (*Stuart v Joy* (1904)) and the original tenant (*Arlesford Trading Co v Servansingh* (1971)) can be sued for failure to perform leasehold covenants irrespective of the time the breach was committed or by whom. This is the principle of continuing liability.

The second[13] major area of difficulty for earlier leases is the requirement that a covenant must 'touch and concern the land' (*Spencer's Case* (1583)) (and the equivalent under statute that it must have 'reference to the subject matter of the lease': **ss 141** and **142** of the **Law of Property Act 1925**), before it can bind successors in title. So, for pre-1996 leases, if privity of estate exists between plaintiff and defendant (that is, they are current landlord and tenant under a legal lease), the assignee of a tenant will acquire the benefit and burden of all those covenants that touch and concern the land (*Spencer's Case*). Likewise, the benefit and the burden of all of the original landlord's covenants will be passed to an assignee of the reversion if they have reference to the subject matter of the lease (**ss 141** and **142** of the **LPA**). Obviously, such a central concept for pre-1996 leases needs to be applied consistently and, if possible, have a core meaning. Despite the guidance provided by the House of Lords in *Swift Investments v Combined English Stores* (1989), it was considered that this was not the case.

Third, there are a number of other matters that attracted criticism and which still operate for pre-1996 leases. It is uncertain whether an assignee of the reversion is liable for breaches of covenants committed by the original landlord before assignment (although see *Celsteel v Alton* (1985)). Again, there is a certain inequality in the fact that landlords lose the right to sue on the covenants when they assign their reversion (*Re King* (1963)), but, according to *City and Metropolitan Properties v Greycroft* (1987), a tenant retains the right to sue the landlord after assigning the lease.

All of this, however, pales into insignificance in the light of the problems that arise when the pre-1996 lease is merely equitable or where a legal lease has been assigned only in equity (that is, not by deed: *Julian v Crago* (1992)). In such cases, although the original parties are bound to each other in contract, there can be no privity of estate between successors in title to those parties. This can cause serious difficulties. Thus, whereas **ss 141** and **142** of the **LPA 1925** operate to transfer the benefit of covenants and the burden of covenants respectively to the equitable assignee of the reversion (as they do with pre-1996 legal leases), the assignee of the equitable tenant does not come under the burden of the covenants due to lack of privity of estate. Thus, we reach the position under a pre-1996 equitable lease that an assignee of the tenant can sue an assignee of the landlord, but not vice versa.[14] Of course, there is some relief for the landlord by virtue of the fact that restrictive covenants may bind under the rule in *Tulk v Moxhay* (1848) and also that the landlord may have the remedy of forfeiture, but this does not address the underlying problem.

The principal provisions of the **1995 Act** then are as follows.[15] First, the Act is applicable both to legal and equitable tenancies granted on or after 1 January 1996 (**s 28(1)** of the **LTCA 1995**). Second, the tenant (whether original or an assignee) is released automatically from the

---

13 Clearly outlining the major problems with the old law will make it easier for the examiner to follow your analysis of the success of the solutions in the new law.

14 It is worth summing up the point briefly, as in this sentence, since it gives it more impact.

15 A summary of the main provisions introduced as a result of legislative reforms allows focus on the most important changes whilst also showing that you are aware of the more minor changes without taking up too much time.

burden of leasehold covenants when they assign the tenancy (s5), subject only to the possibility that they might be required to guarantee performance of the leasehold covenants by the next immediate assignee under an authorised guarantee agreement (AGA) (s16). The exception is for assignments made in breach of covenant or by operation law when the assigning tenant remains liable (s11(2)). Third, the landlord is not released automatically from the burdens of leasehold covenants, but may serve a notice on the tenant applying for release from covenants that have passed to an assignee (s6; *BHP Petroleum v Chesterfield Properties* (2002)), which release will be effective if the notice is not answered within a specified time or on the landlord's application to the county court (s8). A landlord assigning in breach of covenant or by operation of law cannot serve such a notice (s11(3)) (although see the potential effect on this of *London Diocesan Fund v Avonridge* (2005)). Fourth, the rule that covenants must 'touch and concern' the land or 'have reference to the subject matter of the lease' before the benefits and burdens can be passed to assignees of the lease or the reversion is abolished (ss2 and 3). Fifth, the benefit and burden of all leasehold covenants pass automatically to assignees of the lease and the reversion (s3). There is no need to show 'privity of estate' and ss141 and 142 are no longer applicable. There is automatic annexation of all leasehold covenants to the premises comprised in all leases and reversions. Only those covenants that are positively expressed to be personal will not pass to assignees. Sixth, as a counterbalance to the change in the original tenant's liability, the Act permits the landlord to *require* an assigning tenant to enter into an AGA to guarantee performance of the covenants by the person to whom he assigns – s16 LTCA 1995 and *K/S Victoria Street v House of Fraser (Stores Management) Ltd.* (2011). Seventh, an attempt to enforce liability for a 'fixed charge' against a person not in possession must comply with a 'problem notice' procedure. This requires the landlord to serve a notice on the person liable within six months of the charge becoming due. Following payment, this person may go back into the property as tenant under an 'overriding lease' and so attempt to recoup the payment by making use of the land or taking action against the actually defaulting tenant. Failure to serve such a notice within the proper time makes the charge unenforceable.

Clearly, the LTCA rules establish an entirely new system for the enforcement of leasehold covenants. One major feature is that the rights and liabilities of landlord and tenant should be coterminous with possession of the land and that the benefit and burden of all covenants should pass automatically. Likewise, the removal of the distinction between legal and equitable leases is greatly to be welcomed. Additionally, the landlord's position is preserved by the ability to require the assigning tenant to enter into an AGA. This is permissible only as a guarantee of the next immediate assignee (*Good Harvest Partnership LLP v Centaur Services Ltd.* (2010)), but, of course, if the obligation to enter an AGA is itself made a covenant of the lease, it will flow to all assigning tenants.

To conclude, then, there is no doubt that the LTCA has remedied the most serious deficiencies of the old law. Overall, however, there are still doubts about some aspects of the new system.[16] So, the removal of the distinction between 'proprietary' covenants (those that

....

16 This admission that the LTCA did not solve all the difficulties in the previous law brings balance and sophisticated analysis into the answer.

touch and concern) and personal covenants is thought by some to be unnecessary (but see *BHP Petroleum*). Also, even though landlords are not entitled to automatic release from covenants on assignment, two points should be noted. First, it will be rare for tenants to oppose such requests and probably rarer for a court to uphold any objection. Second, the decision in *Avonridge* – whereby a landlord who in the original lease has contractually limited its obligations to the period of his possession of the reversion does *not* actually have to serve a notice to be released because it is a matter of contract – seriously undercuts the idea behind the **LTCA 1995** that tenants should have greater protection. Finally, and most importantly, the AGA concept means the landlord retains another person to sue: the assigning tenant. In residential leases, the landlord cannot refuse to agree to an assignment to a new tenant on the grounds that the existing tenant will not enter an AGA on the landlord's terms unless this would be reasonable in all the circumstances. In commercial leases, however, the long-established obligation that consent to assignment cannot be withheld unreasonably has been abolished, as this was the price extracted by landlords' interest groups for not obstructing the Bill entirely in Parliament. It is a heavy price, for it gives commercial landlords full control over the land by allowing them to deny consent to assignment unless the tenant complies with onerous (and unreasonable) obligations.

Common Pitfalls

❖ This question calls for a comparison between pre-1996 rules and the **LTCA 1995**. It is focused more on the **LTCA 1995**, but do not forget to discuss the deficiencies in the law that it was meant to remedy.

❖ An answer should not be merely descriptive. This is a large topic and should not be attempted unless you have a thorough knowledge of the area and the ability to put it down on paper quickly.

QUESTION 20

(a) Harry is the registered proprietor of a large industrial site on the edge of Shortbridge. In 1992, he lets Unit 1 to Julian on a 21-year lease by deed containing covenants that Julian shall not use the premises for the purpose of the manufacture of household appliances, shall not assign or sub-let the property without Harry's consent, and shall carry out all reasonable external and internal repairs to the property. Seven years later, Julian assigns his interest, with Harry's consent, to Larry, a sporting equipment manufacturer. Larry's business suffers in the recession and he sub-lets to Keith, a manufacturer of portable air-conditioning units, without Harry's knowledge.

(b) Unit 2, title to which is unregistered, is let to Esmeralda on a ten-year lease by deed in 1995 for the purpose of establishing a restaurant on the site to service the estate during working hours. Esmeralda covenants not to open after 8 pm and to sell only beers manufactured by Harry in his brewery. In return, Harry covenants not to carry on any catering business elsewhere on the site. Unfortunately, Esmeralda develops a major alcohol problem and must leave the premises for the sake of her health. She assigns her lease in writing to Nathan, who finds that the only way to make a profit is to open until 11 pm and sell a wider range of beers. Meanwhile, Harry has sold the entire site to Peter, who starts to manufacture chocolate in Unit 3. Peter finds he can make quite a profit selling chocolate cakes to the site workers at lunchtime.

Peter has discovered about Keith and the roof of Unit 1 is leaking. The police are concerned about drunkenness on the estate at night and Nathan is about to sue for breach of covenant.

▶ **Advise the parties as to the enforceability of the covenants.**

How to Read the Question

This question is specifically asking you to consider the enforceability of the covenants, and you must do this, but that does not mean that you should neglect issues such as potential remedies consequent on such enforceability.

How to Answer this Question

- ❖ This is a pre-1996 lease – **LTCA** does not apply.
- ❖ Meaning of 'privity of estate' and the requirement of 'touching and concerning' – *Swift Investments v Combined English Stores* (1989).
- ❖ **Sections 141 and 142 of the LPA 1925.**
- ❖ *Spencer's Case* (1583) and *Re King* (1963).
- ❖ *Tulk v Moxhay* (1848).

Applying the Law

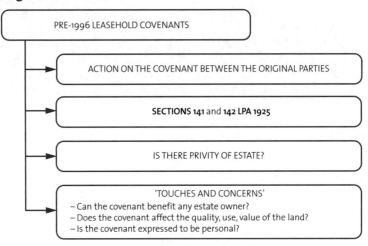

This diagram shows the rules relating to the transmissibility of pre-1996 leasehold covenants.

ANSWER

This question concerns the operation of the rules relating to the enforceability of lease-hold covenants. Importantly, because both leases in this problem were granted before 1 January 1996, the applicable law is the 'old' mix of common law and statute.[17]

---

17 Dates in problem questions are very important – make sure you check them carefully before answering.

On the facts, both the original landlord, Harry, and the original tenants, Julian and Esmeralda, have assigned their leasehold estates. Clearly, the original parties are bound to each other in contract to perform the covenants contained in their lease. Thus, in this problem, Harry can sue Julian, Harry can sue Larry and Larry can sue Harry in contract on all the covenants, whether or not they concern the land. This liability continues throughout the life of the contract, although due to the wording of s 141 of the **LPA 1925**, a landlord will not be able to sue the original tenant after he has parted with the land as that right is statutorily transferred to the new landlord (*Arlesford Trading Co v Servansingh* (1971)).

Of course, for practical purposes, the present landlord, Peter, will wish to enforce the leasehold covenants against the present tenants (and vice versa) and, in this respect, the issue turns on whether the benefit of the covenant (the right to sue on it) has passed to the plaintiff and the burden of the covenant (the obligation to perform it) has passed to the defendant. In simple terms, under pre-1996 law, both burden and benefit will have passed to successors in title of the original landlord and tenant so as to enable an action on the covenant if: (i) there is privity of estate between the parties; and (ii) the covenant touches and concerns the land. In the case of the landlord, these common law conditions are now replicated in slightly modified form in **ss 141** and **142** of the **LPA 1925**.

Before we consider the particular facts in detail, it is wise to determine, as a matter of principle, whether these covenants 'touch and concern' the land. The requirements for determining whether a covenant does 'touch and concern' have been re-stated by the House of Lords in *Swift Investments v Combined English Stores* (1989), namely, whether the covenant could benefit any estate owner as opposed to the particular original covenantee; whether the covenant affected the nature, quality, mode of use or value of the land; and whether the covenant was expressed to be personal.

In our problem, there are six covenants in all.[18]

(i)   The covenant by Julian that the premises shall not be used for the manufacture of household appliances. This is a covenant restrictive of the user of premises and prima facie touches and concerns the land (see, for example, *Williams v Earle* (1868)).
(ii) The covenant by Julian not to assign or sub-let without consent – clearly acceptable, as in *Goldstein v Sanders* (1915).
(iii) The covenant by Julian to undertake all reasonable repairs – clearly acceptable, as in *Martyn v Clue* (1852).
(iv) The covenant by Esmeralda not to open after 8 pm. Although, at first sight, this may seem to be a merely personal covenant, it is clear that it is intended for the benefit of other units on the site. It is not for Harry's personal benefit and does affect the mode of use of the land within the *Swift* formula. It seems to touch and concern.
(v)   The covenant by Esmeralda to buy beer only from Harry – this also touches and concerns the land and is identical to the covenant in *Clegg v Hands* (1890).

....
18 This is a good way to structure questions like this where you need to look at similar law in relation to a variety of fact circumstances.

(vi) The covenant by Harry not to open a catering business. Once again, this covenant affects the mode of use of land and is intended to benefit land granted by him. It is an anti-competition covenant and is also a 'touching and concerning' covenant.[19]

In result, then, all these covenants touch and concern the land.

(a) Unit 1

It is necessary, in respect of Unit 1, to determine a number of issues. First, which parties are within 'privity of estate'? It is only between these parties that 'touching' covenants can run under the pre-1996 leasehold rules. 'Privity of estate' exists where there is a relationship of landlord and tenant under a legal lease. In our case, Peter is in privity of estate with Larry. There is no privity of estate between Peter and Keith because Keith is a sub-tenant. So, presumptively, Peter can sue Larry.

Second, does Peter have the right to sue on the covenants made by Julian to Harry after he (Peter) purchases the reversion: has the benefit run to him? Under s141 of the **LPA 1925**, the benefit of every covenant 'having reference to the subject matter' of the lease is attached to the reversion and passes with it. So, Peter has the right to sue any person with whom he is in privity of estate (Larry) and who is subject to the burden of the covenant. Third, to whom has the burden run? The position here is again clear, following Spencer's Case, that 'touching' covenants are binding on a successor in title to the original tenant in favour of anyone with whom they are in privity of estate. Again, this is Larry.

So, as far as Unit 1 is concerned, Peter can sue Larry on all three covenants if they have been breached. Larry is liable throughout his term, and it is immaterial that the breach in relation to the manufacture of household appliances was actually committed by his own tenant.

Finally, we should also note that, even though Keith and Peter do not share privity of estate, Peter may well be able to enforce any restrictive covenants against Keith under the rule in *Tulk v Moxhay* (1848). Under *Tulk*, restrictive covenants can be enforced against any occupier provided that the person (here, the sub-tenant) has notice of the covenants (unregistered land) or is within s23(1)(a) of the **Land Registration Act 2002** (registered land), which appears to make such covenants automatically binding on a sub-tenant. Also, if Peter is able to utilise the remedy of forfeiture and thereby terminate Larry's lease because of his breaches, the sub-tenancy will also be terminated (*Shiloh Spinners v Harding* (1973)), subject to any claim for relief from forfeiture by Keith.

(b) Unit 2

As above, there is no doubt that Peter, as purchaser, has the benefit of the covenants made to Harry: this is the effect of s141(1) of the **Law of Property Act 1925**. Correspondingly, however, Peter also has the burden of any covenants made by Harry, such as the covenant not to carry on any catering business on the site. This is the effect of s142(1) of the **LPA**. Thus, Peter can sue Esmeralda on the covenants not to open after 8 pm and not

---

19 In these circumstances the majority are determined according to existing case law. This shows the importance of being aware of a range of case law examples.

to sell beer other than the landlord's and Esmeralda's liability continues for the term of the lease even though in fact the breach is committed by Nathan. If Peter does sue Esmeralda, this will not trigger the problem notice procedure under s17 of the **LTCA 1995** because the claim is not for a fixed charge. Likewise, Esmeralda can sue Peter on the covenant to prevent breach of the covenant against catering if as a matter of construction it has been breached. Of course, however, if possible, both the new landlord and the new tenant will wish to secure a direct remedy against the person actually acting in breach.

In this respect, there are some difficulties. For Peter to sue Nathan, the burdens of the covenant must have passed to Nathan. However, even though the original lease is by deed (and, hence, legal), the assignment is only in writing. It is not, therefore, correctly assigned (s52(1) of the **LPA**) and cannot take effect as a legal assignment. Following *Purchase v Lichfield Brewery* (1915), this equitable assignment of a legal lease cannot pass the burdens to Nathan. In essence, there is no privity of the legal estate. However as both of the covenants affecting Nathan's land are restrictive and, given that Nathan should have seen the original lease before taking an assignment of it, he will have notice of the covenants contained therein, and therefore these covenants will be binding under *Tulk*.

The position in respect of Nathan's attempt to sue Peter is not so complicated. We have seen above that Peter is affected by the burden of the covenant made by Harry and there is good reason to suppose that Nathan may well be entitled to the benefit of it. Although the right to sue cannot exist because of lack of privity of estate, it is possible that, as a matter of contract, the benefit of the covenant will have been assigned to Nathan when he purchased the lease. This is a matter of construction of the assignment from Esmeralda. If that were the case, Nathan could sue Peter on this covenant.

Common Pitfalls

❖ Do not write one long answer. The question has to be divided into smaller parts so as to make the answer clearer.

❖ Do not import **LTCA** rules into a pre-1996 problem question.

QUESTION 21

Assess critically the remedies available to landlords for breach of covenant by their tenants. What factors may influence a landlord when deciding which remedy to pursue?

How to Read this Question

The examiner here is asking you to do two things: first, you must assess what remedies are avilable to a landlord; and then, second, you must demonstrate that you are aware of and able to analyse the relative merits of each from the landlord's perspective.

How to Answer this Question

❖ Explain and analyse the various remedies.

❖ Law Commission proposals for forfeiture and distress.

❖   Forfeiture – **s146** of the **LPA 1925**.

❖   Injunction.

❖   Distress.

❖   Action for arrears of rent.

❖   Action for damages.

Up for Debate

The new CRAR scheme, which replaced the remedy of distress from 6 April 2014, applies to commerical leases only. For domestic leases there is now no remedy in the nature of distress. It is worth considering the reasoning behind the abolition and the impacts that this will have on both landlord and tenant.

Applying the Law

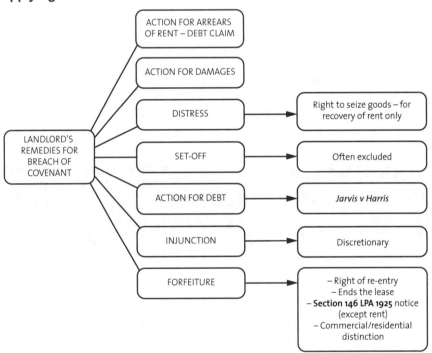

This diagram shows the landlord's remedies for breach of a leasehold covenant.

ANSWER

One of the great advantages of the leasehold estate is that it allows two or more persons to use and enjoy property at the same time. It is, of course, essential if this is to function that all parties are able to preserve the value of their respective interests in the property. This is the purpose of covenants in leases.

From the landlord's point of view, they will wish to ensure that the value of the property and its marketability as an income-generating asset is preserved.[20] Thus, there may be covenants restricting the uses of the premises by the tenant, obliging the tenant to keep the premises in repair, requiring the landlord's consent before any assignment or sub-lease is undertaken and, of course, obliging the tenant to pay rent. The landlord's remedy for breach of covenant by the tenant may well depend on the particular type of covenant that has in fact been broken. In many cases, for example, the landlord will be content to secure performance of the covenant, as with repairing covenants, or simply the payment of outstanding rent. In others, the covenant broken may be so fundamental, or the breach so serious, as to suggest to the landlord that he should end the lease, thereby ridding themselves of an unreliable tenant.

By far the most powerful weapon in the armoury of the landlord in the event of a breach of covenant is the remedy of forfeiture. A successful forfeiture of the lease effectively brings the lease to an end. The right of the landlord to forfeit the lease is strictly controlled by statute.

In general terms, in order for forfeiture to be available the lease must contain a right of re-entry. This is a stipulation that the landlord is entitled to re-enter the premises should the tenant fail to observe their covenants. All professionally drafted leases will contain such a right and one will be implied in all equitable leases (*Shiloh Spinners v Harding* (1973)). Subject to what will be said below, the existence of a right of re-entry gives the landlord two potential paths to a successful forfeiture. First, the landlord may physically re-enter the property by obtaining actual possession. Second, and more frequently, a landlord may seek to exercise his right of re-entry through an action for possession in the courts. At one time, a landlord had a free choice about which path to take, but this is now modified by statute, mainly to protect the tenant from an overzealous landlord using unrestricted force. Thus, a right of re-entry under a residential lease 'while any person is lawfully residing in the premises' must take place through court action (**s 2** of the **Protection from Eviction Act 1977**). Any attempt to physically re-enter will result in criminal liability. Likewise, even if the lease is non-residential (or otherwise outside the scope of **s 2**), it is only peaceful physical re-entry that is permitted.

That, however, is not the end of the statutory code relating to forfeiture. In all cases in which the landlord is seeking to forfeit because of a breach of a covenant, other than a breach of a covenant to pay rent, the procedure specified in **s 146** of the **Law of Property Act 1925** must be strictly followed. **Section 146** requires a landlord to serve a notice on the tenant specifying the breach of covenant of which complaint is made, requesting compensation, if desired, advising the tenant of their rights under the **Leasehold Property (Repairs) Act 1938**, if appropriate, and requesting that the covenant is remedied, if that is possible. If the covenant is capable of remedy (see *Expert Clothing v Hillgate House* (1986)), the landlord must give the tenant a reasonable time to make amends. Only if the covenant cannot be remedied can the landlord proceed to forfeit with reasonable speed. Even then, however, the landlord's remedy is controlled. If the landlord decides to proceed by way of court action, it is clear that the tenant has a right to relief from forfeiture under **s 146(2)** of the **LPA**. This will be granted

---

20 It is a good approach to tie your analysis of the shape of the legal rules to their commercial or practical purpose.

if the tenant has performed the covenants or the court considers that it would be just and reasonable to allow the lease to survive despite the breaches of covenant (see *Shiloh Spinners v Harding*). Likewise, it is now clear after the House of Lords' decision in *Billson v Residential Apartments* (1992) that, even if the landlord proceeds to forfeit by physical re-entry, the tenant can still apply to the court for relief under **s 146(2)**.

Forfeiture for breach of the covenant to pay rent is also controlled. In essence, the landlord must make a formal demand for rent, unless this is excluded by the express terms of the lease or by statute, as where more than six months is in arrears and 'distress' (see below) would be inadequate (**s 210** of the **Common Law Procedure Act 1852**). Additionally, in the case of certain 'long' leases – that is, over 21 years – of a dwelling, certain additional safeguards exist for tenants (**ss 166** and **167** of the **CLPA**). After this, in both county court and High Court, the tenant has a statutory right to have proceedings stayed by payment of rent interests and costs up to a specified time before the hearing date, although, in the High Court, this right arises only if six months' rent is in arrears. However, the High Court has an inherent jurisdiction to grant relief for forfeiture if less than six months is owing and payment is rendered before trial, and may grant relief subsequent to a possession order (or physical re-entry: *Howard v Fanshawe* (1895)), if the tenant pays within six months and probably longer in exceptional cases (*Di Palma v Victoria Square Property* (1984)). In the county court, there is a statutory right to relief if payment is made within four weeks of a possession order and the court has a discretion to grant relief up to six months after possession is obtained (**s 138(3)**, **(9A)** of the **County Courts Act 1984** – see, for example, *Maryland Estates v Joseph* (1998)). The rationale behind these generous provisions is, of course, that the landlord has let the premises in order to generate income and should not be entitled to bring that arrangement to an end when that income is paid.[21]

Indeed, taking all cases of forfeiture together, it is clear that the remedy may well be the most powerful in result, but it is also the one that the courts control most closely.

The remedy of distress used to allow a landlord to seize certain of the tenant's goods present on the property and sell them for the purpose of realising the arrears of rent. It was a remedy for non-payment of rent pure and simple and could not be used in respect of breaches of any other covenant. It was, however, bounded by traditional and often confusing common law conditions and was seen as both complex and harsh for the tenant. For this reason the Law Commission proposed abolishing the remedy. This was enacted in **Part 3** of the **Tribunals, Courts and Enforcement Act 2007** which came into force 6 April 2014. In respect of leases of commercial premises only, the **2007 Act** introduces a statutory scheme – the CRAR scheme – for recovering rent arrears without resort to the courts as a replacement for distress. As noted, it applies only to leases of commercial premises (and never to oral leases of any type of premises) and is, in effect, distress in all but name.

Finally, for covenants other than the covenant to pay rent, there remain two other possible remedies. First, the landlord may sue for damages for breach of covenant. Second, it may be

---

21 This analysis continues the approach earlier of looking at the rules in the light of their commercial reality.

possible for a landlord to obtain an injunction to prevent continued breach of a restrictive covenant under the rules of *Tulk v Moxhay* (1848). In reality, this is just an example of the general rule that equity may intervene to restrain conduct that is contrary to explicitly undertaken obligations. Furthermore, until recently, it was thought that the landlord could not obtain the remedy of specific performance to compel the tenant to perform a covenant to repair. This was thought to be established in *Hill v Barclay* (1810), despite dicta to the contrary in *SEDAC v Tanner* (1982). However, in *Rainbow Estates v Tokenhold* (1999), the judge held that specific performance of a tenant's covenant could be ordered in special circumstances, particularly where the court could supervise the order. This remains a controversial decision and it is unclear what 'special circumstances' justify this unusual step. Nevertheless, it may mark a change in the attitude of the courts when faced with persistent breaches of covenant by a tenant well capable of performing their obligations.

It is indeed true, then, that there is a range of remedies available to the landlord in the event of breach of covenant by the tenant and that the choice of these remedies will depend ultimately on the type of covenant that has been breached and the purpose of the landlord in seeking to enforce it. If the landlord merely wishes to recover rent, there is a range of actions. If, however, the aim is to terminate the tenancy and recover possession, the remedy of forfeiture is available albeit subject to many restrictions. In essence, it will only be available to a landlord when the tenant has behaved in such disregard of the leasehold covenants that they have effectively taken themselves outside the landlord and tenant relationship.

Common Pitfalls

Very recent changes in the law may not be reflected in all the literature. It is important to be aware of these changes and to read older material with the new law in mind.

QUESTION 22

Lyus is the registered proprietor of a dockside warehouse. In 1995, he subdivides the warehouse into two distinct units. The same year, he lets Plot A on a 30-year lease by deed to Tom, an importer of car-tuning kits. Tom covenants not to use the premises for any manufacturing process and to provide Lyus with three free kits each Christmas. Lyus promises 'to maintain in good repair the Premises comprised within Plot A'. In 1996, Tom assigns his lease to Ophelia and she begins to make motorcycle exhaust systems. She continues to store some tuning kits, having purchased Tom's excess stock. In 1997, Ophelia allows her son Jordan, to take over the premises, acknowledging his assumption of the tenancy in a written agreement. Jordan disposes of all the tuning kits and begins large-scale manufacture of motor-cycle exhaust systems. The same year, Lyus assigns his reversion to Ali.

Plot B is let for ten years in 2000 to Charlie, an importer of motorcycle frames. Charlie covenants not to use the premises for any manufacturing process and to supply Lyus with four frames each Christmas. Lyus agrees an identical repairing covenant relating to Plot B to that agreed with Tom concerning Plot A. In January 2001, Charlie is made an offer for his business and assigns his lease to Zoom Ltd. Zoom Ltd use Jordan's exhaust systems in the assembly of motorcycles and no longer import completed machines. In February 2001, Lyus assigns his reversion to Nigel.

Jordan now complains to Ali that the guttering around the building is defective. Zoom Ltd also complains. Ali and Nigel come to you for advice about their leasehold obligations and rights.

How to Read this Question

This question is asking you to apply two different legal regimes to the facts and so you have to be very careful to divide up the issues correctly.

How to Answer this Question

- ❖ Pre-1996 leases and the enforceability of covenants – privity of estate; touching and concerning ss 141 and 142 of the **LPA 1925**.
- ❖ Legal and equitable pre-1996 leases.
- ❖ Leases falling within the **LTCA** – automatic passing of benefit and burdens, personal covenants, no distinction between legal and equitable lease.

Answer Structure

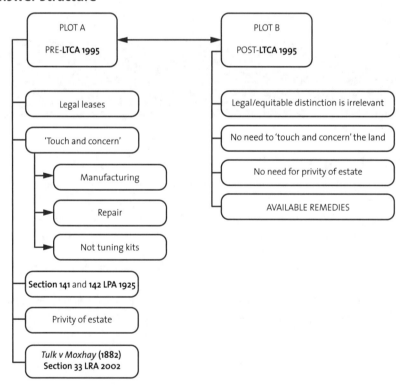

This diagram demonstrates how to apply the pre- and post-**Landlord and Tenant (Covenants) Act 1995** rules to plots A and B.

ANSWER

This problem concerns the enforceability of leasehold covenants between landlords and tenants, and their successors in title, of two separate properties. Importantly, one lease (that of Plot A) is granted before 1 January 1996 and so the covenants are governed by a mix of statute and common law. The second lease, that of Plot B, is granted in 2000 after the coming into force of the **Landlord and Tenant (Covenants) Act 1995** and so falls to be dealt with under this statutory regime.[22]

(a) Plot A

Being a lease governed by pre-**LTCA** principles, the enforceability of covenants is determined by common law principles overlaid by some statutory modifications. The 30-year lease granted by Lyus (L) to Tom (T) is executed by deed. It is therefore a legal lease, which we can assume is registered under the **Land Registration Act 2002** with its own title number. If it were not so registered, it would take effect only as an equitable lease (see *Brown and Root v Sun Alliance* (1996)).

The lease contains three covenants. Two of them – the tenant's covenant prohibiting manufacturing and the landlord's repairing covenant – are clearly proprietary; that is, they 'touch and concern' within the test laid down by Lord Oliver in *Swift Investments v Combined English Stores* (1989). Consequently, they have the potential to run with the land. The third covenant – T's covenant to provide L with tuning kits – is certainly personal in nature and so, for pre-1996 leases, cannot run to any assignee of the tenant: *Spencer's Case* (1583). Consequently, although Ali may have been given the benefit of this personal covenant by contract when he purchased the reversion (because the benefit of contracts/ covenants can be personally assigned), only T (the original tenant) is liable on it.

The remaining two covenants present a different picture. It is possible for the benefit and burden of these two proprietary covenants to pass to assignees of the reversion and the lease in appropriate circumstances. Taking Ali first, we are not told whether the assignment of the reversion to him is by deed or merely in writing. However, although the 'legal' status of his reversion can be maintained only if the assignment is made by deed (*Julian v Crago* (1992)) and he is subsequently registered as proprietor, this does not matter as far as the running of the covenants is concerned. By virtue of **ss 141** and **142** of the **LPA 1925**, the benefit and burden respectively of proprietary leasehold covenants pass to an assignee of the landlord. Thus, we know that Ali may enforce the covenant against manufacture and is potentially liable on the repairing covenant. But whom may he sue, and who may sue him?[23]

Clearly, the original tenant (T) remains liable throughout the entire term of the lease. So, Ali may well wish to sue Tom in damages for breach of the manufacturing covenant if no other remedy is available. Obviously, however, Ali would prefer a remedy against the

22 As with an earlier problem in this chapter, this question shows the crucial importance of dates to problem questions.
23 This hypothetical question is a good way to set up the structure of the ensuing discussion.

person committing the breach. In respect of Ophelia, we are not told whether Tom's assignment to her was by deed. This is critical as the burden of this covenant can run to Ophelia only if she was in privity of estate with Ali and privity of estate depends on the existence of a legal lease (and, hence, an assignment by deed and registration if applicable): *Spencer's Case*; *Julian v Crago*; *Brown and Root*.[24] If such privity existed, Ophelia can be held liable in damages to Ali for the period for which she was in possession under the lease. If the lease is equitable, no such claim arises and Ophelia cannot be liable (*Purchase v Lichfield Brewery* (1915)).

Again, however, damages may not be adequate for Ali. This is difficult as it is clear that Jordan is in possession of the property under an assignment from Ophelia that is merely equitable. Fortunately, however, Ali may be able to rely on *Tulk v Moxhay* (1848). A proprietary restrictive covenant (as here) can be enforced against any person in possession of the land (for example, an equitable tenant, or sub-tenant or squatter) if that person has 'notice' of the covenant. In registered land, which this is, the bindingness of the restrictive covenant on these occupiers is assured by virtue of s 23 of the **LRA 1925** and s 33 of the **LRA 2002**. So, it is possible for Ali to obtain an injunction against Jordan preventing the manufacture of exhaust systems (*Hall v Ewin* (1887)).

Finally, we must determine whether any person has the right to sue Ali on the repairing covenant. In principle, Tom could have maintained a remedy provided that he has not assigned the benefit of the covenant, but not only is it implausible that Tom would wish to sue, he almost certainly has assigned the benefit. Consequently, Ophelia would have enjoyed the benefit of the repairing covenant. Again, however, Ophelia cannot obtain anything other than damages for the loss suffered by her while she was in possession and these are likely to be nominal. That leaves Jordan. As we know, Jordan is an equitable tenant and cannot rely on the 'privity' rules. Again, however, if Ophelia has assigned the benefit of the covenant to Jordan expressly, Jordan may sue Ali. The matter is doubtful as we are told that Ophelia 'acknowledges' Jordan's assumption of the tenancy. All then turns on whether this acknowledgement expressly or impliedly passes the benefit of the repairing covenant. If it does, we must advise Ali that his attempt to obtain an injunction in respect of the manufacturing process may be met with a counter-plea for damages for lack of repair.

(b) Plot B

The enforceability of the three leasehold covenants in respect of Plot B raises similar issues, save that being contained in a lease granted on or after 1 January 1996, the **Landlord and Tenant (Covenants) Act 1995** is applicable. Consequently, some points of importance can be made. First, it matters not whether the leases are legal or equitable. Under the Act, the enforceability of leasehold covenants does not depend on the quality of the lease in which they are contained (s 28(1) of the **LTCA 1995**). Second, all leasehold covenants will run to assignees of the reversion and the lease irrespective of whether they 'touch and concern' or 'have reference to the subject matter of the lease' provided that

---

24 The listing of cases here is a quick way to gain marks in showing knowledge of the case law.

they are not expressed to be personal (**ss 2** and **3** of the **LTCA**). Third, by force of statute, the benefits and burdens of the leasehold covenants pass to assignees. Fourth, the original tenant is released from liability on assignment, subject only to the possibility of being required to guarantee their assignee under an authorised guarantee agreement (**ss 5** and **16** of the **LTCA**). The original landlord is not released automatically, although can request the court to grant such release if the tenant objects on receiving a notice to that effect (**ss 6** and **8** of the **LTCA** and *BHP Petroleum v Chesterfield Properties* (2002)).

So, with these general principles in mind, who is liable to whom and for what under the covenants for Plot B? Clearly, Charlie, the original tenant, is not liable under any of the covenants. He has assigned to Zoom Ltd and there is no suggestion that Lyus extracted an AGA prior to such assignment. Charlie is statutorily released from liability although he cannot enforce any covenants, having gone out of possession (**s 5** of the **LTCA**). However, as Zoom is an assignee of the tenant, and as no covenant is expressed to be personal, it is clear that Zoom is subject to the burden of both covenants (not to manufacture, to provide frames) and enjoys the benefit of the repairing covenant. This is the effect of the **LTCA** irrespective of whether the lease is legal or equitable: the benefits and burdens have passed automatically (**ss 3** and **28** of the **LTCA**). Consequently, we now need to know whom Zoom can sue, and who can sue Zoom.

In principle, Lyus has not escaped liability under the repairing covenant merely by assigning to Nigel. For landlords, the **LTCA** does not provide for automatic release (**s 6**) and we have no suggestion here that Lyus has served a notice requesting such release (**s 8**). However, unless Nigel (L's assignee) is in some way unable to perform the repairing covenant or cannot pay damages, there is no reason for Zoom to sue Lyus. This is simply because Nigel, as assignee, is liable on the repairing covenant under **LTCA**. The burden has passed to him automatically (**s 3**). Similarly, Nigel may also rely on the **LTCA** to pass to him the benefit of both the 'no manufacture' covenant and the covenant to provide frames (**s 3**). Nigel may seek an injunction against Zoom in respect of the former (assuming 'assembling' counts as 'manufacture') and may seek damages or maybe even specific performance for breach of the latter.

Common Pitfalls

❖ Do not attempt this unless you know both sets of rules – pre-1996 and **LTCA** 1995. Examiners do not give extra credit for a great answer on one part of the question and no answer on the next part.

❖ Ensure that you relate the answer to the specific facts of the problem. Do not write generally, but deal with the facts as given.

❖ Do not ignore your statute book. An examiner will not look kindly on misquoting the **LTCA** if you have a copy in front of you.

6 Licences and Proprietary Estoppel

INTRODUCTION

There is no necessary reason why the law of licences and the law of proprietary estoppel should be considered together, but this is a pattern followed in many textbooks and they commonly arise together in problem questions. 'Licences' are one way in which a person may enjoy some right or privilege over the land of another person and many of the issues in this area concern the theoretical and practical distinction between 'licences' and other types of right over land, such as leases and easements. 'Proprietary estoppel', on the other hand, is a method for the creation of rights over land. Viewed in this way, proprietary estoppel is a mechanism that may give rise to licences, easements, leases or any other kind of right connected with the use and enjoyment of land and should be considered as a doctrine in its own right. However, many situations where proprietary estoppel might be applicable arise out of circumstances where the claimant previously had merely a licence over the defendant's land, although there are of course many examples of proprietary estoppel in which the parties previously stood in no prior relationship at all. This chapter will follow the conventional pattern and consider first the law of licences, and then the scope and purpose of the doctrine of proprietary estoppel.

Licences then, involve permission from the owner of land, given to another, to use that land for some purpose. This can be to do anything from attending a cinema, parking a car or occupying premises, to erecting an advertising hoarding. The range of activities that can be covered by a licence are, indeed, virtually limitless and we have already explored this issue in one respect when considering the distinction between 'leases' and occupation licences. Crucially, the orthodox (and correct) view of licences is that they are not proprietary in nature: in other words, they are not interests in land, but rather personal rights over land. As a consequence, a licence can be enforced only against the person who created it. It does not 'run' with the land and, *unlike* easements and restrictive covenants, cannot be enforced against a purchaser of the land over which the licence exists. The licence is a matter of contract, not property law. In the 1970s, this basic point was challenged (although it has been reaffirmed a number of times: *Lloyd v Dugdale* (2002)) and many examination questions still ask students to analyse whether the status of licences has changed over the years. In dealing with both problem and essay questions on licences, students will need to have a firm grasp of what it means to say that something is an 'interest in land'. Case law is particularly important.

Proprietary estoppel is the name given to a doctrine or set of principles whereby an owner of land may be held to have conferred some right or privilege connected with the land on another person. Typically, the right or privilege conferred will arise out of the conduct of the parties, usually because of some assurance made, which is relied upon by the person claiming the right. In other words, proprietary estoppel is a mechanism whereby rights in or over land may be created *informally* in the absence of a deed or signed writing. In this respect, it is close to the doctrine of constructive trusts considered in Chapter 3 and many cases use these doctrines interchangeably. This is not necessarily accurate (see *Stack v Dowden* (2007)), although the precise relationship and any differences between the two doctrines have not yet been worked out. In the law of proprietary estoppel, cases are vital (see especially *Yeoman's Row Management v Cobbe* (2008) and *Thorner v Major* (2009)) as this is a judge-made doctrine, so typical of a court of equity. Proprietary estoppel has similarities with promissory estoppel in the law of contract, but they are different. Promissory estoppel is a defence to an action on a contract; proprietary estoppel is much more powerful and is a means of acquiring rights over land as well as being a defence to an action by the landowner. It is a sword as well as a shield.

QUESTION 23

Are contractual licences interests in land? Why is the issue important?

How to Read this Question

The aim of this question is to test your understanding of what it means to say that something is an 'interest in land' (that it is 'proprietary') and why it matters. It is asking for an analysis of case law to demonstrate how views changed over time.

How to Answer this Question

- ❖ Define an interest in land – Lord Wilberforce in *National Provincial Bank v Ainsworth* (1965).
- ❖ Define a licence – *Thomas v Sorrell* (1673).
- ❖ Identify types of licence and the roles that licences can play in the use of land.
- ❖ What is the relevance of third parties?
- ❖ Focus on judicial developments – *Errington v Errington* (1952); *Binions v Evans* (1972); *Re Sharpe* (1980); *Midland Bank v Farm Pride Hatcheries* (1981); *Ashburn Anstalt v Arnold* (1989); *Kewal Investments v Arthur Maiden* (1990); *Lloyd v Dugdale* (2002); *Chaudhary v Yavuz* (2011); *Groveholt v Hughes* (2012).

Up for Debate

Given that licences can arise in many situations, it is critical to be able to distinguish them from proprietary rights, but are the courts consistent in the practical application of the principle? Some academics argue that certain 'types' of licence do, or should, have the characteristics of a property right because they are so practically important: e.g. contractual occupation licences, licences arising as a result of proprietary estoppel. See Dixon in Tee, ed. Land Law, Themes and Debates (2002), Cullompton: Willan Publishing, Chapter 1.

Applying the Law

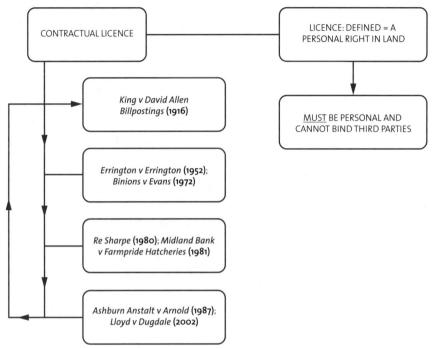

This diagram demonstrates the personal nature of a contractual licence and the relevant case law.

ANSWER

A licence is defined in *Thomas v Sorrell* (1673) as a permission to use land belonging to another that, without such permission, would amount to a trespass. It is the consent of the estate owner to the use of their land by another. Importantly, as Vaughan CJ makes clear in *Sorrell*, the orthodox view of a licence is that it 'properly passeth no interest nor alters or transfers property in any thing'; in other words, licences are not proprietary in nature but personal to the parties that created them.[1] In effect, therefore, they are incapable of binding third parties when the licensor (the grantor of the licence) transfers the affected land.

However, this orthodox view has been subject to attack in some cases and various theories have been advanced to explain why licences are, or should be, regarded as interests in land. The aim is often to ensure that subsequent transferees of the burdened land are bound by the licence. Not least, this is due to the multitude of purposes that licences can serve: for example, entry by ticket to a cinema (*Hurst v Picture Theatres Ltd* (1915));

---

1   In an essay like this where the main argument is very clear, it can be useful to spell it out in the introduction and use the rest of the essay to 'prove' your case.

permission to use facilities for a conference (*Verrall v Great Yarmouth BC* (1981)); permission to erect an advertising hoarding (*Kewal Investments v Arthur Maiden* (1990)); and even permission to occupy premises for residential accommodation (*Ogwr BC v Dykes* (1989); *Gray v Taylor* (1998)).[2]

The various uses of licences are reflected in their traditional categorisation, although it is really only in respect of the last two 'types' that the debate about the proprietary nature of licences has taken place. First, there are 'bare licences', being the most simple form of permission to use land given voluntarily by the owner of property. Typically, such licences allow the 'licensee' to carry on some limited activity on the 'licensor's' land, as where permission is given for children to play. It is intrinsic to this type of licence that the permission may be withdrawn at any time and, because given voluntarily without consideration, it does not give the licensee any claim to damages or other legal remedy when it is withdrawn. Second, there are those licences grouped together because they are 'coupled with an interest in the land'. In essence, these licences enable a person to enjoy some other proprietary right already granted over the land, as where a person is licensed to enter land in order to enjoy (for example) the right to fish, cut turf or gather wood (being 'profits'), as in *James Jones & Son v Earl of Tankerville* (1909). To some extent, however, the label 'licence' is misleading, for the licence is merely incidental to the right that has actually been granted: see, for example, the licence to park given to a tenant in *Donington Park Leisure Ltd v Wheatcroft & Son Ltd* (2006). So, the licence will last for as long as the proprietary right to which it is attached lasts and will be enforceable against whomsoever the proprietary right is enforceable against, being merely ancillary to the greater right.

As noted above, it is with the next two categories that the question of whether a licence can amount to an interest in land has been most commonly posed: contractual licences and licences arising by estoppel. Contractual licences are, in principle, little different in nature from bare licences, save that they are granted to the licensee in return for valuable consideration given to the licensor. The purchase of a cinema ticket is a good example. Such contractual licences are governed by the ordinary rules of contract and it is now clear that, instead of damages for breach, an injunction could be awarded preventing the licensor from revoking the licence before its contractual date of expiry (*Wintergarden Theatres v Millennium Productions Ltd* (1948)) or even a decree of specific performance requiring the licensor to permit the activity authorised by the licence to take place (*Verrall v Great Yarmouth*). It is obvious that the availability of these remedies may make the licence irrevocable between the original parties throughout the contractual period (for example, the theatre performance), and this raises the question whether the licensor should be able to defeat the licence by transferring the land to a third party during that period, even though he might not terminate it himself.[3]

---

2 This section makes good use of the case law and demonstrates a lot of knowledge without spending too long describing the different kinds of licences.

3 This explanation of what it would mean for a licence to take on a 'proprietary' effect shows that the writer understands the distinction between personal and property rights.

In the event, under the influence of Lord Denning's Court of Appeal, two arguments were made in an attempt to enforce licences against third parties. First, in *Errington v Errington* (1952), Lord Denning regarded a contractual licence as binding on a third party who was not a bona fide purchaser for value of a legal estate in the land *simply because* the licensee could have restrained revocation of the licence against the licensor. Of course, this actually assumes that licences are *capable* of binding third parties in the first place and Lord Denning's reasoning is unclear. It seems that he regarded the contractual licence as being supported by 'an equity' that transformed it into a proprietary right. Unfortunately, this ignores the earlier decision of the House of Lords'[4] in *King v David Allen & Sons, Billposting* (1916) which had decided expressly that contractual licences could not bind third parties.

The second line of attack came in *Binions v Evans* (1972) where a purchaser of land over which a licence existed expressly agreed to take the land subject to that licence. The purchaser later sought to evict the licensee. Two judges in the Court of Appeal actually decided that no licence was involved at all; rather, the occupier had a life interest under the **Settled Land Act 1925**. Lord Denning, however, decided that the purchaser was bound to give effect to the licence because he had purchased the property expressly subject to it. This meant that the licence was protected by a constructive trust preventing revocation. This analysis was then adopted in subsequent decisions, for example, *Re Sharpe* (1980).

The two-pronged attack on the orthodox position that licences are not interests in land seemed to represent the law until the decision of the Court of Appeal in *Ashburn Anstalt v Arnold* (1989). In that case, Fox LJ[5] relied on the House of Lords' decision in *King* and *National Provincial Bank v Ainsworth* (1965) and reaffirmed the orthodox view that *as a matter of principle*, licences are not interests in land. In his view, *Errington* was *per incuriam*, because of the existence of the binding authority of *King*. In any event, *Errington* could have been decided on at least three other grounds (the existence of an estate contract binding a non-purchaser, a *Rosset*-type equitable right of ownership or estoppel). This rejection of *Errington* has now been reaffirmed by the Court of Appeal in *Lloyd v Dugdale* (2002) and effectively settles the matter.

However, turning to the *Binions v Evans* argument, Fox LJ in *Ashburn* accepted that in an appropriate case, a contractual licence could *take effect* against a purchaser behind a constructive trust, if the purchaser had so conducted himself that it would be inequitable for the licence to be denied. Such a trust does not exist merely because the purchaser bought the land 'subject to' the licence, but only if there was unconscionable conduct, usually because he pays a lower price as a result of the promise to respect the licence. In any event, the licence is only protected behind a *personal* constructive trust binding on this particular purchaser because of their particular conduct; it has not thereby assumed the status of an interest in land. The possibility of imposing a constructive trust on a purchaser to protect an otherwise unenforceable right (such as a licence or unregistered

---

4   The noting of the court here shows the importance and strength of this authority.
5   Citing a specific judge shows good knowledge of the case law.

property interest) has been confirmed by *Dugdale*, and more recently in *Chaudhary v Yavuz* (2011) and *Groveholt v Hughes* (2012). However, all three cases emphasise that it is difficult to establish this constructive trust because there must be more than a simple promise to respect the right. In all three cases, the attempt failed. The imposition of a constructive trust can be justified only in exceptional circumstances where it would be unconscionable for the purchaser to escape an obligation he has accepted.

The analysis put forward in *Ashburn* and confirmed in later cases represents the law today. It serves to highlight the fundamental distinction between interests in land and purely personal interests to use land. Licences are not interests in land and they never can be. The whole point of a 'licence' is that it is *not* an interest in land. Given the almost infinite ways in which land can be used, there must be some category of right that gives the user permission to be on the land without conferring proprietary status. This is the licence. What is important, therefore, is not to argue about whether licences are interests in land, but where the proper boundary between licences and proprietary rights is to be drawn in any given case.

Common Pitfalls

This is a standard examination question, although it cannot be completed successfully without knowledge of case law. The distinction between the ability of a proprietary right to bind a third party because of its inherent nature and the personal way in which a licence may affect someone because of a purely personal constructive trust is most important. Avoid merely repeating that there are four types of licence and then describing them. The question does not say 'describe four types of licence'.

QUESTION 24

In 2013, Zoe acquired registered title to a small cottage on Dartmoor, formerly part of a large farm and quite close to the old farmhouse. Being fond of animals, she acquires several horses and asks Farmer Roger whether she can keep them on his land. He agrees, but only if he may use the horses to hire to tourists who stay on his farm. Farmer Roger also provides riding holidays for tourists, using his own horses, and Zoe agreed that, if there were insufficient space in the farmhouse, she would accommodate any extra tourists and provide them with breakfast and an evening meal if desired. Zoe also pays Farmer Roger £100 per month to park her car in an old barn on the farm. She also regularly collects firewood from Farmer Roger's land, as her only source of heating is an old wood-burning stove. In 2014, Farmer Roger proposes marriage to Zoe but she refuses. Farmer Roger takes great offence and immediately threatens to turn Zoe's horses out, although he does continue to use them for his riding business. In anger, Zoe refuses to accommodate any of Farmer Roger's tourists and asks those currently staying there to leave. The tourists subsequently sue Roger for a ruined holiday. Roger's response is to sell the barn and fields to Fenland Holidays plc, which immediately refuses Zoe the right to park her car or gather wood.

Zoe comes to you for advice as her car has broken down due to standing in the cold and she cannot live in the cottage without her source of fuel. She hopes to be able to sell the cottage to her friend, Beverley, who would also like to keep horses. It also emerges that Fenland Holidays plc knew of Zoe's activities and paid Farmer Roger a much-reduced price for the land it has purchased. You discover subsequently that Farmer Roger is the major shareholder in Fenland Holidays plc.

How to Read this Question

The question is asking you to apply the case law on the distinction between proprietary rights and personal rights. The examiner is looking for the application of case law to the facts of the problem.

How to Answer this Question

❖   Identify the nature of the claimant's rights over the land – are they licences or proprietary interests?

❖   What is the effect of licences between the original parties – remedies?

❖   What is the effect of licences on third parties?

❖   Is there a role for a constructive trust and the personal protection of licences (*Binions v Evans*; *Chaudhary v Yavuz*)?

❖   Are any new licences created?

Applying the Law

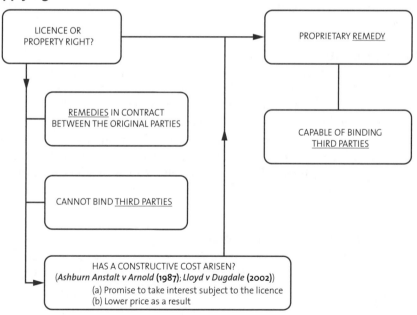

This diagram demonstrates the difference between licences, property rights and constructive trusts.

ANSWER

This problem concerns the creation of rights over land, the identification of the nature of those rights and the consequences that flow from subsequent dealings with the land.[6]

(a) The Horses

Zoe and Farmer Roger have entered into a contract whereby Zoe agrees to allow the horses to be used for Roger's business in return for which Roger allows Zoe to keep the horses on his land. The contract is purely oral and this makes it difficult for Zoe to establish a proprietary interest – s 2 of the **Law of Property (Miscellaneous Provisions) Act 1989**. The only possibility of a proprietary right is if Zoe has a periodic lease of the land (cf. *University of Reading v Johnson-Houghton* (1985)) which would be binding on Roger according to its terms and could be assigned to Beverley by deed (*Julian v Crago* (1992)). However, the lack of exclusive possession and the lack of formality suggest rather that Zoe has a contractual licence over Farmer Roger's land. Presumptively, this is revocable during its term by the licensor, although the licensee (Zoe) would have a claim in damages. However, it is clear from *Wintergarden Theatres v Millennium Productions* (1948) that if, on construction of the contract, a contractual licence was intended to be irrevocable during its term, equity will intervene to restrain breach by the licensor by way of injunction or specific performance as appropriate. Whether the remedy is available to Zoe will depend on many factors, not least her own conduct. Her willingness to continue to allow her horses to be used (that is, that she kept her side of the contract) will be important, although her apparent refusal to cater for the very tourists who would ride will count against. As far as Beverley is concerned, it has always been true that the benefit of a contract can be expressly assigned and Zoe can transfer to Beverley such rights as she has against Roger.[7]

(b) The Tourists

The precise nature of Zoe's liabilities here will depend on the exact terms of the contract she made with Farmer Roger. She could be in breach of contract in evicting the tourists before the end of their holiday and in refusing to accommodate future arrivals. In such a case, Farmer Roger may sue Zoe in contract and recover damages. It is clear that the tourists have no short-term lease over their rooms in Zoe's cottage. Under *Street v Mountford* (1985), these occupiers are lodgers and, therefore, not tenants (see e.g. *Markou v Da Silvaesa* (1986)). The tourists may, of course, have a contractual licence to occupy the cottage (see *Royal Bank of Scotland v Mehta* (1999)), although it is difficult to see on the facts how they could be in direct contract with Zoe.

(c) Car Parking and Collecting Wood

As to the car parking, it is clear from *Moncrieff v Jamieson* (2008) and *R Square Properties v Nissan Motors* (2014) that it is perfectly possible to have an easement giving a right to

---

6 If there is time, set out in the introduction the issues you are going to deal with in the main body of the answer.

7 This shows knowledge of contractual principles going beyond those normally looked at in relation to land law specifically and would therefore receive extra credit.

park on a neighbour's land.[8] However, it is unclear whether an easement can exist where the right to park is in a defined space as opposed to park generally within a larger area – that is, if it gives exclusive or excessive control over the servient land (see *Moncrieff v Jamieson*). In any event, even assuming that this could be an easement, the formality necessary to create a legal or equitable right has not been met and there is little possibility of an estoppel. All in all, this looks as if Zoe has been granted a contractual licence to park her car, which, of course, is enforceable against Roger as the licensor. Further, it is clear from *Ashburn Anstalt v Arnold* (1989) and *Lloyd v Dugdale* (2002) that licences as such are not interests in land and cannot therefore bind a subsequent purchaser of the land. So, subject to what will be said below, at first sight it looks as if Zoe's right to park her car cannot be enforced against Fenland.[9]

The right to collect wood poses different problems because it is possible for a person to be granted a profit *à prendre* to collect wood for the purpose of fuel, otherwise known as a profit of estovers (*AG v Reynolds* (1911)). Profits are proprietary rights and any licences attached to the profit to enter land for the purpose of exercising the profit are merely incidental to the superior proprietary right (*James Jones v Earl of Tankerville* (1909); *Polo Woods v Shelton-Agar* (2009)). Once again, however, in order for the profit to exist and be capable of binding a third party such as Fenland, it must be created in due form. In this case, there is no deed to support a legal profit and no written contract to support an equitable profit. Zoe's only hope is to plead the creation of a profit by estoppel, similar to the creation of an easement by estoppel in *Celsteel v Alton* (1985) and *Joyce v Epsom & Ewell BC* (2012). However, even if that were the case, Zoe would have to register her interest by means of a notice in order for it to be effective against a purchaser – **s 29** of the **Land Registration Act 2002** – for an equitable easement or profit cannot override under the **LRA 2002** (it is not within **Sched 3** to the Act and use of the easement or profit does not amount to 'actual occupation' of the burdened land – *Chaudhary v Yavuz* (2012)).[10] There is no evidence that she has so registered. If, on the other hand, there is no estoppel, Zoe could claim a licence to collect wood. Obviously, this cannot bind Fenland as such – not being an interest in land – but she may gain some remedy via a constructive trust, considered below.

(d) Fenland and Farmer Roger

Although it is clear that any licences could not bind Fenland as a matter of property law, there is the possibility that they could be affected by a personal constructive trust, imposed to give effect to such licences as do exist. This occurs because of the purchaser's unconscionable conduct – see *Ashburn Anstalt v Arnold*, *Lloyd v Dugdale*, *Groveholt v Hughes* (2012) – but *Chaudhary v Yavuz* (2012) makes it clear that this is a very exceptional rule and not easily established. So, it is not enough that the purchaser simply promised to

---

8 Although this is clearly a question about licences in land, it is important to recognise that other topics may come into the answer.

9 This sentence is good because it draws a mini-conclusion in relation to the nature of the car-parking right but shows that this is not the end of the matter.

10 This shows good knowledge of very recent case law.

give effect to the licences – *Ashburn, Yavuz, Groveholt* criticising *Binions v Evans* (1972). In our case, the fact that the purchaser paid a lower price because it knew of the existence of the licences is important (*Dugdale*) and it is arguable that this makes it unconscionable for Fenland to revoke any licences that Zoe might have (to park, to collect wood).

Finally, two further points should be noted. First, Zoe may transfer the benefit of any contract to Beverley irrespective of the nature of the rights created by the contract. That is a matter of contract law. It is not clear, however, whether the transfer of the benefit of the contractual rights to a third party will affect the court's decision to impose a constructive trust on the purchaser of the land over which those rights exists. Second, it may be possible to argue that there is no third party purchaser at all on the grounds that Fenland is just Farmer Roger in another guise. If that were the case, because Roger is the majority shareholder of Fenland, no question of the enforcement of licences against third parties arises. It is more likely, however, given the separate legal personality of companies and their owners, that Roger's majority shareholding will be relevant to the question of the imposition of the constructive trust on the 'third party' rather than in deciding that there was no third party at all (*Jones v Lipman* (1962)).

Common Pitfalls

Do not ignore the formality requirements for the creation of property rights as these also can mean that a claimed right is merely a licence. Remember the connection between easements and licences. Although it is possible to answer this question entirely from the perspective of 'licences', a better answer will consider whether any of the alleged rights might be easements or profits. Land law cannot safely be 'compartmentalised' like some other subjects.

QUESTION 25

'The law relating to proprietary estoppel is flexible and may change over time. It is not possible to identify with certainty when a claim of estoppel might be successful, although it is possible to identify the general principles of the doctrine.'

▶ Do you agree?

How to Read this Question

In this question the examiner is testing your knowledge of the ingredients of a claim of estoppel. In particular, how case law has developed the doctrine since its origin as a defensive claim in equity. The reference to certainty whether a claim will be successful indicates that the examiner wants you to consider whether the doctrine is too vague, or encompasses too much judicial discretion.

How to Answer this Question

❖ Identification of the general nature of proprietary estoppel and its relationship to rules regulating the acquisition of estates and interests in land.

❖ Very briefly, consider the origin of the doctrine and the 'five probanda' for proprietary estoppel (*Willmott v Barber* (1880)).

❖ Consider the modern definition of proprietary estoppel (*Taylor Fashions v Liverpool Victoria Trustees* (1982); *Mathura v Mathura* (1994); *Yeoman's Row Management v Cobbe* (2008); *Thorner v Major* (2009)).

❖ What is the role of unconscionability – *Taylor v Dickens* (1998); *Gillett v Holt* (2001); *Kinane v Conteh* (2005)?

Up for Debate

The role of estoppel in the modern law is controversial, especially how it relates to the formality requirements of statute and the law of constructive trusts. Is it a cover for 'palm-tree' justice or a principled response to unconscionable behaviour? Is there is difference between 'commercial' type cases and 'family' type cases? How does estoppel fit into the relatively rigid requirements of the **Land Registration Act 2002**?

Applying the Law

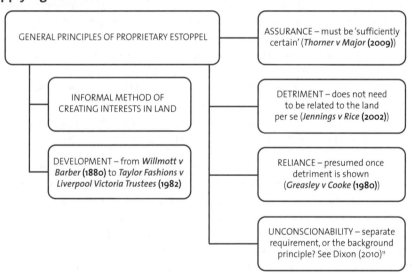

This diagram represents the general principles of proprietary estoppel.

ANSWER

Section 2 of the **Law of Property (Miscellaneous Provisions) Act 1989** establishes the minimum level of formality necessary for the valid creation, acquisition or transfer of estates and interests in land. Since **s2** came into force, purely oral transactions are not in general capable of giving rise to an enforceable proprietary rights in land. Moreover, **s2**

11 Dixon, 'Confining and defining proprietary estoppel: the role of unconscionability' (2010) 30 Legal Studies 408.

stipulates a *minimum* level of formality: legal estates and interests on the whole require the additional formality of a deed and, for registered land, registration under **ss 25** and **27** and **Sched 2** of the **Land Registration Act 2002**. It is in this context, where statute requires a considerable degree of formality for the creation of rights in land, that the doctrine of proprietary estoppel falls to be examined.[12]

The precise role of proprietary estoppel is a matter of some debate. On the one hand, proprietary estoppel can provide a defence to an action by a landowner who seeks to enforce his strict rights against someone who has been promised some right or liberty over the land: e.g. *Mathura v Mathura* (1994). However, a successful plea of proprietary estoppel also can operate positively, in the sense that it can generate new property interests in favour of a claimant: e.g. *Kinane v Conteh* (2005). As is typically stated, proprietary estoppel is both a shield and a sword (*Crabb v Arun DC* (1976)). This means that proprietary estoppel can result in the creation of proprietary rights without a deed, without any writing and without the existence of even an oral contract. It is the generation of proprietary rights by the action of equity on an individual's conscience and is an exception to the normally required formality rules.

The doctrine of proprietary estoppel is not a creation of the modern law, although it certainly has come to the fore in recent times. In *Willmott v Barber* (1880), Fry LJ laid down what was to be regarded for many years as the five 'probanda' of proprietary estoppel, being the five conditions that needed to be established. These were: first, that the claimant should have made some mistake as to their legal rights; second, that the claimant must have expended some money or done some act on the faith of the mistaken belief; third, that the true landowner must know of the existence of their own right and that it is inconsistent with the right claimed by the claimant; fourth, the landowner must know of the claimant's mistaken belief as to their legal rights; and, fifth, that the landowner should have encouraged the expenditure by the claimant, either directly, or by abstaining from enforcing their legal right.

It is obvious that these five conditions are fairly strict and they established a clear framework for ascertaining the likelihood of a successful plea of proprietary estoppel. However, as the doctrine developed, the courts were prepared to accept a plea of proprietary estoppel when one or more of Fry LJ's probanda were missing, largely because the focus had shifted from examining the actions of the landowner to a doctrine that examined the effect of the landowner's actions on the claimant. This is the essence of the modern law first explained in *Taylor Fashions v Liverpool Victoria Trustees* (1982). In that case, Oliver J made it clear that proprietary estoppel is not limited to cases in which the landowner knows of their rights, or their extent, but is indeed a flexible doctrine, springing from equity, which should not be unduly restricted by rigid rules.[13]

The position after *Taylor Fashions* (1982) is that a person may be entitled to claim rights in or over land that belongs to another where it would be unconscionable to deny those

---

12 This introduction explains why the doctrine of proprietary estoppel is so important from the perspective of formalities, and therefore gives the overall angle that the response is taking in addressing the set question.

13 This question in asking about the flexibility of estoppel over time is looking not only for a description of historical developments in the law, but also in terms of its current (and potential future) flexibility.

rights. The claimant must prove an assurance – express or implied – as to the claimant's position in relation to the land, reliance on that assurance by the claimant, and detriment by the claimant as a result of relying on the assurance, although these criteria may well overlap and should not be regarded as completely distinct requirements. The overall aim is to prevent unconscionability (*Gillett v Holt* (2001)), but the claimant must still prove the factual basis for the estoppel. It is not enough simply to argue that it is 'unfair' to deny the claimant certain rights: *Thorner v Major* (2009). Clearly, however, that these criteria are flexible and in some cases little has been required to prove the estoppel. In *Greasley v Cooke* (1980), for example, the court held that if it is clear that assurances have been made, and detriment suffered, it is permissible to assume that reliance has occurred. Likewise, in *JT Developments v Quinn* (1991), it became clear that an estoppel could arise even though there was no intention to create binding obligations.

However, estoppel is not to be regarded as a panacea for *all* problems. There are some circumstances – illustrated by *Yeoman's Row Management v Cobbe* (2008) – where it is not unconscionable for one party to rely on lack of formality as a means of avoiding an oral agreement, especially if both parties were fully aware of the need for formality in their dealings (see also *Herbert v Doyle* (2010)). Thus, while there are some cases (e.g. *Lim Teng Huan v Ang Swee Chuan* (1992); *Flowermix v Site Developments* (2000)) in which estoppel has been used to 'enforce' a contract that is not otherwise valid, *Yeoman's Row* makes it clear that there has to be something *more* than simply a failed bargain. Estoppel is not a device to cure failed contracts, especially in a commercial context. This must be correct, for it is not unconscionable to insist on compliance with *statutory* formalities for the creation of interests in land. Estoppel works outside these formalities, but only where unconscionability exists – *Thorner v Major* (2009).

Thus, proprietary estoppel embodies an ancient equitable jurisdiction that allows for the creation of property rights without needing to fulfil the strict requirements of statute, in cases in which it would be 'unconscionable' to do otherwise. The flexibility this permits is apparent in the ways that a court may 'satisfy' the estoppel. For example, the successful claimant might obtain the freehold (*Dillwyn v Llewellyn* (1862); *Pascoe v Turner* (1979)), or an easement (*Joyce v Epsom & Ewell* (2012)), a mere right of occupation until expenditure is repaid (*Dodsworth v Dodsworth* (1973)), a mortgage (*Kinane* (2005)), a cash sum (*Campbell v Griffin* (2001)) or, simply, dismissal of the paper owner's claim for possession (*Mathura* (1994)).[14] It may even cause a complete readjustment of the parties' rights over the property (*Voyce v Voyce* (1991)) or a remodelling of testamentary dispositions (*Gillett v Holt* (2001)).[15] In fact, the range of remedies is open-ended and, importantly, does not necessarily have to result in the creation or transfer of a proprietary interest at all. In some cases, the remedy will reflect the 'expectation loss' of the claimant (that is, that which they were promised) and in others, it will be their 'reliance loss' (being the value of any detriment incurred) – *Jennings v Rice* (2003) – provided that it is at least the minimum necessary to do justice between the parties.

....

14 This essay calls for discussion of the relevant case law, and listing cases in this way is a good way to show off knowledge whilst managing time effectively.

15 It is important to recognise that flexibility may exist at different levels of application of a particular rule.

The conditions required for establishing an estoppel, and the court's wide discretion in satisfying a successful plea, demonstrate the highly flexible nature of this doctrine. Accompanying such flexibility is a measure of uncertainty, both for any claimant and their legal advisers.[16] Moreover, in so far as the doctrine allows the creation of rights over property by entirely informal means, it provides an escape route for the claimant who has failed to observe the statutory requirements for the creation of proprietary rights. That said, the existence of a doctrine that enables a court to resolve matters according to the conscience of the parties involved, rather than according to the strict forms of a statute, is a necessary adjunct to any legal system that stipulates formalities as a means to certainty. The key is, however, not to go too far. There is merit in certainty, especially in relation to transactions concerning land, and policy considerations should not be forgotten when considering the informal and flexible doctrine of proprietary estoppel.

Common Pitfalls

Do not avoid the apparent differences between *Yeomans Row v Cobbe* (2008) and *Thorner v Major* (2009). Try not to simply state that there are four conditions for estoppel. The examiner is asking you to assess how the conditions relate to wider issues about formality and certainty in land law. Hence, ignoring the formality rules for the creation of property rights leads to a weak answer.

QUESTION 26

In 2013, Leroy, McGee and Tony live in Nos 1, 2 and 3 Navy Street respectively, an area of registered land. Each house has a large garden, although Leroy has concreted over his and uses it to store spare parts connected with his carpentry business. Last year, Leroy asked McGee (who lives in No 2) whether he would mind if he (Leroy) constructed a small shed to store some more valuable equipment, even though this meant building some foundations in McGee's garden. McGee readily agreed and helped Leroy construct the shed. A little later, before the shed was complete, Leroy promised that McGee could store some of his (McGee's) own goods in the shed. McGee also asked if Leroy would mind if his wife's mother, Ziva, parked her mobility scooter in the shed.

Leroy readily agreed, not realising that Ziva drove a very large scooter that would occupy considerable space. Meanwhile, Tony has been negotiating with McGee over the purchase of some land owned by McGee at the back of Navy Street. McGee is unwilling to sell, but permits Tony to occupy the land pending the negotiation of a long lease. McGee asks Tony to pay him £600 per month as 'a down payment' for the lease, but, when Tony comes to pay, McGee tells him to keep his money as he (McGee) has decided to sell and will give him a full price later. Tony subsequently seeks planning permission from the local council to build a coffee house on his new land and gets Leroy and McGee's guarantee that they will not oppose planning permission. However, just as he is about to instruct a local builder, McGee informs him that he has sold the property to CaffPow plc.

---

16 This conclusion is good because it goes beyond summarising what has been established in the course of the essay and examines instead the merits of the flexibility of the rules.

Leroy is distraught at the prospect of a large coffee house behind his house and manages to sell to Ducky. Ducky has just discovered Ziva's scooter in the shed and has removed it, along with McGee's property. In retaliation, McGee is about to knock down that part of the shed that stands on his land. Tony wants to know whether he has any rights that can be enforced against CaffPow plc.

▶ **Advise generally.**

How to Read this Question

In this question the examiner is testing your ability to identify rights to use land and how they might affect third parties. The examiner will expect you first to identify the nature of the right claimed and then whether it will affect the new owner of the land. The informal nature of the arrangements indicates that proprietary estoppel is relevant.

How to Answer this Question

- ❖ What rights, if any, are created by the actions of the parties – proprietary estoppel?
- ❖ What are the nature of those rights – how is the equity satisfied?
- ❖ How, if at all, do those rights affect subsequent purchasers of the land?

Answer Structure

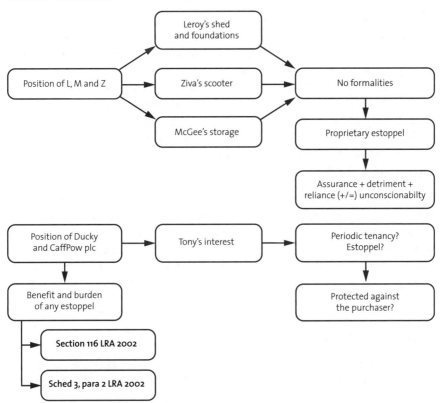

This diagram shows how to apply the rules relating to proprietary estoppel to the parties.

ANSWER

This problem essentially revolves around two central issues. First, it is necessary to determine the nature and extent of any interests created by the actions of the parties in favour of each other. Second, it is necessary to establish whether any or all of those interests are rights binding on the subsequent purchasers of the plots.

(a) Leroy and the Shed; McGee and the Storage; Ziva and the Scooter

The facts indicate that none of the arrangements between the parties have been recorded in writing. This means that unless the activities fall within one of the recognised exceptions to the formality requirements found in **s 2** of the **Law of Property (Miscellaneous Provisions) Act 1989**, then any interests they may have will be void as property rights.

The absence of writing means that Leroy, McGee and Ziva will have to rely on proprietary estoppel if they are to claim property rights which could be enforceable against Ducky and CaffPow. Failing that, their rights might amount to contractual licences but they would be incapable of binding any third party (*Ashburn Anstalt v Arnold* (1989); *Lloyd v Dugdale* (2002)).

(i) The Shed

McGee, the owner of the land over which the shed will protrude, has agreed that Leroy can build that shed in the full knowledge that use of his own land will thereby be diminished. In such circumstances, Leroy will have a reasonable chance of establishing that McGee is bound by proprietary estoppel from demolishing the shed. Following *Taylor Fashions v Liverpool Victoria Trustees* (1982), McGee made an assurance to Leroy that the shed could be built, which was relied upon by Leroy to his detriment. The fact that McGee assisted in the building can only reinforce this presumption. In such circumstances, following cases such as *Crabb v Arun DC* (1976) and *Ives v High* (1967), it is unlikely that McGee will be able to renege on his promise and destroy the shed. Equity will intervene by way of an injunction.

What is not clear, however, is what happens when Leroy sells his land to Ducky. There is authority that the *benefit* of the estoppel cannot be transferred to a successor in title (*Fryer v Brook* (1984)) because it is merely personal to the promisee, although this appears to have been contradicted by Lord Denning in *Ives v High*. Indeed, it is difficult to see why the alleged personal nature of an estoppel (even *if* this were true) should stop the *benefit* passing to another, as contractual benefits may pass under the general law unless the contract prohibits it.[17]

(ii) The Storage of McGee's Goods

On one view of the facts, Leroy has simply agreed that McGee can store goods in his shed. This may have been done as a personal favour – in which case McGee has a bare

---

17 It is perfectly acceptable to argue that a rule is unclear or unsettled.

licence – or it may have been done as a counterpart to McGee's promise and assistance with the shed – in which case it may be a contractual licence. If it is a bare licence, it is revocable at will by Leroy (*Thomas v Sorrell* (1673)), although, if it is contractual, it may be irrevocable by Leroy according to its terms (*Wintergarden Theatres v Millennium Productions Ltd* (1948)). However, in either case, the licence as such cannot be binding on a third party (Ducky) (*Ashburn Anstalt v Arnold*; *Lloyd v Dugdale*).

An alternative view is, however, that there has been some form of estoppel generated in McGee's favour by Leroy's conduct in relation to the storage. It would be necessary to establish that there was an assurance, reliance and detriment (*Taylor Fashions*), although it might well be difficult on the facts as there appears to be little in the way of detriment suffered by McGee in reliance on the promise (and such detriment is crucial: *Gillett v Holt* (2001)). However, if the estoppel is made out, McGee could go on to argue that it is enforceable against Ducky as an interest in land (**s 116** of the **LRA 2002**): either because it might be protected by an entry on the register (a notice: **s 29** of the **LRA 2002**);[18] or as an overriding interest under **Sched 3, para 2** to the **LRA 2002** on the basis of discoverable actual occupation – *Henry v Henry* (2010).

(iii) The Shed and the Storage

We have assumed above that the shed building and the storage were separate events. It might be possible to argue that they are so interconnected that, at least for Leroy and McGee, they must be taken together. Hence, by analogy with *Ives v High*, it could be argued that, if Leroy wants the benefit of the shed, he must be subject to the burden of the storage of McGee's goods. This would, of course, prevent either of the original parties from reneging on their agreement. But, even then it is doubtful if the 'burden' of Leroy's obligations could be passed to Ducky. There is no evidence that Ducky purchased Leroy's land with express knowledge of McGee's rights (or in an inequitable manner), so as to subject him to a personal constructive trust within *Ashburn Anstalt v Arnold*, *Lloyd v Dugdale* and *Chaudhary v Yavuz*.[19]

(iv) The Mobility Scooter

The issue of Ziva's motorcycle is very similar to that concerning McGee's goods and it may well be just as difficult to establish anything other than a bare or contractual licence to support the parking/storage. Even if we were to approach this issue on a benefit/burden analysis, it could be decisive that the 'benefit' is given to someone (Ziva) other than the person who is subject to the burden of the shed (McGee). This makes it highly unlikely that Ducky would be bound by this obligation when he purchases Leroy's land.

....

18 Never forget about registration requirements!

19 Even in problem questions it is important to analyse the merits of any solution as well as applying the law to the facts.

(b) Tony, the Plot of Land and CaffPow Plc

Tony and McGee start off by negotiating the terms of a lease following McGee's initial refusal to sell the land. When they fail to reach agreement on the terms of the long lease, Tony is let into occupation by McGee pending successful conclusion of negotiations and provided that he pays £600. At first sight, this raises the possibility of a periodic tenancy. If this could be established then Tony would have an overriding interest against the purchaser CaffPow (**Sched 3, para 1** to the **LRA 2002**), who would be bound by the terms of the lease. Unfortunately for Tony, however, it appears from *Javad v Aqil* (1991) and *Erimus Housing v Barclays Wealth Trustees* (2014) that occupation and payment of rent will not give rise to a periodic tenancy if the occupation can be attributed to negotiations pending the grant of a 'real' lease. This is Tony's position and he will be a 'tenant at will', which, even if it is binding on CaffPow, can be terminated on reasonable notice. Circumstances then take a different turn. McGee makes it clear that he will now sell to Tony and Tony, acting in reliance on this, begins to make plans for his coffee house. McGee even re-enforces this by promising not to oppose a planning application (see the similarity with *Yeoman's Row v Cobbe* (2008)). This may, then, raise a proprietary estoppel in Tony's favour, provided that he can establish assurance, reliance and detriment. On the facts, McGee will argue that he simply made an offer to sell that he has now withdrawn (*Ravenocean v Gardner* (2001)), whereas Tony will argue that he has relied on the promise to such an extent as to make its withdrawal unconscionable, as in *Thorner v Major* (2009). In fact, it is a marginal case, as Tony does not suffer the same degree of detriment as the promisees in other cases such as *Re Basham* (1986), and *Pascoe v Turner* (1979) and, although the cases of *Lim Teng Huan v Chuan* (1992) and *Flowermix v Site Development* (2000) offer some support, it may be that the estoppel cannot be made out because the promise is legitimately withdrawn (*Canty v Broad*; *Taylor v Dickens* (1998); *Yeoman's Row v Cobbe* (2008)).[20] However, were it to be accepted that Tony had an estoppel in his favour, it might be binding against CaffPow in the same way that McGee's estoppel might have been enforceable against Ducky: via an entry on the register or as an overriding interest.

Common Pitfalls

Do not write a general answer on estoppel. This question is about specific facts and specific claimants. Always relate your law to the facts you are given – not to those you would like to be there. Examiners give marks for applying law to facts. Failure to refer to the specific facts will lose marks. If the answer is uncertain, say so. Do not make assumptions to make the question easier.

---

20 This section demonstrates that the writer has very good knowledge of the case law and would receive a lot of credit in the exam.

7

Easements

INTRODUCTION

Easements comprise those rights that one landowner may exercise over the land of their neighbour. Common examples are the right of way, the right of light and the right of support. It is essential to the understanding of the law of easements that the student appreciates that every easement has two aspects: one landowner will enjoy the benefit of an easement and another will be subject to its burden. This is just another way of saying that easements exist over a servient tenement for the benefit of a dominant tenement. It is important to remember the dual nature of an easement as this will make problems concerning the transmission of easements to third parties easier to understand. It is often said that easements can either be 'positive' or 'negative' in character. The former are those that allow the dominant tenement owner (the person who has the benefit) to do something on the servient land, such as enjoy a right of way, while the latter prevent the servient tenement owner (the person subject to the burden) from doing something on their own land, such as building new premises. However, it is obvious that most easements have a positive and negative aspect, depending on how you look at it, and the distinction is not of great practical use. Its one advantage is that it illustrates that many so-called negative easements are similar to restrictive covenants and perhaps their subject matter would be more appropriate to the legal regime of the latter rather than the former.

Checklist
Questions on the law of easements can come in either problem or essay form and the student should be aware of the following issues:

- the nature of easements;
- the creation of easements;
- the distinction between legal and equitable easements;
- the transmissibility of easements to third parties, both benefit and burden;
- the conveyancing dimension;
- reform of the law of easements.

QUESTION 27

'The law of easements is constrained by the innately conservative principle that the categories of admissible easement must not dramatically overstep the boundaries of the kinds of easements already recognised.'

(Gray and Gray, *Elements of Land Law* (5th edn, 2009) Oxford: Oxford University Press, p. 617)

▶ **How far is the above statement accurate, and is there any consistent policy evident in the rights that the courts have recognised as easements?**

How to Read this Question

The examiner is expecting an essay on the nature of easements. This does not mean simply repetition of the 'four criteria' for the existence of an easement. It means examining the case law and highlighting inconsistencies.

How to Answer this Question

The answer should discuss the general requirements for an easement found in *Re Ellenborough Park* (1956), the existence of positive and negative easements and (briefly) their relationship to restrictive covenants. It should highlight inconsistencies in the case law and focus on how the law of easements changes over time – *Moncrieff v Jameson* (2007) and *Coventry v Lawrence* (2014). Questions of public policy – how far the use of land is to be controlled by easements – are also relevant.

Up for Debate

The Law Commission has proposed significant reform of the law of easements, but this does not include a statutory formula for defining what might be an easement. Nor is there a 'bright line' distinction between easements and covenants. Should there be? See Law Commission Report No 327 (2011) 'Making land work: easements, covenants and profits à prendre'.

Applying the Law

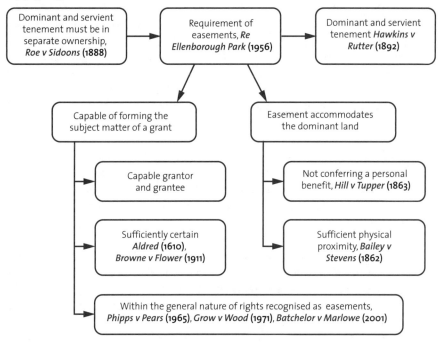

ANSWER

An easement is essentially a right of property that is enjoyed or exercised over land belonging to another. In one sense, the law of easements can be regarded as the private law equivalent to public planning law as where an easement prevents the owner of land from doing something on their own property. For example, if land is subject to an easement of light, this effectively prevents the owner of that land from building so as to obstruct that light. However, easements are not only negative in nature. Many easements authorise a neighbour to use the land subject to the ease-ment in a way that would otherwise be a trespass. Thus, a right of way enables the owner of the easement to walk across their neighbour's land. Indeed, this distinction between 'negative' and 'positive' easements is often said to be one of the most important factors in the law of easements, since case law establishes that the law should be wary of accepting new negative easements, as in *Phipps v Pears* (1965), in which it was alleged (and rejected) that the servient owner was under a negative ease-ment preventing him from demolishing his premises. In fact, it is inherent in the nature of all easements that they comprise both a positive and a negative aspect, for what the dominant owner is allowed to do, the servient owner must suffer. In this sense, irre-spective of whether the easement is positive or negative, all easements comprise a benefit and a burden. The land subject to the easement (the servient tenement) bears the burden of that easement whilst the owner of the land entitled to enjoy the ease-ment (the dominant tenement) has the benefit of it.

The essential characteristics of an easement were listed in the judgment in *Re Ellenborough Park* (1956), a decision which at the time challenged existing notions of what could be an easement. The case proposed a four-fold test. First, there must be a dominant and a servient tenement. Second, an easement must accommodate (that is, benefit) the dominant tenement. Third, the dominant and servient tenement owners must be owned or occupied by different persons and, fourth, the easement must be capable of being the subject matter of a grant. If the alleged right satisfies these conditions, it is most likely to be recognised as an easement irrespective of the name given to it by the parties that created it.

The essential duality of an easement is evident from the first condition. It is crucial that if an easement is to exist, there must be a dominant and servient tenement. The easement must burden land, but it must also benefit land, and in technical terms the easement cannot exist in gross (*Hawkins v Rutter* (1892)). The easement runs with the land, both the benefit and the burden.

The second condition essentially makes it clear than an alleged easement must confer a benefit on the dominant tenement: it must 'accommodate' it. Easements are proprietary rights and therefore confer benefits on land, not persons (*Manson v Shrewsbury Railway* (1871)). Rather like covenants that touch and concern the land, easements must benefit the user of land, the value of land or the mode of occupation of land. Thus, the servient tenement must be sufficiently close to the dominant tenement to be able to confer the benefit on it (*Bailey v Stevens* (1862)) and must not confer what is merely a personal advantage. So, in *Hill v Tupper* (1863), the claimant's right to put pleasure boats on the canal could not amount to an easement as it was not to be sufficiently connected to a dominant tenement. It is not, however, authority for the proposition that mere commercial advantages cannot be easements: examples of easements supporting commercial activity include *Moody v Steggles* (1879) (hanging a pub sign) and *Platt v Crouch* (2003) (mooring boats to facilitate access to an hotel). Perhaps *Hill* is also an example of the impact of public policy on the definition of easements – would it be in the public interest to give one person the right to put boats on a waterway that existed for the benefit of the public at large?[1]

Given that an easement is a right over *another's* land, the third *Ellenborough* condition stipulates that the dominant and servient tenements must not be both owned and occupied by the same person (*Roe v Siddons* (1888)). Indeed, should the dominant and servient tenements come into the ownership and possession of the same person, any easement over the servient land could be extinguished. This means that a person cannot have an easement against themselves, although due to the operation of the rule in *Wheeldon v Burrows* (1879) an easement may be created when part of a plot of land is sold off, thereby creating two tenements.

Finally, no right may amount to an easement unless it is 'capable of forming the subject matter of a grant' or, in other words, an easement must be capable of being

---

1   It is good to point out the potential downsides of a flexible jurisdiction like this.

expressly conveyed by deed. This has various aspects.[2] First, an easement cannot exist unless there is a capable grantor – that is, somebody legally competent to create an easement – and a capable grantee. So, for example, no easement can exist where purportedly granted or received by a limited company having no power to grant or receive easements under its articles of association. Second, all rights that are capable of forming the subject matter of a grant must be sufficiently definite. In the case of an easement, therefore, the right must be capable of clear description and precise definition: for example, a right to a good view cannot exist as an easement (*Re Aldred* (1610)), although mere practical difficulties in definition will not prevent an easement from arising (*Coventry v Lawrence* (2014) – easement to make a noise possible, when permitted noise can be quantified). Third, only those interests that are capable of being granted may be easements: in other words, the right must be within the general nature of rights recognised as easements or be rights by close analogy thereto. This does not mean, of course, that new easements for new times cannot exist. Thus, there can be an easement to use a letterbox (*Goldberg v Edwards* (1950)), an easement to use an airfield (*Re Bolton Paul* (1976)) and an easement to park many cars on neighbouring land (*R Square Properties v Nissan Motors* (2014)). But, it does mean that the courts will strike down alleged easements that do not appear to be within the class of rights that should be recognised as such.[3] Of course, some general principles have developed and it is often said that no new easement will be recognised that requires the servient owner to spend money (*Phipps v Pears*) or unduly controls the servient owner in the use of his land (*Batchelor v Marlowe* (2003)). Such alleged new 'negative easements' are more properly to be regarded as within the sphere of restrictive covenants. It is also said that no right will be recognised as an easement that gives the dominant tenement owner the right to use exclusively the servient tenement. So, in *Copeland v Greenhalf* (1952), no easement could exist to store tools of the trade on the servient land and, in *Grigsby v Melville* (1974), a right of storage in a cellar could not be accepted. But, we cannot be rigid about this. So, in *Batchelor v Marlow* a right to park many cars could not be an easement, but this was permitted in *R Square Properties* (2014).[4] The position here is, however, somewhat policy-orientated, for, as *Wright v Macadam* shows, the particular facts of a case may require the granting of an easement so as to facilitate commodious living. In that case, the tenant successfully claimed an easement of storage of coal in a small part of the landlord's coal shed. There is no real distinction that can be sensibly drawn between this and *Copeland* and *Melville*, other than to say that the court in *Macadam* believed that the tenant deserved the right claimed. Such flexibility is inherent in the *Ellenborough* conditions and it would be unfortunate if the development of the law of easements were hindered by too exacting and rigorously applied conditions.

---

2 Being explicit that this is really more than one rule is both clearer, and analytically more convincing, than attempting to discuss all aspects of this rule simultaneously.

3 Splitting up the paragraphs like this gives each section a definite focus and shows that the answer is a clear response to the question.

4 There has been a lot of academic commentary on this line of cases which could be brought in here.

At present, the *Re Ellenborough* rules provide an envelope outside which a judge usually will not go, but inside which he may recognise an easement or not according to the circumstances of the case, the needs of the property and, indeed, the behaviour of the parties. In this sense, of course, the law is uncertain as it becomes difficult to predict whether a new right will be regarded as an easement: for example, the recognition of the possibility of an easement to make a noise by the Supreme Court in *Coventry v Lawrence* (2014) surprised many. To some extent, perhaps some of these issues would be better dealt with by the law of restrictive covenants or local planning regulations.

Common Pitfalls

This is one of the most textbook-based questions any examiner can ask. It is straightforward and easy to score a 'safe' mark. But try not to repeat the *Re Ellenborough* conditions as if they were a list. It is difficult not to but any attempt at criticism and comparison will be rewarded.

QUESTION 28

Aside from the law of prescription, analyse how easements may be created, especially when the parties have failed to stipulate clearly that an easement should exist.

How to Read this Question

It is common – but not universal – for a land law syllabus to exclude prescription, hence the exclusion in this question. The examiner wants you to analyse the methods for the creation of easements with special reference to implied grant and reservation.

How to Answer this Question

The answer needs to include a discussion of the distinction between 'grant' and 'reservation' and 'legal' and 'equitable' easements; a brief discussion of express creation and a fuller analysis of the ways in which easements might arise impliedly: necessity; by reason of common intention; under the rule in *Wheeldon v Burrows* (1879); and by reason of **s 62** of the **Law of Property Act 1925**.

Up for Debate

The Law Commission's Report on Easements and Covenants proposes abolition of the existing 'methods' of implied creation of easements and their replacement with a single statutory test. Is this a good idea and will it bring certainty. Is the law currently uncertain? See Law Commission Report No 327 (2011) 'Making land work: easements, covenants and profits à prendre'.

Applying the Law

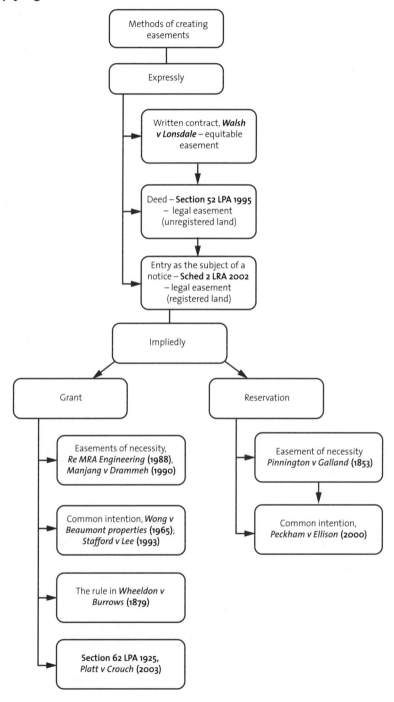

This diagram demonstrates the different methods of creating easements.

ANSWER

Easements are proprietary rights that one landowner enjoys over the land of another. Moreover, like restrictive covenants, easements have a dual aspect. They confer a benefit on one piece of land to be enjoyed by the owners for the time being thereof and they impose a burden on land that must be accepted by the owners for the time being of the servient land. It is intrinsic in this duality that the benefit and the burden of an easement can be transmitted independently along with the land they affect. The ability of easements to bind third parties is one reason, perhaps the most important, why it is necessary to have clear rules governing both the creation of easements and the conditions that must be fulfilled before an easement can be regarded as legal or equitable.

All easements are either created expressly, impliedly or by long user under the law of prescription, although the latter is outside the scope of this question. Generally speaking, and putting prescription on one side, the creation of easements is either by express or implied grant or express or implied reservation. A grant is where the owner of the servient tenement grants an easement to the owner of what will become the dominant tenement. A reservation is the opposite. It is where the transferor of land reserves to themselves an easement over the land they are transferring

Turning first to reservation.[5] If A sells land to B, A may expressly reserve to himself an easement over the land sold. The easement will be legal if it is reserved in a deed and it will be equitable if it is reserved in a written document. Further, an easement implied by reason of necessity (*Pinnington v Galland* (1853)) or one implied from the common intention of the parties (*Peckham v Ellison* (2000)) also can be reserved by the vendor. It should be noted that impliedly reserved easements may also be legal or equitable. The easement will arise by reservation because it is implied into a sale of land by A to B (in favour of A). If, therefore, the sale is by deed, the easement is implied into a deed and is legal. If the sale is by written document for valuable consideration, the easement is implied into that document and will be equitable. In other words, the easement carries the character of the document into which it is implied.[6]

Turning now to easements by grant, in most cases this is done expressly, as where one landowner (A) expressly grants an easement to his neighbour B, either by deed or in writing, or where A sells some land to B and as part of that sale deliberately grants B an easement over the land retained by themselves. In such cases, the easement will be legal or equitable according to the form the transaction takes, although in practice a deed is usually used resulting in a legal easement (assuming registration if required takes place: **ss 25** and **27** of the **LRA 2002**). Further, where the sale of land is involved this may give rise to the implied grant of easements and if the easement is implied into a deed, the

---

5   The distinction between reservation and grant is crucial with regard to implied easements and should always be at the front of your mind.

6   This is an important idea to get to grips with and it is useful to state it explicitly in an easements answer so that the examiner is aware of your understanding of this point.

easement will be legal and, if it is implied into a written transfer, it will be equitable. First, easements may be impliedly granted by way of necessity. So, if the land granted cannot be used except by, say, access over the land retained by the vendor, an easement of necessity will exist, providing a real necessity exists, rather than that it would be more convenient to have the easement – *Re MRA Engineering* (1987), *Walby v Walby* (2012).

The second method by which easements may be impliedly granted is where they arise from the 'common intention' of the parties. An example is provided by *Stafford v Lee* (1992), where the Court of Appeal held that an easement of way could be implied by reason of common intention into the original sale by deed of the land to the plaintiff because the easement was required to put into effect the purpose for which the land was sold (building a house), which purpose was the point of the sale. So too in *Donovan v Rana* (2014) where the easement was for service utilities for a house built on land sold by one party to the other, which was the common intention of the sale. As both these cases illustrate, easements arising through common intention are quite distinct from easements of necessity, for the only requirements are that there was in fact a common intention to use land in a certain way and that an easement is required to give effect to that purpose. Of course, the plaintiff in such cases bears a heavy burden of proof, having to explain why, if there was such a clear common intention, the easement was not expressly inserted into the conveyance in the first place.[7]

Third, easements may be impliedly granted under the rule in *Wheeldon v Burrows* (1879). As we know, no easement can exist where the dominant and the servient tenement are owned and occupied by the same person. However, it often happens that a landowner will use one part of their land for the benefit of another, as where a landowner walks across a field to get to their house. These are sometimes known as 'quasi-easements' because they would be easements had the land been in separate ownership or possession. So, if it should happen that the owner of the entire plot of land should sell the quasi-dominant part of his land (in the previous example, the house), the rule in *Wheeldon v Burrows* stipulates that the vendor might impliedly grant that right to a purchaser. This rule, which is based upon the idea that a person cannot derogate from their grant, can be expressly excluded and, of course, applies only to uses that are capable of being easements. Furthermore, it appears from *Wheeldon* itself that the rights that are implied granted must have been used by the vendor at the time of the grant for the benefit of the part sold and the easement must be continuous and apparent and necessary for the reasonable enjoyment of the part granted (*Wood v Waddington* (2014).[8] Again, the right may be legal if the conveyance of the land was by deed or equitable as in *Borman v Griffith* (1930), in which the grant of the land was under an equitable lease. Although the rule in *Wheeldon* does not apply to reservations of easements (confirmed in *Ellison*), it is obvious that any owner of land who intends to sell land in parts may well find their own land bound by easements they have impliedly granted. It is, in fact, a very powerful means of creating easements.

....

7   Thinking about what a person claiming an implied easement would actually need to argue had taken place in the run up to the acquisition of the estate in land is a useful way of approaching problem questions as well as essays and helps to point you in the right direction.

8   It is now clear that both these conditions must be met – *Wood v Waddington*.

Fourth, easements may be implicitly granted under **s 62** of the **LPA 1925**. At the outset, however, it should be noted that **s 62** only applies to 'conveyances' and these are defined in the **LPA 1925** as transfers by deed. Thus, **s 62** can operate only to create legal easements because it only operates when there has been a transfer of land by deed or its registered land equivalent, the registered disposition. In fact, **s 62** is a very wide-ranging statutory provision and it will apply in two sets of circumstances. First, if land is owned by one person, but split into parts so that he (the owner) occupies one part and a different person occupies the other; if there is then a conveyance of part, the purchaser will acquire as easements all those rights enjoyed at the time of sale for the benefit of the part sold. This is known as a situation of 'prior diversity of occupation' and it does not matter whether the new easement was 'continuous and apparent' or 'reasonably necessary' at the time of the sale: *Sovmots Investments v Secretary of State for the Environment* (1979) (following *Long v Gowlett* (1923)). Practically, this means that, before the land is sold to the person acquiring the easement, it must have been used by either a tenant or a licensee of the vendor who enjoyed rights over that land. If, then, the land is conveyed to that person (or possibly any other person) by deed, that person will be implicitly granted the rights previously enjoyed: so, in *Goldberg v Edwards* (1950), a licensee enjoyed a right over her 'landlord's' land and when a new tenancy by deed was granted to her, that licence was transformed into an easement. Second, however, even if there is no prior diversity of occupation, **s 62** will create easements in favour of the part sold if the use was 'continuous and apparent' at the time of sale: *Platt v Crouch* (2003) and *Wood v Waddington* (2014).[9] Obviously, this creates overlap with *Wheeldon* and the best advice to a person selling land is to expressly exclude the effect of both *Wheeldon* and **s 62**.

Common Pitfalls

Although relatively straightforward, try to avoid merely describing the methods of implied grant. Instead, assess how they react with each other and do not ignore the question of whether implied easements will be legal or equitable. Students commonly confuse 'grant' and 'reservation': be clear.

QUESTION 29

In 1993, Gerald, the owner of three adjacent terraced houses, title to which was registered, decided to realise some capital and resolved to sell two of his properties whilst remaining in the third. In the conveyance of No 20 to Frank, Gerald promised to allow Frank to park his 20-foot horsebox in his (Gerald's) garden, in return for which Frank allowed Gerald to site a satellite dish on his (Frank's) roof. Gerald also agreed orally that Frank could hang a small sign advertising his horsebox building business (which was based on an industrial estate some five miles away) on his end wall. When negotiating a sale of No 22 to Ivor, the latter insisted that he be given the right to temporarily store some roofing materials in Gerald's garden (next to the horsebox), should he run out of space in his yard opposite. This was agreed in the conveyance.

---

9   It is now settled that 'prior diversity' is not always needed, as controversially decided in *Platt v Crouch*.

Gerald has just sold his house (No 21) to Ben, who is unhappy with the elaborate sign that Frank had erected and with the horsebox taking up most of his garden. Frank, however, has just retired and sold his business, the horsebox and house to Christine, who is threatening to remove the satellite dish unless the horsebox and the sign are allowed to stay. Meanwhile, Ivor has been storing materials on a permanent basis in the garden of No 21, and Ben decides to remove them.

▶ **Discuss.**

How to Read this Question

The examiner is expecting a discussion of the nature of easements and how they might be created. Notice the date of the original sale by Gerald – this is before the entry into force of the **Land Registration Act 2002**.

How to Answer this Question

The following areas need to be discussed: the nature of easements, the creation of easements and the formalities required for legal and equitable easements. In turn, this will determine the effect of the easements on third parties.

Applying the Law

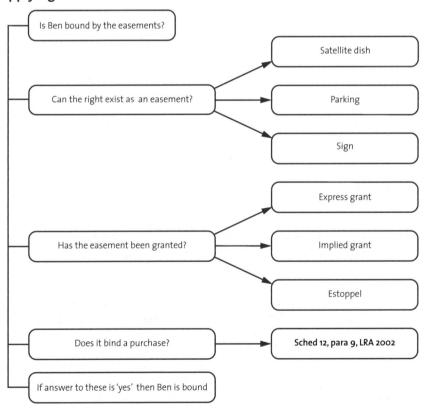

This diagram shows how to establish whether Ben is bound by the various easements.

ANSWER

This problem concerns the acquisition of easements and their effects on persons who subsequently come into possession of the servient and dominant land. It is first necessary to determine whether the alleged rights are capable of existing as easements, then whether any easement that does exist is legal or equitable and then, finally, their effect on a purchaser of the dominant or servient tenement, as the case may be.[10]

(a) Gerald, Frank and the Sales of Both Houses

In this situation, there are three rights that it is alleged may amount to easements: the erection of the satellite dish in favour of Gerald's property, and the parking of the caravan and erection of the sign on Gerald's property in favour of Frank's property. If they do not amount to easements, they will be personal licences between the original parties, which cannot bind on successors in title (*Ashburn Anstalt v Arnold* (1989)). Clearly, in respect of all the rights, there is a capable grantor and grantee, there are two properties that could be the dominant and servient tenements, and both tenements are not owned or occupied by the same person: see *Re Ellenborough Park* (1956).[11] However, some difficulty may exist in the need to show that the alleged rights benefit the dominant tenement *qua* tenement, and whether they fall within the general nature of rights capable of being created as easements.

(i) The Erection of the Satellite Dish

It is highly likely that such a right is of benefit to the dominant tenement in much the same way as the easement to run telephone lines over neighbouring land was accepted in *Lancashire and Cheshire Telephone Exchange Co v Manchester Overseers* (1885).[12] There is no expenditure required of the servient owner and no exclusive occupation of his premises and the right is sufficiently definite. It would seem to be able to qualify as an easement.

Further, the facts make it quite clear that the right was expressly reserved by Gerald when he sold the house to Frank. There is, then, no difficulty over its creation and, because it is expressly reserved in a conveyance (that is, a transfer by deed), this is a legal easement. Finally, given that this is registered land and the easement was created expressly it would have been registered against Frank's title when he became registered proprietor. If it were not, as an expressly created legal easement it would have been an overriding interest under **s 70(1)(a)** of the **LRA 1925** (which was then in force) and such rights are 'preserved' as interests which override under the **Land Registration Act 2002**, thus binding the servient land automatically (**Sched 12, para 9** to the **LRA 2002**). In either case, therefore, Christine is bound to give effect to the easement allowing erection of the satellite dish. It should be noted finally that, when Gerald conveys the dominant tenement to Ben, the benefit of the easement is transferred to Ben under the general rule that a benefit of an easement becomes annexed to each and every part of the legal estate of the dominant tenement and passes with it.

---

10 Highlighting your approach to the structure of the problem question in the introduction makes your answer easy to follow and clear for the examiner.

11 Where certain aspects of the problem are straightforward, do not spend too much time on them, as that is not where the high marks are to be found.

12 Easements is one topic where facts of other cases can be very useful for drawing parallels, as here, and good answers will analyse why certain facts are relevantly similar.

(ii) Can Frank (and then Christine) Claim an Easement of Parking of the Horsebox?

This particular claim raises difficulties for the owners of the alleged dominant tenement. There is no doubt that an easement of parking does exist (*London and Blenheim Estates v Ladbroke* (1994); *Moncrieff v Jamieson* (2008)). However, it is also clear that easements in general must not amount to exclusive use of the servient land (*Copeland v Greenhalf* (1952)) and, for this reason, it is uncertain whether a right to park in a defined space can be an easement.[13] Certainly, a right to *store* many cars cannot (*Batchelor v Marlowe* (2003)) although a right to *park* many can be (*R Square Properties v Nissan Motors* (2014)). On balance, but only on balance, it seems that this right amounts only to a personal permission between Frank and Gerald: in other words, a contractual licence. So, even if the benefit of this contract has passed to Christine, the burden of it is incapable of binding a successor in title of the alleged servient tenement (*Ashburn Anstalt v Arnold*). Ben will not be bound.

(iii) The Sign

There is no doubt that erecting a sign on a neighbour's property can amount to an easement: *Moody v Steggles* (1879). It matters not that this is to advertise some commercial activity on the land, so long as the activity is intimately connected with the land and not a 'pure' commercial venture (*Hill v Tupper* (1863)). Moreover, there is no objection in principle to a grant of an easement to a landowner on the occasion of a conveyance of property X (the house), where the easement is to benefit property Y (the horsebox factory). After all, easements can be created by deed between landowners irrespective of any sale, as where a freeholder grants a right of way to their neighbour.

However, every easement must accommodate the dominant tenement and, in this case, when the land was sold to Frank, the business was undertaken on property some five miles away. While the dominant and servient tenement need not be adjacent, there must be proximity between them (*Pugh v Savage* (1970)). This will be a question of fact in each case. Yet, even if the right is capable of existing as an easement, there is a further problem over its creation. This is not a case of implied grant (there is no necessity, little evidence of common intention, no claim under **s 62** and no quasi-easement within *Wheeldon v Burrows* (1879)) and, in any event, the aim of the parties seems to have been to create the easement expressly. Also, as we are told that the intended right is not expressly included in the conveyance to Frank, it cannot be legal: not being made by deed (more accurately, not by registered disposition, as this is registered land). Of course, easements can be expressly granted by other means (assuming relevant formality), but then they will be only equitable. In order to be equitable, the easement would have to have been granted by a specifically enforceable valid contract (*Walsh v Lonsdale* (1882)), but the 'contract' in this case is not in writing as required by **s 2** of the **Law of Property (Miscellaneous Provisions) Act 1989**. The remaining possibility is that Frank can claim an easement by proprietary estoppel: *Joyce v Epsom & Ewell* (2012). There appears to have been a promise made and we are told that Frank erects an elaborate (and hence expensive?) sign. This may be detrimental reliance.

---

13 It might be useful to bring some academic commentary in here.

Further, it is no objection to the existence of an estoppel that it did indeed arise out of a failed explicit bargain (*Flowermix v Site Developments* (2000)), although *Thorner v Major* (2009) is critical of this. If an estoppel is established, Christine will have obtained the benefit of it under the normal rule that it is annexed to the land. Ben, the purchaser of the servient tenement, would be bound by the estoppel easement as an overriding interest because of the decision in *Celsteel v Alton* (1985) (followed in *Thatcher v Douglas* (1995)) under the then applicable **Land Registration Act 1925 (s 70(1)(a))**.[14]

(b) Gerald, Ivor, the Roofing Materials and Ben

Whether the right to store is capable of being an easement again depends on the case law. It must not amount to exclusive use of the servient tenement (*Copeland v Greenhalf; Batchelor v Marlowe*) but we are told here that the right expressly granted was a right to store temporarily when the need should arise. There are many easements (for example, a right to use a lavatory: *Miller v Emcer Products* (1956)) that, when being exercised by the dominant tenement owner on the servient land, exclude any other use by the servient owner. One view is that the right of temporary storage is analogous to the right to park generally on a piece of land and, in any event, a right to store trade produce has been accepted as an easement in *AG of Southern Nigeria v John Holt and Co* (1915). Thus, it is a matter for argument whether this can exist as an easement. If it does, it seems that Ivor is going beyond its explicit terms and, of course, this can be restrained by injunction. Finally, if the easement does exist, it is clear that it has been expressly created by the conveyance (that is, by deed/registered disposition) and is legal. As with the legal easements considered above, this will bind Ben, the purchaser of the servient tenement, whether as being registered against his title or as an overriding interest under **s 70(1)(a)** of the **LRA 1925** given continuing validity by the transitional provisions of the **LRA 2002**.

Common Pitfalls

It is crucial to use case law other than *Re Ellenborough Park* to explain why you think these rights might be easements. Then, you must determine whether they are legal or equitable as this determines how any easements affect purchasers of the servient land. Do not forget to explain how the benefit of easements pass.

QUESTION 30

In 2005, John became the registered leasehold proprietor of No 35 Main Street. Title to this property included the alleyway between No 35 and No 37. Alan was the registered leasehold proprietor of No 37 and he accessed the upper floor of No 37 by a staircase that he had installed in the alleyway following a written agreement with John. In 2008 John sold No 35 to Bob. In 2009, Alan granted a lease of the first floor of No 37 to Claire and Claire was duly registered proprietor of the leasehold estate. Bob does not wish Claire to use the staircase.

14 For the sake of completeness we can note that, if created after 13 October 2003, equitable easements cannot now be interests which override and must be protected by notice on the register.

In addition, Claire decided to set up a beauty salon on the first floor of No 37. Before transferring the lease of the first floor Alan had run a ventilation system from the first floor to the ground floor. Claire wishes to use this system as she needs to keep her salon at just the right temperature. Alan had also been using the hot tub on the roof of Claire's flat. The lease to Claire included the roof space. Alan has now sold the lease of the ground floor to David who wants to block off the ventilation shaft although he was aware of Claire's use of the ventilation shaft at the time of sale. Claire is refusing to let David use the hot tub whilst the dispute goes on, but David insists that he is entitled to use the hot tub.

▶ Advise Claire.

How to Read this Question

The examiner is looking for you to demonstrate your knowledge of how easements are created and the effect of unconscionable conduct on the parties. It brings together easements, estoppel and licences.

How to Answer this Question

The answer needs to include a discussion of the following: leasehold estates and easements; the creation of easements and their effect on purchasers; the relevance of inequitable conduct and constructive trusts – *Lloyd v Dugdale* (2002). The key is to state the law, then apply it to the actual facts of the problem.

Applying the Law

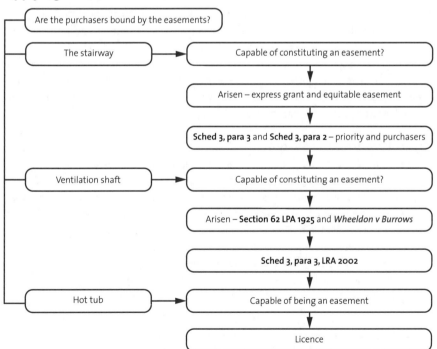

This diagram demonstrates how to determine whether the easements in this problem are binding on the purchasers of the servient land.

ANSWER

In order to assess it is necessary to analyse the types of rights that can constitute easements, as well as the methods of creation of such rights, and the effects of these rights on third parties. Even though the relevant estates are leasehold, and Alan is Claire's landlord, this does not affect the operation of the easements and as long as there is a dominant and servient tenement in separate ownership.[15]

(a) The Stairway

The use of a stairway to access property is capable of being an easement (*Liverpool CC v Irwin* (1976); *Chaudhary v Yavuz* (2011)).[16] There is also a dominant and a servient tenement and these are in separate ownership. It does not matter for this that the properties may (or may not) have the same freeholder. It clearly benefits the dominant land allowing easy access to the upper floor. This right is capable of being an easement in these circumstances.

The next question then is whether such an easement arose between the original parties, Alan and John. John had agreed with Alan *in writing* that Alan could use the stairway and so this easement is equitable by virtue of the doctrine in *Walsh v Lonsdale* (1882) and compliance with **s 2 Law of Property (Miscellaneous Provisions) Act 1989**. As successor in title to Alan, Claire is entitled to the benefit of any property rights which ran with the land. But, being an unregistered equitable easement means that there is some difficulty in showing that John's successor, Bob, is bound by that easement. Whether or not he is so bound will depend on the priority rules in **s 29 LRA 2002**. The easement, not being the subject of a notice, can only bind Bob as a purchaser if it amounts to an overriding interest under **Sched 3 LRA 2002**. It does not, as decided in *Chaudhary v Yavuz*.[17] Claire cannot therefore continue to use the staircase to access the property. It is also important to note that there is no mechanism on these facts whereby the court will 'imply' an easement of necessity. There needs to be a conveyance into which such an easement can be implied between potential grantor and grantee, which is not the case.

(b) The Ventilation System

The first thing to note here is that the passage of air through a defined channel, such as a ventilation shaft, is a recognised easement (*Wong v Beaumont Properties* (1964)). But the question remains whether one has been created in Claire's favour. There is no expressly granted easement, and so we must see whether one of the four methods of implying easements will assist Claire. These are: easements of necessity, common intention, the rule in *Wheeldon v Burrows* (1879) and the operation of **s 62 LPA 1925**. First, the rules on easements of necessity will not assist Claire here, as there is no evidence of genuine necessity, as opposed to convenience (*MRA Engineering v Trimster* (1987); *Manjang v Drammah* (1999)).

---

15 Dealing with this primary issue here saves time later on.

16 Although you may feel as though you are repeating yourself when outlining the structure of your answer overall, and then of each section, it is likely to lead to a better quality answer.

17 The facts of this case are so similar to the facts of the problem that it can be relied on to a large extent in addressing the issue of actual occupation.

Second, implication by common intention may be relevant because Alan was aware that Claire wanted to use the top flat as a beauty salon. But the test for 'common intention' is strict (*Stafford v Lee* (1993); *Chaffe v Kingsley* (2000)) and most importantly the intention must be one shared by the parties. The most plausible explanation of Alan's action here is that although he knew Claire wanted to set up a beauty salon, he was not party to the plan, as long as she could pay him for the leasehold interest. There was nothing in the nature of a joint enterprise here, suggesting that the rules on common intention easements would not assist Claire.

Third, the rule in *Wheeldon v Burrows* operates so as to imply an easement into a deed of grant of an estate in land where the grantor had previously used the land in such a way as to amount to a quasi-easement. Here, since Alan had been using the ventilation shaft himself for the passage of air, Claire can rely on the rule. *Wheeldon* also requires that the use of the quasi-easement be 'continuous and apparent' and also 'reasonably necessary' for the enjoyment of the dominant tenement (*Wood v Waddington* (2014)). The passage of air through the system is likely to be continuous and the existence of the ventilation shaft is likely to have been obvious. So too ventilation is certainly 'reasonably' necessary for use of the land as a beauty salon. Consequently, an argument based on *Wheeldon v Burrows* has a reasonable chance of success

Claire may also wish to use **s 62 LPA 1925** which will imply easements into conveyances of a legal estate. *Sovmots Investments v Secretary of State for the Environment* (1979) stipulated that in order to transform a mere permission into an easement, usually there must have been prior diversity of occupation of that land. That was not the case here. However, *Platt v Crouch* (2003), followed in *Wood v Waddington* (2014) determines that as long as the usage was continual and apparent (as here) there is no need for prior diversity of occupation. Thus Claire may also rely on **s 62**: there is a conveyance as her lease was 'granted' as a legal estate.[18] As a result, Alan would be subject to an easement of passage of air through a defined channel as a result of the rule in *Wheeldon v Burrows* and/or **s 62 LPA 1925**. Does David have to respect this easement? As an implied legal easement, it will fall under **Sched 3, para 3 LRA 2002** and will override a purchaser under **s 29 LRA 2002** if: it was known to the purchaser at the time of the disposition;, or was obvious on a reasonably careful inspection of the land; or had been used at any time in the 12 months prior to the disposition. The last of these certainly applies and causes the easement to override David's estate and be enforceable.

(c) The Hot Tub

The final issue concerns the hot tub and whether Claire must permit David to use it. However, it is uncertain whether the use of a hot tub can constitute an easement. According to *Re Ellenborough Park*, a right that is *purely* recreational is not capable of being an easement, but the right to use a park was considered capable. The possibility of the use of a swimming pool being a valid easement was approved in the Canadian case of *Grant v*

---

18 After *Waddington*, *Platt* now represents the law despite being controversial when first decided.

MacDonald (1992)[19] but frowned on in the Scottish decision in *Moncreiff v Jamieson*. Perhaps, however, the use of a hot tub is even less 'easement like' than use of a swimming pool and more likely would amount to a mere licence. As a result, being a licence, it would be incapable of binding a third party (*Ashburn Anstalt v Arnold* (1989)). There is no reason to believe that a constructive trust would have arisen in David's favour either (see *Ashburn Anstalt*). Further, and in any event, there is no express of implied creation of the alleged easement – the 'agreement' is entirely oral and there is nothing to suggest an estoppel. It is a precarious personal permission and there is nothing to suggest that David has been given this right.

Common Pitfalls

Take care to adopt a structured approach. Ensure that, for each right claimed, you have considered both whether it can be an easement – that is, has it the necessary characteristics – and also by what method it can be acquired. Then, in order to complete the answer, consider the impact of any right on third parties.

---

19 This case would not be binding in an English or Welsh court, but overseas cases provide some useful discussion of the very issues you are looking at and certainly credit will be given for considering them, as long as they are not relied on too heavily.

8

Freehold Covenants

INTRODUCTION

In Chapter 5 on leases, we examined the law surrounding the operation of leasehold covenants. However, it is not only landlord and tenant who may wish to enter into promises affecting the mode of use of their property. Freeholders may also wish to control the use that neighbours may make of their land, as where owners of residential property may wish to preserve the non-business character of their area, or the owners of an industrial estate may wish to limit the type of activity carried on there. Obviously, freeholders do not stand in a relationship of landlord and tenant with each other and the rules of leasehold covenants are inapplicable. Consequently, a set of principles have developed – mainly in connection with restrictive covenants – that govern the running of covenants between freeholders. Like leasehold covenants (and easements), each freehold covenant comprises a 'benefit' and a 'burden'. It is always necessary, when considering problems in this particular area, to remember that before a claimant can sue a defendant on a particular covenant, the benefit must have passed to the claimant and the burden must have passed to the defendant. Indeed, it can quite easily happen that the benefit of a covenant has passed, but the burden has not, or vice versa. So it is imperative when dealing with these issues to consider the issue of the benefit of a covenant separately from questions relating to the burden.

Checklist

- Be clear about the rules for passing the benefit and burden of covenants. They are different.
- Understand the limited relevance of a claim 'at law' and a claim 'in equity'.
- Understand the avoidance techniques currently employed.
- Be aware of the Law Commission's proposals for the reform of the law of covenants – Report No 327 (2011), 'Making land work: easements, covenants and profits à prendre'.
- In problem questions, it is wiser to tackle the issue of passing the burden first, and then move to the benefit. Identify your defendant first and why they are liable, and this will define who can be the claimant.

QUESTION 31

'The case of *Crest Nicholson Residential (South) Ltd v McAllister* (2004) EWCA Civ 410 is an important milestone in the lengthy development through the case law of the law of restrictive covenants. When these are read collectively judicial decisions in the area provide one of the richest areas of fantasy in written English. *Crest Nicholson*, though tediously lengthy as is the way with contemporary judgments, blows a breath of fresh air into the gloom created by the mysterious judgment in *Federated Homes Ltd v Mill Lodge Properties.*'

(Kenny, 'Drafting restrictive covenants' (2005) 69 Conv 2)

In the light of the above statement, consider whether the rules relating to the running of freehold covenants adequately ensure that successors in title can enforce the benefits obtained by an original covenantee.

How to Read this Question

This asks you to consider the passing of the benefit of freehold covenants. In particular, the effect that *Federated Homes* had on this area of law. The examiner will expect you to consider whether the rules are fit for purpose, rather than just repeat the rules.

How to Answer this Question

Consider the meaning of 'benefit'. Remember that **s78 LPA 1925** identifies who is a 'successors in title' and this is where case law has an impact. Identify how the rules for the passing of the benefit differ 'at law' and 'in equity': annexation, assignment and building schemes. Relevant cases include *Federated Homes v Mill Lodge* (1980); *Whitgift Homes v Stocks* (2001); *Crest Nicholson Residential (South) Ltd v McAllister* (2004).

Up for Debate

Is it necessary to have different rules for passing the benefit 'at law' and 'in equity'? How will the Law Commission's proposals affect this issue? See Law Commission Report No 327 (2011), 'Making land work: easements, covenants and profits à prendre'.

Aim Higher

Consider the limitations on the *Federated Homes* principle, particularly how the rule may be excluded and the extent to which the land has to be identified in the covenant. Also, assess the effect that the Law Commission's proposals might have on the application of the *Federated Homes* rule.

Applying the Law

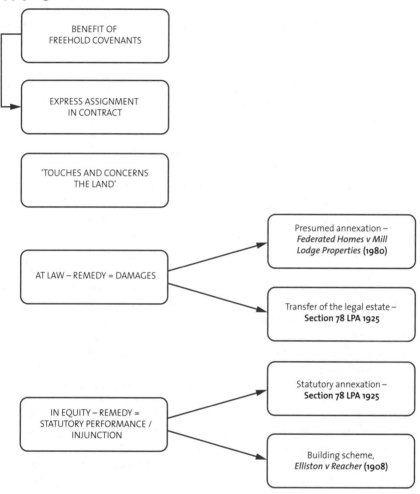

This diagram shows the rules relating to the transmissibility of the benefit of a freehold covenant.

ANSWER

The law of real property has developed rules and principles that allow one landowner to control the use to which their neighbour may put their own land. As well as being achieved through the law of easements, it can also be achieved by the use of covenants. The law relating to freehold covenants applies in all of those circumstances where there is no privity of estate between the parties and each covenant will confer a benefit and a corresponding burden on the relevant parties. Indeed, the rules relating to the transmission of the benefit of a freehold covenant – that is, to somebody who buys the land from the original covenantee (the person to whom the covenant was made) – are entirely independent from the rules relating to the transmission of the burdens of the covenant – that is, to a person who buys land from the original covenantor (the person who made the promise). It is quite possible, therefore, for the benefit of a covenant to run to a successor in title of the original covenantee, but for the burden of that covenant to have been destroyed or to bind only the original covenantor, and vice versa.[1]

This question raises issues concerning the transmission of the benefit of freehold covenants or, more accurately, whether a successor in title to land of the original covenantee gains the right to enforce covenants made for the benefit of land when he acquires that land. In very general terms, apart from situations in which there has been an express assignment of contractual rights (see below), the benefit of a covenant will pass provided that the covenant 'touches and concerns' the land of the original covenantee when it was made. This is simply another way of saying that property law is concerned with the transmission of proprietary rights, not personal advantages. So, it is essential to determine whether the covenant 'touches and concerns' according to the flexible guidelines put forward by Lord Oliver in *Swift Investments v Combined English Stores* (1989). If the freehold covenant does 'touch and concern' the land, then it is possible that the right to sue on the covenant may pass either 'at law' or 'in equity' to a successor to the original covenantee. The methods by which this benefit may pass in law or in equity are very similar, save that the requirements of equity are slightly less demanding. If a claimant had the choice of suing on the benefit of the covenant at law or in equity (which occurs frequently), much would depend on which remedy the claimant required.[2] A suit at law usually would result in the award of damages, whereas in equity the discretionary remedies of injunction to prevent breach of a restrictive covenant or order of specific performance to compel performance of a positive covenant would be available.

Ultimately, once the 'touching and concerning' requirement has been met, it seems that three further conditions must be satisfied if the benefit is to run to the successor in law. First, the person seeking to enforce the covenant must own some legal estate in the land. This may be the same legal estate as the original covenantee or a derivative legal estate – s 78 LPA 1925 – such as where the original covenantee being a freeholder lets the land to a successor on a lease by deed. This has clearly made the transmission of the benefit at law slightly simpler. Second, the covenant must benefit the land of the original covenantee. In most cases, it will be enough that the covenant touches and concerns the land because, from this, the fact of benefit will be presumed (*Whitgift Homes v Stocks* (2001)). However, it is open to somebody disputing the fact that the benefit has run at law to claim that the land of the original covenantee never could have benefited from the particular covenant made and therefore cannot pass to a successor in title: see *Wrotham Park Estate v Parkside Homes* (1974). Third, and most importantly of all, the covenant must have been annexed to the land in order for the

---

1   This introduction puts the discussion as to the running of the benefit of a restrictive covenant into context.

2   It is important in a question like this to be aware of the practical consequences of the benefit running in law as opposed to equity and vice versa, not just the different rules governing the passing of the benefit.

benefit to run with the land.[3] In this respect, the decision in *Federated Homes v Mill Lodge Properties Ltd* (1980) has made the position much simpler. According to the Court of Appeal decision in that case, now fully confirmed in *Whitgift Homes v Stocks* and *Crest Nicholson v McAllister* (2004), the benefit of every covenant whether positive or negative and whether in law or in equity will be annexed to the land and, indeed, to every part of it, provided that the land is identified in the covenant (*Crest*). Later cases (*Roake v Chadha* (1984); *Crest Nicholson*) have made it clear that this statutory annexation can be excluded by clear contrary intention, but the decision in *Federated Homes* has clearly provided successors in title to original covenantees with a safe and certain method of claiming that they are entitled to the benefit of a covenant. The decision in *Federated Homes* has been subject to criticism: for example, it has been pointed out that **s 78** does not precisely say what the Court of Appeal alleges and that it is a decision favouring certainty at the expense of individuality. Nevertheless, as noted above, it has been confirmed by a strong Court of Appeal in *Whitgift Homes v Stocks* and, unless overruled by the House of Lords (which seems most unlikely), this decision will govern the running of the benefit of covenants both at law and in equity.[4]

Turning now to the position in equity, we will see that if the covenant touches and concerns the land, the person seeking to enforce the covenant must have *some* estate or interest in the land, although of course this may now only be equitable. Thereafter, there are three methods by which the benefit may transfer in equity. The first of these is under the rule of statutory annexation that we have just considered in relation to covenants at law. As noted, *Federated Homes* applies with equal vigour to the annexation of covenants in equity, so a covenant will be statutorily annexed to each and every part of the land provided that it is clear what land is intended to be benefited. Indeed, the efficacy of the *Federated Homes* principle is such that the other two methods of transferring the benefit in equity may now be largely redundant, except perhaps in the limited circumstances of express contrary intention (*Roake*) or when the advantages of a building scheme are required.

The building scheme is the second method by which the benefit may be transferred in equity. This is a rule based upon common intention and practicality. It allows a common vendor (such as a property developer) to transfer the benefit of the covenants received by them from every purchaser of a plot of land to every other purchaser of a plot of land. It is an attempt to create mutually enforceable obligations and the advantage of a building scheme is that it allows the benefit of later purchasers' covenants to be given to earlier purchasers. The requirements for a valid building scheme were laid down in *Elliston v Reacher* (1908). There must be a common vendor, the land must be laid out in definable plots, the benefits must be intended to be mutually enforceable and these must be the conditions upon which all purchasers buy. These are, however, not inflexible and later

---

3   This paragraph does a good job of providing a clear and coherent structure to the rules being discussed. It is important to be systematic in this way.

4   This sort of analysis of the continuing strength of an authority and its acceptance in the courts is a good approach to take to controversial decisions.

cases such as *Re Dolphins Conveyance* (1970) and *Baxter v Four Oaks* (1965) illustrate that the benefit will run under a building scheme even though all of the requirements have not been met.[5] Importantly, however, no building scheme can exist unless it is clear what land is subject to the scheme (*Whitgift Homes v Stocks*).

Finally, the third method of transmitting the benefit of covenants is the assignment. It is trite law that the benefit of a contract (that is, a covenant) may be expressly assigned. So, for example, if a purchaser of the covenantee's land is expressly assigned the benefit of that covenant, they will be able to enforce it. However, this method does have some disadvantages. It seems that this is a method of transferring the benefit personally. So, following *Re Pinewood* (1958), where there has been an assignment of the covenant to the first successor of the original covenantee, a chain of assignments is required if the benefit is to be assigned to subsequent assignees. Of course, after *Federated Homes*, such a method is largely redundant.

It should be apparent from the above that it is relatively straightforward to transmit the benefit of a covenant both at law and in equity. The decision in *Federated Homes* has made this even more likely and the only real limit (except possibly for personal assignment) seems to be that the covenant must touch and concern the land. Of course, having the benefit of a covenant is useless unless there is somebody who is subject to the burden. In this respect, the rule that the burden of restrictive covenants only may run, and then only in equity, is a real limitation on the practical enforcement of covenants.

Common Pitfalls

Do not ignore the differences between enforcement at law and in equity and remember that case law might not be consistent: *Federated Homes* has been qualified by *Crest Nicholson*.

QUESTION 32

In what circumstances may the burden of a freehold covenant pass to a successor in title of the original covenantor?

How to Read this Question

This is the counterpart of the question above and calls for an examination of the passing of the burden of freehold covenants. The examiner is looking for clearly stated rules, supported by case law, with some analysis of their practical effect.

How to Answer this Question

Identify the original covenantor and explain the effect of 'law' and 'equity'. Identify the application of s79 of the LPA 1925. Crucially, consider the impact of registration requirements.

---

5 This paragraph makes good use of case law to show the flexibility of the rules relating to building schemes.

Applying the Law

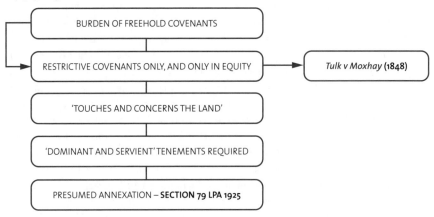

BURDEN OF FREEHOLD COVENANTS
RESTRICTIVE COVENANTS ONLY, AND ONLY IN EQUITY	→	*Tulk v Moxhay* (1848)
'TOUCHES AND CONCERNS THE LAND'
'DOMINANT AND SERVIENT' TENEMENTS REQUIRED
PRESUMED ANNEXATION – **SECTION 79 LPA 1925**

This diagram shows the options for the running of the burden of a freehold covenant.

ANSWER

It is a general principle of English law that, while the benefit of a contract can be assigned to a third party, the burden of a contract cannot. In the law of real property, this can cause serious difficulties, for it means that when an owner of land makes a promise by covenant to do or not to do something on their land (in other words, imposing a burden on that land), then any successor in title to that original covenantor may well be able to acquire the land free of the burden placed upon it. Obviously, this is of great advantage to the successor to the original covenantor, but it is of no use to those persons who enjoy the benefit of the covenant, for they may see the benefits that they so carefully extracted destroyed on the first sale of the burdened land. Fortunately, the law of real property has mitigated the harshness of the contractual rule by providing that, in some circumstances, burdens attached to land by way of covenant may assume a proprietary nature and may be passed on to any person who subsequently acquires that land. If the covenant was made between freeholders, the rules commonly known as the rules of freehold covenants come into play. Not surprisingly, the rules allowing the transmission of burdens in non-leasehold cases are quite strict, as it is a general policy requirement that title to land should not be unduly cluttered.

The starting point for a discussion of the transmission of the burden of freehold covenants is the decision in *Tulk v Moxhay* (1848). In that case, concerning a restrictive covenant not to build in Leicester Square, it was decided that if a covenant touched and concerned the land, it could, as a matter of conscience and equity, be binding on any purchaser of the land burdened by the covenant who had notice of its existence. Although the principles have developed considerably since *Tulk*, the limits put on the doctrine by that case still exist. Thus, it is clear that burdens of covenants may only run in equity and, as an equitable doctrine, there are all of the attendant problems associated with equitable rights, including the fact that remedies are discretionary. Moreover, despite some attempts to argue the contrary, it is clear that only the burden of restrictive or negative covenants may run in equity (*Rhone v Stephens* (1994)).

The conditions for the transmission of the burden of a covenant are as follows. First, the covenant must touch and concern the land and therefore pass the test in *Swift Investments v Combined English Stores* (1989). Second, the covenant must be negative in nature and this is a question of substance not a question of form, normally resolved by asking whether the owner of the burdened land is required to expend money. Third, the doctrine takes effect in equity only thus opening up the possibility that the equitable interests (that is, the negative covenants) may be defeated by a sale to a purchaser of a legal estate for value. Of course, in many cases, these hurdles are not formidable and, in most cases, the restrictive covenant will satisfy these initial tests. If it does, there are further matters that must be satisfied before a burden will run to a successor in title. First, and most importantly of all, the covenant must have been made for the benefit of land owned by the covenantee. In other words, the burden cannot run unless it is a burden that benefits the land of the covenantee. Like easements, there must be a dominant and servient tenement. In effect, this means that not only must the original covenantee have owned land at the time the covenant was created but also that the particular covenant must have been capable of benefiting that land (*Whitgift Homes v Stocks* (2001)). This is a question of fact, although the onus is on the person seeking to deny the covenant to prove that the land of the covenantee was not in fact benefited (*Wrotham Park Estates v Parkside Homes* (1974)) and may often be presumed from the fact that the covenant touches and concerns (*Whitgift*).[6] The meaning of benefit is crucial in these circumstances and, according to *Re Gadd's Transfer* (1966), it has several components: for example, does it affect the value or mode of use of the land? Next, it is necessary to establish that the burden of the covenant is annexed to the land. Express words of annexation can, of course, be used. So, for example, a covenant expressed to be for X and their heirs and successors in title would effectively annex the covenant to the land. However, such long-windedness is no longer needed because of **s 79** of the **LPA**. This provision effectively incorporates words of annexation into every deed of covenant. The net effect is that the burden of restrictive covenants will be automatically annexed to the land unless the deed of covenant expressly contains a provision to the contrary. The position is effectively the same as that achieved for the benefit of the covenant under **s 78** of the **LPA**, as interpreted in *Federated Homes v Mill Lodge* (1980).[7]

Assuming these conditions are established, the covenant now has a proprietary nature. This means that the burden of the covenant can, in principle, bind successors in title to the original covenantor's land. However, as we have noted above, these restrictive covenants take effect in equity and, like all equitable rights, they are capable of being defeated by a sale to a purchaser of a legal estate for value. Before 1925, as *Tulk* itself makes clear, a purchaser of the covenantor's land would only be bound by restrictive covenants, even if they had passed the above tests, if they purchased that land with notice of the covenants. Now, of course, notice has been replaced by registration, both in registered and unregistered land. Thus, in order for a proprietary restrictive covenant to bind *a purchaser*, it must be registered in the relevant way. In registered land, the covenant will, under **ss 29** and **33** of the **Land Registration Act 2002**, need to be protected by the entry of either an Agreed or Unilateral Notice

---

6   This description of the burden of proof here shows that the writer is aware of the detail of the rule and its operation in practice.

7   This comparison with the rules relating to burden adds an extra dimension of analysis to the discussion.

against the title of the burdened land. In unregistered land, the restrictive covenant is classi-fied as a Class D(ii) land charge under the **Land Charges Act 1972** and must be registered accordingly against the name of the original estate owner. It should be noted, however, that the requirement of registration is needed only to bind purchasers of the legal estate. Thus, because these covenants are already proprietary, if the covenantor's land comes into the possession of somebody who is not a purchaser of a legal estate (such as a squatter or an equitable tenant or a person receiving the property by way of gift), then a restrictive cove-nant will be binding, whether registered or not.

These, then, are the conditions upon which the burden of a restrictive covenant may be binding. As is obvious, the rules are quite strict, applying only to restrictive covenants and only operating in equity, thereby making covenants subject to a requirement of registration. Obviously, the burden of positive covenants cannot run and of course this can cause hard-ship. For this reason, there are a number of avoidance devices that may be used. None of these are entirely satisfactory[8] and, in particular, the concept of 'mutual benefit and burden' has been restricted by case law (*Thamesmead Town v Allotey* (1998), but see recently *Wilkin-son v Kerndene* (2013) and *Goodman v Elwood* (2014)). Consequently, it is only if the Law Com-mission's 2011 proposals for reform are adopted (and this seems unlikely at present) that the situation will change substantially. Those proposals would ensure that a covenant could be either positive or negative in substance, whose benefit and burden would run if registered against the title of the covenantee's and covenantor's titles respectively.[9] Clearly, this would solve some of the present problems in the law and make the avoidance devices unnecessary.

Common Pitfalls

Be very clear that, here, you are being asked to write about the person who gave the covenant – that is, the covenantor – and who will subsequently be bound by that covenant. You are not being asked to discuss the right to sue on or enforce that same covenant. Do not confuse benefit and burden.

QUESTION 33

Wordsworth was the freehold owner, registered with absolute title, of five shops in Par-nassus Road, Redbridge. No 5 sold bread and cakes, No 6 general hardware, No 7 was a chemist and Nos 8 and 9 were empty. Two years ago, Wordsworth sold No 8 to Virginia, who covenanted that she would not carry on any trade other than a hair salon at No 8. Just after, Wordsworth sold No 9 to Marlowe who covenanted 'with Wordsworth and the owners for the time being of the shops in Parnassus Road' that he would use No 9 for no other purpose than the breeding and wholesale of pet chinchilla rabbits and would erect and maintain a fence to protect his neighbours in the event of an escape.

8   This section takes the essay beyond the main focus of the passing of the burden of negative covenants giving an extra dimension to the answer.

9   It is always good to show that you are aware of reform proposals, especially where they are recent, and that you know some of the specifics of those proposals.

Last week, Wordsworth let No 5 on a four-year lease in writing to Chaucer, who immediately sub-let to Betjeman. At the same time, Wordsworth sold No 6 by registered disposition to Keats, who turned the premises into a garden centre. Wordsworth has since discovered that his original tenant of No 7, the chemist, left the property some months ago and it is now occupied by Trevelyan, a squatter, who is selling second-hand electrical goods.

In the course of her hairdressing, Virginia has invented a new miracle shampoo and has begun a small-scale manufacturing and retail outlet from her premises. Meanwhile, Marlowe found that chinchilla breeding was not profitable and has turned to breeding parrots and budgerigars. Unfortunately, this has got out of hand and Parnassus Road is overrun with birds escaping from No 9. Keat's entire stock is threatened.

▶ Advise the occupants of Parnassus Road as to their respective rights and obligations.

How to Read this Question

The examiner is asking you *to apply* the rules concerning the passing of freehold covenants, with particular emphasis in this problem on passing the benefit.

How to Answer this Question

Set out the law and apply the law. Thus what is the position of the original covenantors and covenantees and will the benefit pass at law and/or in equity. Consider **s 78** of the **LPA 1925** and *Federated Homes* (1980); *Whitgift Homes v Stocks* (2001); *Crest Nicholson v McAllister* (2004). Note also the effect of **s 56** of the **LPA 1925** and *Amsprop Trading v Harris* (1997). Note also the position of squatters.

Applying the Law

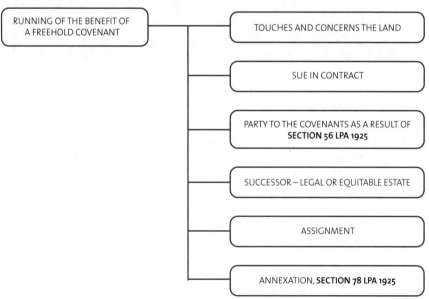

This diagram shows the options for the running of the benefit of a freehold covenant.

ANSWER

The problem concerns the law of freehold covenants. There is no issue here of the running of the burden of the covenant: both the original covenantors (Virginia and Marlowe) are still in occupation of the burdened land and it is against them that an action for breach of the covenants will be directed.[10] Turning first to the nature of these covenants, the covenant by Virginia is clearly restrictive in nature and without doubt touches and concerns the land. Likewise, Marlowe's covenant to keep only chinchilla rabbits is restrictive and, because it affects the mode of use of the land (*Swift Investments v Combined English Stores* (1989)), it also touches and concerns. Marlowe's second covenant – to erect and maintain a fence – does touch and concern, but it is positive in nature, requiring expenditure by the owner of the burdened land. However, the fact that one covenant is positive is not crucial in this case, as it is only successors in title that cannot be made liable on the burden of positive covenants. Here, the defendants are the original covenantors and there is nothing to prevent the benefit of a positive covenant passing to successors of the original covenantee.

First, we need to identify the original parties to the covenants, for they will be able to sue on the benefit of the covenant against Virginia and Marlowe (the original covenantors), irrespective of any question of the passing of the benefit under land law rules. This would be simply a matter of contract. Clearly, Wordsworth, the original freeholder (and now the landlord of No 5 and owner of No 7), has the benefit of all covenants by both Virginia and Marlowe, being an original covenantee: he can sue on all the covenants at law and on those covenants in equity where he is still in possession of the land (*Chambers v Randall* (1923)). Of course, the remedy at law will be damages and they will be nominal if Wordsworth does not possess the land at the time of any breach of covenant. In practice, he will wish to obtain an injunction for breach of both restrictive covenants and a decree of specific performance in respect of the positive covenant to build a fence.[11] This will require him to sue in equity and, therefore, he should sue as freeholder of No 7. It is clear also, however, that Virginia, the purchaser of No 8 (and an original covenantor to Wordsworth), is actually an original covenantee of the covenants made by Marlowe. As we are told, Marlowe's covenants are made with his vendor (Wordsworth) but also the 'owners for the time being of the shops in Parnassus Road'.[12] This description includes Virginia who, by then, is an owner of a shop in Parnassus Road: s 56 of the **Law of Property Act 1925**. That section allows a person 'to take the benefit' of any covenant as an original party to it so long as they are in existence at the date of the covenant and the covenant is intended to benefit them as a party (*Amsprop Trading v Harris* (1997)). Thus, Virginia may enforce both the positive and negative covenants against Marlowe in law or in equity, being an original covenantee.

10 The introduction to a problem question is a good place to close off 'blind alleys' and to show that you are aware of the precise issues arising in the problem.

11 It is important to show the practical remedial consequences of the continuing distinction between law and equity in relation to freehold covenants.

12 Where a problem question gives you the precise wording of an agreement, as here, it is likely that the wording itself is going to be relevant to the answer, and so it is worth analysing that wording closely.

We can now turn to the position of successors in title to the original covenantees (Wordsworth). It is trite law that the benefit of a covenant may be transmitted to a successor either at law or in equity, provided that the covenant touches and concerns the land (except possibly in cases of contractual assignment).[13]

(a) The Successors to Shop No 5: Chaucer and Betjeman

It is clear that Chaucer and Betjeman will be able to claim the benefit of these covenants only in equity. Chaucer's estate in the land is under a four-year lease in writing – not by deed – and so it must amount to an equitable lease (*Walsh v Lonsdale* (1882)). Chaucer has only an equitable estate and thus his tenant Betjeman can be in no better position. So, both have equitable interests and we need to consider whether the benefit of the covenant has passed in equity (*Mellon v Sinclair* (1996)).

Clearly, all covenants touch and concern the land, and both Chaucer and Betjeman have some interest in the land, entitling them to sue. We may note here that neither of them has to have the same interest in the land as the original covenantee (Wordsworth), so long as they have some interest: s78 of the **LPA 1925**. Moreover, the covenants will be presumed to benefit the land (*Whitgift Homes v Stocks* (2001)) and, in any event, seem to be within the meaning of 'benefit' in *Re Gadd* (1966). However, has the benefit passed under one of the three ways recognised by equity: assignment, a building scheme or annexation? There is no evidence of the first, and the second is clearly inappropriate on the facts. However, after *Federated Homes v Mill Lodge Properties* (1980), it is established that the effect of s78 of the **LPA 1925** is to attach the benefit of a covenant automatically to the land, provided that the land is readily identifiable from the covenant (*Crest Nicholson v McAllister* (2004)), unless this is explicitly precluded, as in *Roake v Chadha* (1984).[14] There is no such exclusion in this case. Further, it is immaterial that the present claimants have an interest in only part of the land originally benefited by these covenants. Under *Federated Homes*, a covenant is attached to each and every part of the land, so long as each and every part is capable of benefiting from it. That is clearly the case here. It should also be noted that *Federated Homes* applies to positive covenants in exactly the same way as negative covenants and so no distinction can be drawn between the covenants made by Virginia and those made by Marlowe. Thus, the benefit of all three covenants has run in principle to Chaucer and Betjeman and they can take action to restrain unlawful use of No 8 and No 9 as well as force Marlowe to build a secure fence, subject to the court's discretion in respect of equitable remedies (*Gafford v Graham* (1998)). The action will be commenced by Betjeman, the present occupant of No 5 and Chaucer will be permitted to sue in respect of his reversionary interest only if Betjeman does not take action.

(b) The Successor to Shop No 6: Wordsworth

The position with Keats is much the same as above, except that Keats has a legal estate in the land. He may sue, therefore, either at law or in equity depending on whether he

---

13 The answer here is made much easier to follow by the use of sub-headings.

14 This section demonstrates a wide knowledge of the case law.

wishes damages or an injunction and specific performance. To recap: there is no doubt that Keats has an estate in the land, that the covenants touch and concern the land and that the benefit has been annexed to his part of the land under *Federated Homes*.[15] He may enforce all three covenants against Virginia and Marlowe respectively.

(c) The Successor/Occupier to Shop No 7: Wordsworth and the Squatter

As noted above, Wordsworth is an original covenantee and may sue on all three covenants as a matter of contract. Moreover, he is still in possession of No 7 so may sue for a legal or equitable remedy at his choosing. Yet, what of the squatter, Trevelyan (the person actually in occupation), for he may wish to enforce the covenants if his occupation and use of the property is being disrupted? Once again, the covenants touch and concern the land and, under *Federated Homes*, they are annexed to each and every part of it. Further, it is not fatal that Trevelyan is a squatter. **Section 78** of the **LPA 1925** declares that successors in title may obtain the benefit of covenants and then says that 'in connection with covenants restrictive of the use of land successors in title shall be deemed to include owners and occupiers for the time being of the land'. This means that even a squatter, being an occupier, can obtain the benefit of a *restrictive* covenant if all of the other conditions are met. Thus, Trevelyan can sue on the covenants restricting the use of premises and so can prevent Virginia from manufacturing shampoo and Marlowe from breeding parrots and budgerigars.

Common Pitfalls

Do not confuse the law of freehold and leasehold covenants. A leasehold covenant must be in a lease, not simply that one of the parties is a tenant or sub-tenant.

QUESTION 34

In 2003, Hubert, a businessman from the town of Casterbridge, decided to purchase a country house in the nearby village of Melchester. Finding a farm cottage with a paddock in a small private road, he offered to buy it from Bertram Belcher, the owner of the farm of which it was part. The sale was completed by deed and contained covenants by Hubert, to contribute to the cost of the upkeep of the road, to maintain the paddock as an open space, to use the premises for residential occupation only and not to alter the external appearance of the cottage. These covenants are expressed to be made with 'the vendor and the owners for the time being of No 2 and No 3 Hazel Lane, being similar properties'.

Five years later, Hubert's business has suffered a number of setbacks and he finds he can no longer afford the cottage in Melchester. He sells the property to Durbeyfield, a builder, who announces that he is going to subdivide the cottage into a flat and a workshop,

---

15 This shows how to summarise the relevant law quickly to justify the conclusion reached without wasting time going over material already covered in the answer.

adding a small studio at the back. He has no use for the field and Tess a squatter, starts to build herself a small wooden cabin. Farmer Belcher has already lost several sheep due to holes in the fence and the residents of Hazel Lane wish to resurface the road.

▶ Discuss.

How to Read this Question

The examiner is looking for an application of the rules concerning the burden of covenants. The examiner will expect the law to be applied to the specific facts, rather than read a general essay on the law.

How to Answer this Question

Consider the original covenantees, **s 56** of the **LPA**, *Amsprop Trading v Harris* (1997) and identify the nature of the covenants. Explain the law concerning the running of the burden in equity. Examine and apply the requirements of registration. Is there the possibility of the application of the mutual benefit and burden rules: *Thamesmead Town v Allotey* (1998)?

Applying the Law

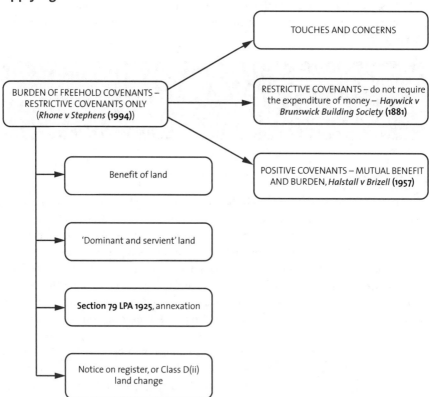

This diagram shows the rules relating to the transfer of the burden of restrictive freehold covenants.

ANSWER

In this problem, a landowner has entered into various covenants in respect of his land for the benefit of adjoining properties. Unfortunately, when the land subject to those covenants was sold to a third person – that is, someone not a party to the covenants – it appears that the covenants were broken. Consequently, the owners of the adjoining land, who have the benefit of those covenants, will wish to enforce them against the successor in title to the original covenantor. The issue thus revolves around the transmission of the burden of freehold covenants.

Before we can deal with the substance of the matter in more detail, two preliminary points must be addressed. First, irrespective of all other matters, only the burden of those covenants that touch and concern the land are capable of being transmitted to purchasers from the original covenantor (*Rogers v Hosegood* (1900)). In our case, there are five covenants and it would seem that all satisfy Lord Oliver's test for 'touching and concerning' put forward in *Swift Investments v Combined English Stores* (1989).[16] The only doubt may be over the covenant to pay for the upkeep of the private road, as this seems to be related to property other than land owned by the surrounding occupants. However, in itself this is not fatal, for the benefit is in the use of this road for surrounding properties, rather than the facility of a well-made road for its own sake. For that reason, this covenant also 'touches and concerns' (see also *Thamesmead Town v Allotey* (1998)). Second, it is trite law (*Austerberry v Corp of Oldham* (1885); *Rhone v Stephens* (1994))[17] that it is only the burden of restrictive covenants that may run, and then only in equity. It is necessary, therefore, to determine which covenants are restrictive, and this is done by examining their substance, rather than the form in which they are expressed (*Tulk v Moxhay* (1848)). In substance (and one test is whether the covenantor is required to spend money: *Hayward v Brunswick Permanent Benefit Building Society* (1881)), the covenant to contribute to the cost of the road is positive in nature. So, subject to what will be said below about avoidance devices, this covenant cannot be enforced against the purchaser Durbeyfield or the squatter Tess. All the other covenants are restrictive.

In essence, whether the burden of a restrictive covenant will run against a successor in title to the original covenantor will depend on two further factors, as supplemented by the requirements of registration under the **Land Registration Act 2002** or **Land Charges Act 1972** depending on whether the land is registered or unregistered. First, at the date of the covenant, the covenantee must have had land capable of benefiting from the covenant. In other words, the burden will run only if the covenant was made for the benefit of other land and that other land is in fact benefited (*London and South Western Railway v Gomm* (1882)). In our problem, there was in existence at the time of the covenant land owned by the covenantee – Farmer Belcher – and it is a question of fact

---

16 Where an issue is relatively straightforward in a problem, it is good to deal with it quickly to leave time in the exam for covering the complicated issues in more detail.

17 Citing both cases here shows the strength of this rule.

whether that land is benefited by these covenants, with the onus on the defendant to prove that it does not (*Whitgift Homes v Stocks* (2001); *Crest Nicholson v McAllister* (2004)). In any event, even if it was thought that these covenants do not benefit land retained by Farmer Eves because they are 'residence' oriented (which is highly unlikely), it is clear that the covenants are also made with the owners of No 2 and No 3 Hazel Lane. Although not parties to the deed, these owners are intended to be benefited by the covenants as parties and, under s56 of the LPA, they are therefore deemed to be in the position of original covenantees (*Amsprop Trading v Harris* (1997)). Their properties are also benefited. Thus, the first criterion is satisfied.

Second, the burden of the restrictive covenant must be annexed to the land of the original covenantor. Fortunately, this condition is easily satisfied, as s79 of the LPA effectively annexes the burden of all restrictive covenants unless a contrary intention is expressed in the deed of creation. There is no contrary intention here and so all four restrictive covenants are annexed.[18]

Presumably, then, the burden of these covenants is capable of running with the land. However, it is inherent in the *Tulk* rules that such covenants – being equitable – in practice will bind only a purchaser of a legal estate who has notice of them. Notice has, of course, been replaced by registration.[19] Thus, if this is registered land, these covenants will be interests that need to be protected by the placing of a notice on the register to bind the purchaser Durbeyfield (s33 **Land Registration Act 2002**) as he is a purchaser of a legal estate: s29 **Land Registration Act 2002**. If they are not so registered, they may not be enforced against him and all future successors because they will have lost priority. Likewise, in (the admittedly now rare) case of unregistered land, the covenants must be registered as Class D(ii) land charges under s4 of the **Land Charges Act 1972** in order to bind a purchaser of a legal estate. In short, only if this requirement is satisfied is Durbeyfield bound in practice by these restrictive covenants. The squatter, Tess, is however in a different position. A squatter is not a purchaser of a legal estate in the land and, therefore, it is immaterial whether the covenants are registered or not (*Re Nisbet and Potts Contract* (1905)). So long as the restrictive covenants fulfil all other requirements, they become proprietary in nature and will bind. The squatter cannot plead lack of registration, because she is not a purchaser and she at least will not be able to build on the paddock.

Finally, we should note that there is one way in which Durbeyfield might be forced to pay for the upkeep of the road, even though this is a positive covenant entered into by his predecessor in title. Under *Halsall v Brizell* (1957), if a person wishes to take the benefit of certain rights, they can be compelled to honour his obligation to contribute to the cost

---

18 'Mini-conclusions' like this throughout the answer help to show the reader where the answer has got to and what the position is so far.

19 The discussion of the relevance of notice here shows the origins of the rules whilst recognising the change in approach represented by land registration.

of their provision. This is the principle of mutual benefit and burden: for example, he who takes the benefit of a private road must take the burden of the obligation to pay for its upkeep. The validity of this principle has been affirmed in *Thamesmead Town v Allotey* in which it was held that an obligation to contribute to the upkeep of certain common facilities (the burden) was enforceable as the counterpart of enjoying those facilities (the benefit), provided that the person liable actually chose to take advantage of the benefit in practice: see also *Wilkinson v Kerndene* (2013) and *Goodman v Elwood* (2014). So, if Durbeyfield wishes to use the road, he can be made liable for a share of the cost of its maintenance.[20]

Common Pitfalls

Do not look for difficulties where there are none: this question demonstrates that the passing of the 'burden' of a restrictive covenant is reasonably easily achieved although the requirements of registration are vital. Do not confuse claims in equity with claims at law.

QUESTION 35

The Boxfield Housing Company has just completed the redevelopment of a large inner city estate in Westhampton. It is Boxfield's intention to ensure that the entire estate should be for residential occupation only and it proposes to impose restrictive covenants on all purchasers to ensure this. It does not wish to retain any interest in the property. It also wishes to impose an obligation on all purchasers to keep the properties in good repair, so as to preserve the character of the neighbourhood.

▶ **Advise Boxfield of the various methods by which this can be achieved, if at all.**

How to Read this Question

This looks like a problem question, but it can be answered as if it were an essay on the establishment of mutually enforceable covenant obligations, including ways in which a positive covenant might be enforced. That said, the examiner will expect the law to be related to the facts.

How to Answer this Question

Identify the original covenantees and original covenantors and consider the passing the benefit under s56 of the LPA and *Federated Homes* (1980); *Crest Nicholson v McAllister* (2004). Consider the requirements for passing the benefit of covenants under a building scheme, *Whitgift Homes v Stocks* (2001), and note how the burden may pass negative covenants and requirements of registration. Conclude with a discussion of the mechanisms to pass positive burdens and their effectiveness.

20 It would be easy in the exam to forget about the road covenant once it had been established as being a positive covenant but it is important to consider all aspects of the problem in full.

Applying the Law

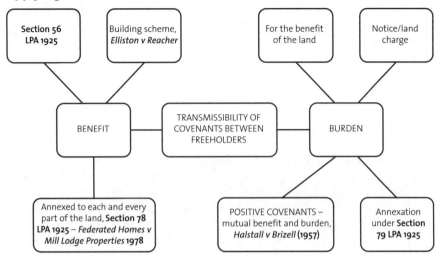

This diagram shows the structure of the rules relating to the transmissibility of covenants between freeholders.

ANSWER

This question invites consideration of the law relating to the transmissibility of covenants between freeholders. Given that the Boxfield Housing Company has no wish to retain an interest in the property, the relatively easy method of establishing leasehold obligations cannot be used.

The development company wishes to ensure two things: first, that each purchaser from it is placed under the burden of a covenant against non-residential use and the burden of a positive obligation to repair; and, second, that each purchaser obtains the right to enforce every other purchaser's covenant. There is, in other words, a need to ensure mutuality of obligation between all the purchasers of properties on the estate.

(a) The Benefit

In this problem, there is both a positive and a negative covenant, although, as regards transmission of the benefit to successors in title from the original covenantee, there is no need to make a distinction between the two types of covenant. However, since it is the stated objective to ensure that there is mutuality of obligation amongst the prospective purchasers of the properties, it is clear that we are really concerned with transmission of the benefit in equity. The reason is, quite simply, that the burdens of covenants (at least restrictive ones) can be transmitted in equity only.[21]

---

21 This is an unusual problem question in that it is asking advice on how to achieve a certain end, rather than in establishing what the position of the parties is following certain facts, and it is important to recognise the angle from which you are being asked to discuss the problem.

Clearly, there is no difficulty with the requirement that the covenants must touch and concern the land (*Rogers v Hosegood* (1900)) or that the covenants do in fact benefit the land (*Re Earl of Leicester* (1863)). Likewise, each intending purchaser will have an estate in the land benefited and the original covenantee will have land capable of benefiting at the time the covenant was made (although note the problem of the last sale, considered below). The difficulty is, however, with the remaining requirement – namely, that the benefit must be transmitted by one of the methods recognised by equity. The position is not straightforward for one simple reason. The developer owns all the land prior to any sale. On sale to the first purchaser, that purchaser will make the required covenants for the benefit of the land retained by the developer. In fact, under the *Federated Homes v Mill Lodge Properties* (1980) interpretation of **s78** of the **LPA**, as confirmed in *Whitgift Homes v Stocks* (2001), and *Crest Nicholson v McAllister* (2004), the benefit of the covenant will be annexed to each and every part of the retained land. So, when the second purchaser comes along, and buys a piece of the retained land, they will clearly obtain the benefit of the first purchaser's covenants. Their own covenants will, of course, then go to benefit the retained land in the same way as those of the first purchaser. The difficulty is, however, that on this analysis, it is impossible for the first purchaser to gain the benefit of the second purchaser's covenants and, indeed, for the second purchaser to gain the benefit of the third's and so on. In fact, although later purchasers always get the benefit of earlier purchaser's covenants, previous purchasers never get the benefit of those who buy later because, when the subsequent purchasers actually buy the land, the previous purchasers have already bought their plots, which are, consequently, no longer part of the developer's retained land. This problem, which is essentially one of timing, can be solved in two ways.[22]

First, when subsequent purchasers purchase their property, they can expressly include all previous purchasers as original covenantees. This will put those previous purchasers in the same position as the developer and **s56** of the **LPA 1925** can be utilised to achieve (*Amsprop Trading v Harris* (1997)). There may be some difficulty with the last purchaser from the developer, as after that purchase the original covenantee (the developer) will have no interest in the land and this is required for transfer of the benefit in equity. However, this problem can be avoided by ensuring that one of the previous purchasers who does have land capable of benefiting is actually made a party to the deed. Clearly, this is a cumbersome method of achieving the desired effect, but it would ensure that the benefit of every purchaser's covenant – negative and positive – was transmitted to every other purchaser.

A much simpler way to achieve the same result is to ensure that the transfer of benefit takes place under a building scheme. This is a rule of limited effect that allows a common vendor (for example, Boxfield) to achieve the mutuality of benefit desired without having to worry about timing, or lack of land for the final sale or even the use of **s56** of the **LPA 1925**. Under *Elliston v Reacher* (1908), if there is a common vendor, an allotted plan for the building site wherein the land is laid out in lots, a well-defined area (see *Whitgift*) and an

---

22 The identification o f this practical problem is the key to this question.

intention that each purchaser shall be under the same obligation, then the benefit of all covenants can be given to all purchasers without more and irrespective of the time they purchase their own individual plot. Indeed, as later cases show, it may even be possible to omit some of the *Elliston* conditions, as where there is no allotted plan (*Baxter v Four Oaks Properties* (1965)) and where, as in *Re Dolphin's Conveyance* (1970), there is no common vendor. The advice to Boxfield is, then, to follow this reliable and accepted method of ensuring mutuality of benefit and, in this connection, to ensure that the land that is to be subject to a building scheme is clearly identified so that all purchasers know the extent of their mutual rights (*Whitgift*).

(b) The Burden

This is not inherently difficult; rather, it is that the present state of the law allows the burden to flow in only limited circumstances. Thus, it is only the burden of restrictive covenants that can pass to successors in title of the original covenantor (*Austerberry v Corporation of Oldham* (1885); *Rhone v Stephens* (1994)). To ensure this, the covenant must touch and concern the land, the covenantees must at the time of the covenant have had land capable of benefiting from the covenant and the burden must be attached to the land. The first two requirements are clearly satisfied, as each purchaser will make a covenant with the developer as they purchase the land. (On sale of the last plot, the developer is treated as having land because of the special rules relating to a building scheme.) Moreover, annexation of the covenant will occur automatically under s79 of the **LPA** and there will be no problem of this effect being deliberately excluded. Of course, if the covenants are to bind successors in title from the original purchasers/covenantors, they must be either protected by a notice on the register in registered land (s29 **Land Registration 2002**) or Class D(ii) land charges in unregistered land (s4 **Land Charges Act 1972**). The developer must ensure this takes place as otherwise the covenants will be unenforceable after the first sale of each burdened plot.

As to the positive covenant to repair, there is little the developer can do. It could decide to let the property as a leasehold development and rely on the rules relating to leasehold enfranchisement in respect of leasehold covenants, but this is cumbersome and expensive and not what Boxfield wants to do.[23] Neither is there any scope for the doctrine of mutual benefit and burden under *Halsall v Brizell* (1957) and *Wilkinson v Kerndene* (2013). That principle applies only in cases in which there is some shared utility or service, such as a road or sewer. It would be possible for each original covenantor/purchaser (who, of course, is under the obligation to repair as matter of contract) to extract a covenant to repair from any purchaser from them, thus creating a chain of covenants. But, this 'chain of indemnity' is only as strong as its weakest link and depends on the ability and desire of the original covenantor to impose such an obligation on a successor.[24] A final chance – at least if this were registered land – would be for each purchaser of a plot to permit the entry of a restriction against their title, requiring any future purchaser from them to enter

---

23 The analysis of this alternative solution shows creativity which will be given credit in the exam.

24 Recognising the practical limitations of a valid 'legal' solution shows that you are analysing the law throughout, rather than simply describing it.

a direct covenant with the remaining owners to pay for the upkeep of the property. Such a covenant would then be a condition of purchasing the land. This would work, but it is also cumbersome and might well deter prospective purchasers from buying from Boxfield in the first place.

To conclude, it is reasonably straightforward for Boxfield to achieve the desired effect of giving each purchaser a right to sue on these covenants. The burden is, however, more problematical and it is only the burden of the restrictive covenants that could be guaranteed to run.

Common Pitfalls

Ensure that you relate the rules to the facts of the case. Marks can be easily lost by failing to take this simple step.

QUESTION 36

Tastee Ltd, a frozen food manufacturer, owns large premises on an industrial estate just outside Grandtown. Title is unregistered. In 1995, it decides to sell off parts of its property in order to meet mounting company debts. Unit 1 is sold to Michael, who covenants not to carry on any trade or business in food manufacture on the site and to require his staff to use the catering facilities established by Tastee Ltd on the estate. Later that year, Tastee Ltd sells Unit 2 to Neil on a seven-year lease in writing. Neil makes identical covenants as to those made by Michael and immediately sub-lets the property to Otto by a lease in writing on the same terms. Otto has since inherited a fortune and makes a gift of the premises to his nephew Henry, a major confectionary manufacturer. Subsequently, Michael sells his property to Priscilla who begins to make birthday cakes and opens a small cafeteria for her staff. Meanwhile, Tastee Ltd has sold its remaining property to Titanic Foods Inc, which immediately contemplates litigation. Unfortunately, Neil has disappeared and it transpires that none of these covenants were registered.

▶ Advise how would your advice differ if the covenants had been registered?

How to Read this Question

The examiner is expecting an unfussy application of the freehold covenant rules. This means a logical progression through the facts. Set out first any issues concerning the burden, and then those for the benefit. The existence of a lease does not mean this is a question about leasehold covenants.

How to Answer this Question

Consider whether the covenants that touch and concern the land and whether the burden and/or the benefit may run with the land. Note the lack of privity of estate in a *pre-1996 lease*, indicating that freehold covenant rules apply. Consider the requirements of registration and their effect on purchasers and others.

Answer Structure

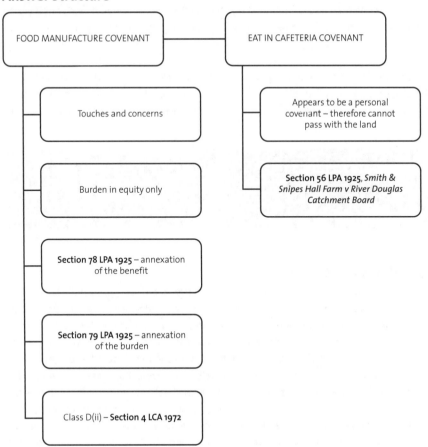

This diagram shows how to apply the rules relating to restrictive covenants to the food manufacture and cafeteria covenants.

ANSWER

It is clear that in this problem there are difficulties concerning both the transfer of the benefit and the transfer of the burden to successors in title of the original parties in respect of covenants affecting freehold land. In order to consider this problem in detail, it is first necessary to determine the nature of these two covenants – the covenant not to carry on any food manufacture and the covenant to ensure that staff working on the burdened land eat at the covenantee's cafeteria.

The first point is whether these covenants touch and concern the land. There is no difficulty with the covenant restrictive of use, as this is a type of covenant often employed to control the use of land (*Re Gadd* (1966)). On the other hand, there is a serious doubt whether the covenant to use the cafeteria of the covenantee does touch and concern the land. It is doubtful whether it affects the value or mode of use of the land (*Swift Investments v Combined English*

Stores (1989)) and appears to be only personal in nature. If this is the case, then this particular covenant can bind only the original parties, being Michael and Neil. It is a matter of contract. In addition, if, as a matter of construction, Otto's covenant with Neil in the sub-lease was intended to be made with Tastee Ltd (the head landlord) under **s56** of the **Law of Property Act 1925**, Otto will be bound in contract with Tastee as well as Neil (**s56** applies even to covenants that do not touch and concern). That apart, this covenant binds no successor in title, being personal in nature. So, Priscilla cannot be sued on this covenant even if it were negative and fulfilled all the other conditions relating to the transmission of the burden of freehold covenants (or leasehold covenants in a pre-1996 lease). Likewise, its benefit cannot be transferred automatically to Titanic Foods under property law principles when it buys the original covenantee's land. Of course, the benefit of it can be expressly assigned as a matter of contract, under the rule that contractual benefits can be assigned personally.[25]

That leaves us, then, with the restrictive covenant against certain types of user. First, does the benefit of this run in equity to Titanic Foods? (Note the position at law is not relevant as the burden of the covenant can only be transmitted in equity and thus the claimant must sue in equity.[26]) For the benefit to run in equity, the claimant must have some estate in the land within **s78** of the **LPA 1925** and the covenant must have benefited land of the original covenantee. The fact of benefit will be presumed (*Whitgift Homes v Stocks* (2001); *Crest Nicholson v McAllister* (2004)) unless the contrary is shown. In any event, there is clear benefit within the definition of *Re Gadd* because the covenant affects the mode of use of the land. There is no difficulty with either of these conditions. In addition, however, the benefit of the covenant must have been transmitted in a method accepted by equity. In this case, there is clearly no building scheme and no evidence of an express assignment of the benefit. We must, therefore, rely on annexation. Clearly, there has been no express annexation but this is much less important after the decision of *Federated Homes v Mill Lodge Properties* (1980), which makes it clear that this covenant will be statutorily annexed under **s78** of the **LPA** unless the covenant contains a contrary intention, which this does not. In fact, the covenant is attached to each and every part of the land, so it is not only Titanic Foods that can enforce the covenant, but also Neil and Henry, the first of whom purchased an estate in part of the benefited land before Michael's covenant and the second is an occupier of that land entitled to the benefit of a restrictive covenant within **s78** of the **LPA 1925**. However, it is likely that only Titanic Foods will wish to enforce this covenant and Neil (if he could be found) will be prevented from doing so unless Henry refuses to act.

Second, what of the burden of this covenant, for it appears that it has been broken in respect of both Unit 1 and Unit 2? Turning first to Unit 1,[27] can this restrictive covenant bind Priscilla? It seems clear that the conditions required to give the burden of this covenant a proprietary

---

25 The personal nature of this covenant makes the solution here quite straightforward – it is important not to look for 'more' in a question than is really there.

26 This demonstrates to the examiner that the writer is aware of these rules without wasting time going through them when they cannot help in the instant case.

27 If you are clear and precise about exactly what you are considering and when, it makes the answer easier to follow for the examiner, and also makes it more likely that you will not miss an issue.

nature have been satisfied. On the one hand, at the time of the covenant, there was land owned by the covenantee (Tastee Ltd) that was capable of benefiting from the covenant, as required by *London and South Western Railway v Gomm* (1882). Similarly, the burden of the covenant appears to have been annexed to the land under **s79** of the **LPA 1925**: there is no contrary intention expressed. So, the covenant is proprietary within the rules of *Tulk v Moxhay* (1848). However, this means only that the covenant is *capable* of binding a successor in title to the original covenantor, not that it actually does so. In order for it to bind a purchaser of a *legal* estate in the land – which presumably Priscilla is – it must be registered as a Class D(ii) land charge in unregistered land under **s4** of the **Land Charges Act 1972**. We are told that it is not and so even this covenant is not binding on her, nor can it be binding on any subsequent purchasers having been statutorily voided by the **Land Charges Act 1972**. Obviously, if the covenant had been registered, it would have been enforceable.

Third, what of the successors in title to Unit 2, being Neil and now Henry (via a gift of Otto's lease)? The position concerning whether the covenant is proprietary is, not surprisingly, the same as with Unit 1: the covenant was made for the benefit of land of the covenantee and it is annexed to that land. However, it also is unregistered. Yet, in this case it is not necessarily the case that the covenant is void for lack of registration. Under **s4** of the **LCA 1972**, a Class D(ii) land charge is void for lack of registration against a purchaser for money or money's worth of a legal estate in the land. When Neil acquires the land, he acquires it by virtue of a lease in writing – not by deed – so he purchases only an equitable estate (*Walsh v Lonsdale*).[28] Moreover, Henry does not even purchase the land, for he obtains the land by gift. Consequently, both Neil and Henry are bound by the covenant even though it may not be registered. Of course, had registration occurred, this would make the covenant safe against any future purchaser of a legal estate, but such registration is not necessary on these facts.

Finally, for the sake of completeness, it should be noted that Neil could enforce all covenants against Otto, his tenant, under privity of contract. Likewise, Tastee Ltd, and then Titanic Foods, can proceed to forfeit Neil's lease for breach of covenant if the lease contained a right of re-entry. Subject to the normal safeguards surrounding forfeiture, this would terminate Henry's occupation also and would result in de facto enforcement of the covenant against user (*Pennell v Payne* (1995)).

Common Pitfalls

Do not consider the burden and the benefit together. Deal with them separately. The claimant can sue if they have the benefit, and the defendant is liable if they have the burden (and if there has been a breach). However, both these need to be true in order for there to be an action on the covenant.

---

28 Sometimes where a problem question focuses on a particular topic, here, freehold covenants, it is easy to forget about formality and registration rules. It is a good habit to check whether these have been complied with at each and every stage in all problem questions.

9

The Law of Mortgages

INTRODUCTION

There is no doubt that, for the ordinary person, the purchase of a house is their most direct contact with the law of real property. For this event most people require a mortgage, and the subsequent repayment of the mortgage becomes one of their most pressing economic concerns. However, the use of the mortgage as a device to *acquire* property is a relatively modern development. In fact, for so long as people have been capable of owning land (or more precisely, an interest in it), the mortgage has been a way of converting a fixed economic asset (the land) into a flexible economic asset (its monetary value). The mortgage is, in essence, a way of realising and releasing the capital value of the land. Fundamentally, therefore, a mortgage is a security for a loan. This rather bland statement hides a multitude of consequences, not least the idea that a mortgage – being a proprietary right – is subject to controls not otherwise found in 'ordinary' loan contracts. Indeed, one of the most frequent examination questions asks the student to assess the extent to which a mortgage really is a right in property or just another species of contract.

Checklist
In order to deal with mortgage issues, three reasonably distinct areas have to be addressed. First, how are mortgages created, both legal and equitable, and are there any specific reasons for choosing a particular method? Second, what are the rights of a mortgagor (the borrower) under a mortgage and in particular what is the nature and extent of the 'equity of redemption'? Third, what are the rights of the mortgagee (the lender) under a mortgage and what remedies may be suitably employed in the event of a defaulting mortgagor? These questions largely depend on the application of traditional equitable principles, as supplemented by statute where appropriate. A good knowledge of case law is invaluable.

QUESTION 37

Analyse the methods by which legal and equitable mortgages might be created since 1925. What was the purpose of the 1925 reforms?

How to Read this Question

The examiner is asking you to demonstrate that you understand how mortgages are created, and therefore what they are. It is just as important to explain the point behind the reforms as it is to state the law itself.

How to Answer this Question

The following areas need to be discussed: the definition of a mortgage – *Santley v Wilde* (1899); the use of the charge, ss 85 and 86 of the LPA 1925; s 23 of the LRA 2002; equitable mortgages, including s 53(1)(c) of the LPA 1925, *Walsh v Lonsdale* (1882), s 2 of the **Law of Property (Miscellaneous Provisions) Act 1989**; and proprietary estoppel. Note the purpose of reform – protection of the borrower; ease and inexpensive creation.

Up for Debate

There is not much uncertainty about the law in this area. Consider whether it should be compulsory for every mortgage to be made by the 'charge' method and the potential impact of electronic creation of mortgages under the e-conveyancing provisions of the **LRA 2002**.

Applying the Law

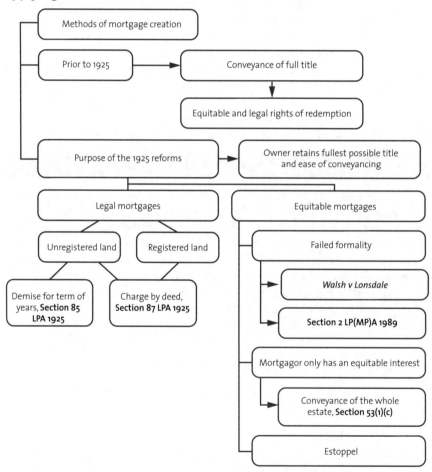

This diagram shows the different methods of creating mortgages.

ANSWER

Although today the mortgage is most commonly employed to enable the purchase of land in the first place, the true nature of a mortgage is that it is a lender's security for money lent to the borrower. The mortgage is much more than a simple contract of loan, for the mortgagee will acquire an interest in the land over which the mortgage operates. In technical terms, a mortgage is regarded as a conveyance of an estate in the land to the mortgagee, with a provision that the mortgagee's interest shall lapse upon repayment of the loan plus interest and costs. It is one of the most important aspects of the mortgage that the lender obtains not only a right to have the money repaid but also a proprietary interest in the land charged as security for that loan.

Before 1925, if an owner of a legal or equitable interest in land sought to raise money on security of that land, the borrower's interest in the property was usually conveyed in full to the lender. In his turn, the mortgagee promised to re-convey the estate on repayment of principal, interest and costs. Moreover, originally, not only did the mortgagee have the actual estate of the borrower vested in them, the contract also made provision for the lender to retain that interest if the borrower failed to repay the loan on the date stipulated in the contract. This date, known as the 'legal date of redemption', became crucial, and the consequences for the borrower of missing payment on that date were severe: the borrower lost their estate entirely. Fortunately, equity was soon to intervene. Adopting the policy position of 'once a mortgage always a mortgage', equity developed the 'equity of redemption' and its counterpart, the 'equitable right to redeem'. Essentially, this meant that the borrower was entitled to a re-conveyance of their property should they pay the full charges due under the mortgage, even though the legal date for payment had passed. This then was the background to the changes made by the **Law of Property Act (LPA) 1925** to the methods by which mortgages could be created.[1]

The general principle underlying the 1925 property reforms is that, as far as possible, the owner of land should retain the fullest interest possible in their own property even when seeking a mortgage of it. Hence, since 1926, freeholds can no longer be mortgaged by a conveyance of the fee simple to the mortgagee and the mortgagee is limited to receiving some lesser right in the land. With obvious and necessary modifications, this principle also applies to mortgages of leaseholds.

The position of legal mortgages of freeholds is now as follows. In respect of *unregistered land only*,[2] under **s 85(1)** of the **LPA 1925**, there are two methods only of creating a legal mortgage of a freehold. First, the borrower may demise a term of years absolute to the lender and no mortgage may take effect by absolute conveyance of the legal estate (**s 85(2)**). In effect, this is the granting of a long lease to the mortgagee with a provision for cesser on redemption (that is, that the term of years shall cease when the loan is repaid). In the typical case, the term granted is usually long, such as 3,000 years. The demised

---

1 In a question like this, it is always useful to give background to the reforms being discussed to put your discussion into some context.

2 Always be clear about the scope of the rules that you are discussing.

term will also fix a contractual date for redemption, being the legal right to redeem, and that is usually six months after the date of the mortgage or later if the mortgage is payable by instalment. However, as was the case before 1926, the mortgagor has an equitable right to redeem on the payment of the loan at any time after this legal date has passed. The clear effect of these provisions is that the mortgagor retains their legal fee simple and the mortgage is more clearly regarded as the security for a loan.[3] Moreover, this approach has one major practical advantage. Since 1925, it has been possible for the mortgagor to create further legal mortgages of their land, in order to raise further sums. So, because the mortgagor retains the legal fee simple, it is perfectly possible to grant another mortgage for another term to a second lender, as where the first mortgage was for a relatively small sum. The second term granted will necessarily be longer than the first, so as to give the second mortgagee a notional legal interest in the property distinct from that of the first mortgagee.

The second method of creating a mortgage of a legal freehold of unregistered land since 1925 is the charge by deed expressed to be by way of legal mortgage. This is an invention of s 87 of the **LPA 1925**: the legal charge is simply a statutory form of mortgage that is easier and less expensive to execute than a formal demise of a term of years. In fact, the legal charge is the main method of mortgaging legal estates currently in use. Under s 87, this charge must be made by deed and it must be expressed to be by way of legal mortgage but, that done, it is clear that a legal chargee (a lender) gets exactly the same protection, powers and remedies as if they had been given a term of 3,000 years in the normal way (s 87 of the **LPA**; *Regent Oil Company v Gregory* (1996)). For all practical purposes, therefore, the legal charge is as effective as a mortgage by way of demise of term of years. It is, however, cheaper, shorter and more efficient. Consequently, in respect of registered land – which, of course, now comprises the majority of titles – the **Land Registration Act 2002** provides that the charge is the only way of mortgaging a legal estate in registered land (s 23 of the **LRA 2002**) and that it must be registered to complete the legal formalities (**Sched 2** to the **LRA 1925**). In reality, the mandatory use of the charge for registered land merely reflects the practical position before the **2002 Act**.

As far as leaseholds are concerned, the position is substantially similar. Before 1925, the leaseholder (the tenant) would assign their lease to the mortgagee just as the freeholder would transfer their fee simple. Now, however, by virtue of s 86 of the **LPA 1925**, a legal mortgage of a leasehold of *unregistered title* can be created by two methods only. The first is the charge by deed expressed to be by way of legal mortgage, as above. The second is by a sub-lease for a term of years to the mortgagee. This sub-lease will necessarily be shorter than the term of years that the leaseholder actually has and, in practice, the mortgagee's term will be ten days shorter than the original leaseholder's. This is to ensure that the leaseholder can grant subsequent legal mortgages of their leasehold by creating a term longer than the first mortgagee's but shorter than their own. Any attempt to avoid these provisions by assigning a lease will operate only as a sub-lease for a term shorter

---

3 Although this question does not specifically ask whether the reforms meet their purpose, approaching your analysis from this angle is a good way to integrate both aspects of the question into the answer.

than that of the tenant (*Grangeside Securities v Collingwood Securities Ltd* (1964)). Of course, as far as registered leasehold titles are concerned, the charge method is now compulsory (s 23 of the **LRA 2002**).

Turning now to equitable mortgages, these can be split conveniently into two categories. First, it may well be that the borrower only has an equitable interest and it necessarily follows that any mortgage of that equitable interest will itself be equitable. The **LPA 1925** and the **LRA 2002** have not affected this matter to any great extent[4] and mortgages of equitable interests (such as a beneficiary's rights under a trust) are still carried into effect by a conveyance of the whole equitable interest to the mortgagee. As far as formality requirements are concerned, there is no need to use a deed, but because this mortgage will amount to a disposition of a subsisting equitable interest (that is, that of the mortgagor), it must comply with s 53(1)(c) of the **LPA**. This requires the mortgage of the equitable interest to be in writing, on penalty of voidness, unless saved by estoppel (*Kinane v Conteh* (2005)).[5]

The second issue is the creation of the informal mortgage or, in other words, a mortgage that does not comply with the formality requirements necessary for the creation of a legal mortgage. As with many other equitable interests in land, an informal mortgage commences life as a contract to create a legal mortgage that, if capable of specific performance, will be treated as an equitable mortgage along the same lines as equitable leases in *Walsh v Lonsdale* (1882). It is vital, however, for this informal mortgage that the contract be in writing under s 2 of the **LPA 1989** (*United Bank of Kuwait v Sahib* (1997))[6] and be specifically enforceable. It is also possible for an equitable mortgage to arise by estoppel under *Taylor Fashions v Liverpool Victoria Trustees* (1982). Thus, if a lender has actually advanced money on the basis of a promise, it is possible that the mortgage will be enforced under estoppel despite the absence of any formality, provided that there is evidence of unconscionability: see *Kinane v Conteh*. Finally, mention must also be made of the equitable charge, a completely informal way of securing a loan over property. This requires no special form of words, only an intention to charge property with a debt (*National Provincial and Union Bank of England v Charnley* (1924)). Such a method is extremely precarious and is rarely used in either commercial or residential mortgages.

Common Pitfalls

This is as straightforward a question as it is possible to get on mortgages. Good use of case law will reinforce knowledge of the statutory provisions. Be clear that a mortgage over registered land will not actually exist as a legal charge until it is entered on the register, as with all dispositions of a registered estate: ss 25 and 27 of and Sched 2 to the **LRA 2002**.

---

4   As well as showing what the reforms of 1925 onwards did achieve, it is important to outline what they did not do, in order to demonstrate the breadth of any changes.
5   'Side points' like this show that you understand the inevitable limitations of formality requirements.
6   You need to be aware that it is not just the 1925 reforms, and the **2002 Act** that have had profound effects on the law in this area.

QUESTION 38

To what extent do the rights of a mortgagor under a legal mortgage provide sufficient protection for the borrower?

How to Read this Question

The examiner is expecting an analysis of the protection afforded to borrowers by the modern law of mortgages. Case law is critical.

How to Answer this Question

The following areas need to be discussed: the nature of the mortgagor's rights (the legal right to redeem, the equitable right to redeem and the equity of redemption); the doctrine of clogs and fetters (options, collateral advantages, oppressive terms, unconscionable conduct, *Jones v Morgan* (2002)).

Up for Debate

Should the law of mortgages be reformed? Does the current law weigh too heavily in favour of the borrower? Is there a potential for a human rights defence?

Applying the Law

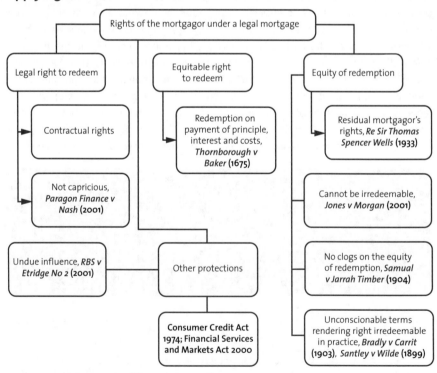

This diagram shows the rights of the mortgagor under a legal mortgage.

ANSWER

The mortgage is one of the most versatile and unique of property law concepts. It is, on the one hand, a simple contract of loan between lender and borrower and, on the other, it creates a valuable and powerful proprietary right in land. It is a concept governed by contract law and property law and the different philosophies of each can sometimes cause confusion and difficulties.

In the normal course of events, a legal mortgage of a registered estate will be created by the execution of a legal charge by way of mortgage: s 23 of the **Land Registration Act 2002**. This is deemed to be the creation of a proprietary interest under s 87 of the **Law of Property Act 1925** and has the same effect as if the mortgage was created by the old method of demise. This means that the mortgagor retains their interest in the land subject, of course, to the rights of the mortgagee. As the mortgage is also a contract of loan, there are stipulations relating to the repayment of the loan and certain remedies that the mortgagee may pursue in the event of default on the loan. However, the mortgage remains at all times security for a debt and this means that the mortgagor does have a considerable degree of protection, both of their interest in the land and in respect of their position under the loan contract *if they repay the loan*.

As a matter of contract, the mortgagor has a contractual right to redeem on the date specified in the contract. Traditionally, this was six months from the date of the mortgage, but may be at any date specified by the parties and will often be later in instalment mortgages. At one time, if the mortgagor did not redeem on this date, they lost their security even though redemption could have been made at a later date, but now equity allows redemption after this date, on payment of principal, interests and costs (*Thornborough v Baker* (1675)). This is the 'equitable right to redeem' and, without doubt, is a valuable part of the mortgagor's protection under a mortgage. In fact, the equitable right to redeem is just part of the wider rights that the mortgagor has under the mortgage.

In equity, the mortgagor is protected by the equity of redemption.[7] This equity of redemption represents the sum total of the mortgagor's rights in the property: in essence, the residual rights of ownership that the mortgagor has, both in virtue of his paramount legal estate in the land and the protection that equity affords them (*Re Sir Thomas Spencer Wells* (1933)). The equity of redemption is valuable in itself for it represents the mortgagor's right to the property (or its monetary equivalent) when the mortgage is discharged or the property sold. In fact, on subsequent mortgages, the second and third lenders are able and willing to grant further loans precisely because the mortgagor has this valuable right.

The inherent quality of the equity of redemption is demonstrated by the fact that equity will intervene to protect the mortgagor and their equity of redemption against encroachment by the mortgagee: *Jones v Morgan* (2002). As noted above, equity regards the

---

7   It is important to explain clearly the difference between the equity of redemption and the equitable right to redeem.

mortgage as a loan, which can be redeemed, and not as an opportunity for the lender to acquire the mortgagor's property. This protection manifests itself in various ways.[8]

First, it is a general principle that a mortgage cannot be made irredeemable: it is a security, not a conveyance, and the right to redeem cannot be limited to certain people or certain periods of time (*Re Wells*). However, a provision postponing the date of redemption may be valid where the mortgage is not otherwise harsh and unconscionable, so long as the right to redeem is not made illusory (*Knightsbridge Estates v Byrne* (1939); *Fairclough v Swan Brewery* (1912)). Again, a provision in a mortgage that provides that the property shall become the mortgagee's or which gives the mortgagee an option to purchase the property is void (*Samuel v Jarrah Timber* (1904); *Jones v Morgan*). The rationale is that the mortgagor needs protection when negotiating for a loan, often being in a vulnerable position. Thus, an option to purchase given to the mortgagee in a separate and independent transaction can be valid, as not forming part of the mortgage itself (*Reeve v Lisle* (1902)).

Second, as a matter of principle, the mortgagor should be able to redeem the mortgage and have the mortgagee's rights extinguished free from any ancillary conditions in the mortgage other than the payment of principal, interests and costs. The basic principle is, again, the mortgage as a security that ends when its reason – the money – is repaid. Formerly, the courts struck down these 'collateral advantages' made in favour of a mortgagee, as where the mortgage contract stipulates that the mortgagor should fulfil some other obligation as a condition of the mortgage (cf. *Bradley v Carritt* (1903)). However, it is now clear that there is no objection to a collateral advantage that ceases when the mortgage is redeemed (*Santley v Wilde* (1899)). This is a matter of contract between the parties and, provided that the terms are not unconscionable or do not in fact restrict the right to redeem, they will be valid (*Biggs v Hoddinot* (1898)). Indeed, at least with commercial mortgages made between equal parties at arm's length, *Kreglinger v New Patagonia Meat and Cold Storage Company* (1914) suggests that even a collateral advantage that is meant to continue after redemption may be acceptable so long as the mortgagor's property returns to the mortgagor in the same form that it was mortgaged. Clearly, this is a flexible principle that can be used to invalidate harsh, unreasonable terms as the situation demands. On the other hand, courts are aware that the parties' business dealings should be upheld as far as possible in the absence of unconscionable conduct (e.g. *Brighton & Hove City Council v Audus* (2009)).[9]

Third, the court has the power to strike down any term that, in effect, destroys the equity of redemption. Thus, a high interest rate might render the mortgagor's equity of redemption valueless (*Cityland and Property (Holdings) v Dabrah* (1968)) or the terms of the mortgage might be so oppressive as to make it harsh and unconscionable, although it must be more than merely unreasonable or unfair (*Multiservice Bookbinding v Marden* (1979); *Jones v Morgan*).

....

8   Using sentences like this helps the examiner to follow your structure and allows a clear presentation of the arguments.

9   Putting in extra information like this shows that you are aware of the context of recent case law.

Fourth, the mortgage may be struck down in whole or in part on the ground that the mortgagor's consent was obtained by undue influence.[10] It is rare for the mortgagee themselves to have exerted the undue influence, but the mortgagee can be tainted with the undue influence of the person who persuaded the mortgagor to sign (such as a co-mortgagor, a husband or lover). This will occur if the person exercising the undue influence can be said to be the agent of the mortgagee (rare) or if the mortgagee has notice of the undue influence (*Barclays Bank v O'Brien* (1994); *Royal Bank of Scotland v Etridge* (2002)). Formerly, 'undue influence' was a favourite defence for a mortgagor resisting the possession claims of the mortgagee but recent case law (especially *Etridge*) has confined the plea to manageable and defensible limits.

Finally, it is also clear that mortgages, being contracts, are subject to normal contractual rules governing credit relationships and related matters. The vast majority of first mortgages on residential property offered by banks, building societies, local authorities and other similar lenders will be regulated by the **Financial Services and Markets Act 2000**.[11] Even if the mortgage is not covered by that Act – for example because it is a second mortgage or mortgage of business premises – if the borrower is an individual, he or she might still gain protection under **s140A–C** of the **Consumer Credit Act 2006** if the court is satisfied that there is an unfair credit relationship between the borrower and the lender. A mortgage transaction may also set aside as being in restraint of trade (*Esso Petroleum v Harper's Garage* (1968)).

All in all then, the mortgagor does benefit from a degree of protection, both by virtue of equity protecting the equity of redemption and by statute and general common law principles applicable to contracts per se. In addition to these, when the mortgagee seeks to exercise their remedies under the mortgage, statute intervenes to restrain, exclude or modify those remedies, particularly in the case of mortgagees seeking to obtain possession by court order of a dwelling house (**s36** of the **Administration of Justice Act 1970**). Also, in relation to mortgages of residential property, there is the potential for a human rights defence to a lender seeking to sell the property, but this has not yet materialised, see *Horsham Properties v Beech* (2008).

Common Pitfalls

Much of the law in this area is case based. Answers that do not exhibit sufficient knowledge and use of case law will lose considerable marks.

QUESTION 39

How extensive are the remedies available to a legal mortgagee?

10 Strictly speaking, this can be seen as a matter of contract, but it interacts uniquely with the position of mortgagor as both contracting party, and institutional lender.

11 Although a problem question, or indeed an essay, may not ask you to go into detail regarding the consumer protection legislation, it is worth being familiar with the requirements.

How to Read this Question

The question asks how 'extensive' the remedies are: not merely what they are. The examiner is expecting an assessment of the remedies in the light of the mortgagee's aim to recover the money lent.

How to Answer this Question

The remedies of a legal mortgagee need to be discussed: the action on the contract for debt, possibly leading to bankruptcy; the appointment of a receiver; the power of sale; the right to possession; foreclosure (briefly). The answer should note that the degree of protection for the mortgagor varies according to the type of mortgage and the circumstances of default.

Up for Debate

Does the mortgagee need all of these remedies? In particular, why should possession be a right and why can it be obtained without a court order? Does the lender always meet his duties when selling and are the mortgagor's remedies for breach of these duties effective?

Applying the Law

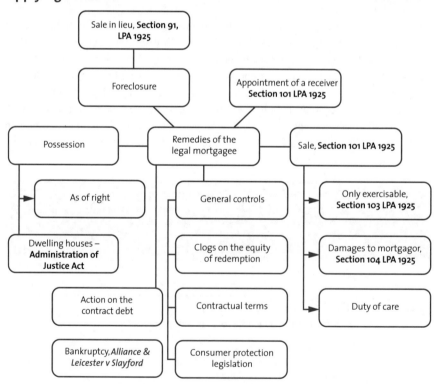

This diagram shows the remedies of the legal mortgagee.

ANSWER

Given the importance of mortgages to the general economy, it is apparent that a mortgagee should have effective means by which it can protect and/or enforce its security in the case of a breach of any of the terms of the mortgage by the mortgagor, particularly those in respect of repayment. The fact that a mortgage is both a contract of loan and springs from the grant of a proprietary right means that the mortgagee enjoys a range of remedies. The particular remedy or remedies employed by the mortgagee (for they are cumulative and not mutually exclusive *Alliance & Leicester v Slayford* (2001)) will depend on the precise nature of the default of the mortgagor and the requirements of the mortgagee. Some are more suitable for recovery of unpaid interest, while others are more suitable for recovery of the entire loan and the ending of the charge.

The first and most straightforward of the mortgagee's remedies arises because the mortgage is a contract of loan between the parties. The mortgagee has an action on the express covenant given by the mortgagor for repayment of the sum due on a certain date plus interest. Of course, this remedy may be of little practical use if the mortgagor has no funds other than those tied up in the secured property, but it is often an adjunct to possession proceedings against them. It may, however, lead to the mortgagor becoming bankrupt and this, in turn, can lead to a sale of the property at the request of the trustee in bankruptcy (*Alliance & Leicester v Slayford*).

A second way of recovering the whole sum due and ending the mortgage occurs if the mortgagee should seek to exercise his power of sale. In most cases a mortgage will contain an express power of sale, although by virtue of **s 101(1)(i)** of the **Law of Property Act 1925** a power of sale is implied into every mortgage made by deed unless a contrary intention appears. This power arises as soon as the legal (contractual) date for redemption has passed or, in the case of instalment mortgages, when one instalment is in arrears (*Twentieth Century Banking v Wilkinson* (1977)). However, under **s 103** of the **LPA** the power only becomes exercisable when either: (a) notice requiring payment of the mortgage money has been served and the mortgagor is three months in arrears since the notice; or (b) interest under the mortgage is two months in arrears and unpaid; or (c) the mortgagor has breached some covenant in the mortgage (other than the covenant to pay) or some provision of the **LPA 1925**. Any sale then conveys the land to the purchaser free from the mortgagee's mortgage, all subsequent mortgages (which are paid off in order, before the mortgagor) and the equity of redemption (**ss 88** and **113** of the **LPA**) and subject only to any previous mortgages. Obviously, a sale of the mortgaged property is calamitous for the mortgagor, and equity offers some protection.[12] Thus, the selling mortgagee is under a duty of care to the mortgagor to obtain the best price reasonably obtainable (*Standard Chartered Bank v Walker* (1982)), although an open sale by auction, even when prices are low, satisfies this rule (*Cuckmere Brick Co v Mutual Finance* (1971)).[13] If the mortgagee is negligent and thereby obtains a lower price than it would otherwise have obtained, it is liable to the mortgagor (*Cuckmere*) and the mortgagee cannot sell to himself or his agent (*Williams v Wellingborough Council* (1975)). However, this duty is

---

12 Thus limiting the practical scope of the mortgagees' powers.
13 Although simply relying on a reputable estate agent may not be enough.

owed to the mortgagor only and not to a person having merely an equitable interest in the property (*Parker-Tweedale v Dunbar* (1990)). Likewise, the mortgagee is not trustee of the power of sale and its motives in choosing to exercise the power of sale are irrelevant.

Usually, of course, the mortgagee will wish to sell the property in order to realise its security and to do this effectively,[14] the property must be sold with vacant possession. In practice, therefore, before sale, a mortgagee may wish to exercise its third remedy: the right of possession. Taking possession of the mortgaged property can also be used as a method of securing recovery of any outstanding interest on the loan, as where a mortgagee in possession sub-lets or runs the business over which the mortgage exists. Possession then does not necessarily mean the end of the mortgage. By virtue of the way in which mortgages are created, the mortgagee will have an estate in the land and an immediate right to possession of the property the moment the ink is dry on the mortgage, irrespective of any fault on the part of the mortgagor (*Four-Maids v Dudley Marshall* (1957); *Ropaigealach v Barclays Bank* (1999)), although normally the mortgagee will not exercise its right of possession and might even promise not to seek possession unless the mortgagor defaults on the interest repayments or breaches some other term of the mortgage. There is a positive disincentive for a mortgagee to take possession, as a mortgagee in possession will be called strictly to account for any income generated by its possession (*White v City of London Brewery* (1889)). This is why most commercial mortgagees desist from seeking possession.[15]

In the residential context, possession is further regulated. Under **s 36** of the **Administration of Justice Act (AJA) 1970** (as amended by **s 8** of the **AJA 1973**), a mortgagee's application for possession of a dwelling house may be suspended, adjourned or postponed by the court, in its discretion, if it appears that the mortgagor would be able to pay within a reasonable period any sums due under the mortgage. Due to **s 8** of the **AJA 1973** (reversing *Halifax BS v Clark* (1973)),[16] 'any sums due' may be treated only as those instalments missed and not the whole sum once one mortgage payment is missed. Note, however that the power under **s 36** is not available if the mortgagee takes possession under its common law right without a court order (*Ropaigealach v Barclays Bank*). In addition, while it is clear that the 'reasonable period' that the mortgagor is given to repay his arrears might actually be the rest of the mortgage – so as to spread the debt evenly (*Cheltenham and Gloucester BS v Norgan* (1996)) – there is no discretion if there is no prospect of the mortgagor making a reasonable attempt to actually repay the accumulated debt, let alone meet future repayments (*Guarantee v Zacaria* (1993)). However, the courts do show considerable sympathy to mortgagors pleading **s 36** and *Cheltenham and Gloucester BS v Norgan* suggests that the court will postpone possession if it appears that the mortgagor will be able to repay at some future time and not within an arbitrary period chosen by the court. Clearly, this is a generous interpretation[17] of **s 36** and, while it is understandable given the social utility of protecting residential occupiers, it does compromise significantly the undoubted right of the mortgagee to seek such possession.

---

14 In practice, possession is not a legal prerequisite to sale.
15 The right of possession highlights the public interest in strong remedies for the lender.
16 The use of this case in this way shows the examiner a good depth of knowledge of the relevant case law.
17 It is always good to express clearly your own view on the case law.

The fourth of the mortgagee's remedies may also be used to recover the interest owed rather than ending the mortgage. The mortgagee's right to appoint a receiver is often expressly included in a mortgage but, in any event, such a power will be implied into every mortgage by deed (**s 101** of the **LPA**). Any express power is exercisable according to its terms, although the statutory power becomes exercisable only in those circumstances in which the statutory power of sale becomes exercisable and is often an alternative to that remedy. The great advantage of the appointment of a receiver as opposed to the mortgagee taking possession of the property is that the receiver is deemed to be the agent of the mortgagor, not the mortgagee (*Chatsworth Properties v Effiom* (1971)), with the consequence that any negligence on the part of the receiver is not attributable to the latter.

Finally, the largely defunct remedy of foreclosure will extinguish the equity of redemption and cause the transfer of the property to the mortgagee, entirely free of any rights of the mortgagor. In view of the powerful nature of foreclosure, the court has power under **s 91(2)** of the **LPA** to order sale in lieu of a foreclosure (and in other circumstances: *Palk v Mortgage Services Funding* (1993)) and this means that any surplus funds after redemption of the mortgage will be paid to the mortgagor. In modern times, foreclosure is unheard of and a court would order sale instead. It could be safely abolished.[18]

Common Pitfalls

The question is about remedies, not about general protection. Remember to evaluate the remedies. Hence, there is no need to talk at length about foreclosure.

QUESTION 40

In 2004 Angus and Coleen combined their life savings of £80,000 in order to purchase No 1 High Street with the assistance of a mortgage advance of £250,000 provided by the Scotsdale Bank. Title to the house was registered in the name of Coleen subject to a registered charge in favour of the Bank. Angus had agreed to the mortgage and had met with the Bank to discuss this with his own solicitor. The agreement meant that the interest rate was variable at the discretion of the Bank, and, in 2007, the Bank quadrupled its interest rate for all customers with red hair, including Coleen.

Angus and Coleen (who had both been contributing to the mortgage) could not make these payments and went on holiday. While they were away, the Scotsdale Bank sent a letter addressed to No 1 High Street to Coleen, informing her that the Bank proposed to take possession of the house and offer it for sale at auction in three days' time.

A month later Angus returned to discover that the Bank had sold the house for £305,000 to a bidder who turned out to be the brother-in-law of the manager of the local branch of

18 If time permitted, there could be brief mention of the borrower's protection under the general law: clogs, fetters, undue influence and controlled credit bargains.

the Bank. Coleen, by this time, had run off with a waiter she met on holiday, and wished to sell and keep the proceeds of the sale once the bank had been paid all for herself in order to buy a new property on the Costa Brava.

▶ **Advise Angus and Coleen.**

How to Read this Question

The question combines issues about ownership of land with mortgagee's remedies. This is very common in the land law examination.

How to Answer this Question

First, establish who owns the land at law and in equity. Then, consider whether the lender has priority such that it can exercise remedies. Third, consider the remedies: possession and sale. This order of issues is critical.

Answer Structure

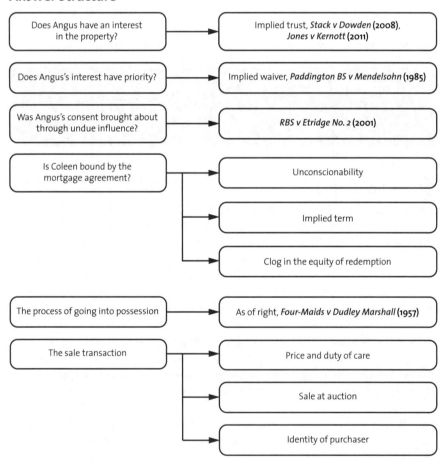

Does Angus have an interest in the property?	Implied trust, *Stack v Dowden* (2008), *Jones v Kernott* (2011)
Does Angus's interest have priority?	Implied waiver, *Paddington BS v Mendelsohn* (1985)
Was Angus's consent brought about through undue influence?	*RBS v Etridge No. 2* (2001)
Is Coleen bound by the mortgage agreement?	Unconscionability
	Implied term
	Clog in the equity of redemption
The process of going into possession	As of right, *Four-Maids v Dudley Marshall* (1957)
The sale transaction	Price and duty of care
	Sale at auction
	Identity of purchaser

This diagram shows how to apply the rules relating to trusts and mortgages in the situation involving Angus and Coleen.

ANSWER

Angus (A) wishes to establish an interest in the property which takes priority over the Bank's interest. Coleen (C) will wish to maximise the proceeds of sale by challenging the interest rate rise, as well as seeking damages for loss suffered.

Angus's Interest in the Property

As a preliminary issue, as a result of the registration of Coleen (C) as sole registered owner, A, under the approach outlined in *Stack v Dowden* (2007) and *Jones v Kernott* (2012) is presumed to have no interest in the property unless an express or implied common intention to the effect that he is to have such an interest can be demonstrated. Although this is a sole names case, and the extent to which *Kernott* etc. covers this case is therefore uncertain,[19] we can be fairly sure that A would be entitled to an equitable interest in this property as a result of his contribution to the purchase price and mortgage.

Once it is established that A does have an interest, it is necessary to determine the size of his equitable share, as outlined by Baroness Hale in *Stack*. If no express intention as to the size of the share is demonstrable, then such an intention can be either implied or imputed (*Kernott*). In this case, without information as to the proportions contributed by each to the deposit, or the mortgage, we cannot be certain as to quantity, but given the mutually communal nature of this relationship (see Gardner, 'Family property today' (2008) 124 LQR 422; Gardner and Davidson, 'The future of Stack v Dowden' (2011) 127 LQR 13; Gardner and Davidson, 'The Supreme Court on family homes' (2012) 128 LQR 178),[20] somewhere in the region of a 50 per cent share seems reasonable.

Priority Over Angus's Share

C holds on trust for herself and A and so B will have to demonstrate that its charge takes priority over A's interest. Although it is likely that A's interest would override under **Sched 3, para 2 LRA 2002**), it seems as if he has impliedly waived his priority – *Paddington BS v Mendelsohn* (1985). The only potential caveat to this is if A's consent to the mortgage was obtained as a result of C bringing pressure to bear on A such that he was put at a manifest disadvantage to bring the rules of undue influence into play (*RBS v Etridge No. 2* (2001)). There is no evidence of that and so B has priority over A (consent) and over C (mortgagee).

The Interest Rate Rise

The Bank quadrupled its interest rates for all customers with red hair, including C. C herself may wish to challenge this increase on the grounds that it: is unconscionable; is in breach of an implied term; is a fetter on the equity of redemption; and/or is regulated by the consumer protection legislation so as to increase her sale proceeds.

---

19 Where, as here, it is relatively straightforward to demonstrate that A is likely to have a share in the property, you need to make a judgment as to how much detail to provide in relation to co-ownership issues and the relevant case law, including the uncertainties in that case law.

20 Mentioning academic commentators in an answer like this not only avoids the risk of plagiarising others' ideas, it also shows that you have read around the topic and are aware of the ongoing academic debates in the field.

(a) Unconscionability

The general principle is that the parties are free to decide whatever mortgage terms they wish, and there are doubts whether judicial intervention in this is to be welcomed.[21] Perhaps, this term could be struck down because it 'shocks the conscience of the court' (*Multiservice Bookbinding v Marden* (1977); *Jones v Morgan* (2001)), but the test is high: *Alec Lobb* (1984) and *Jones v Morgan*. Given that the circumstances in *Jones v Morgan* did not give rise to a sufficient degree of unconscionability to allow the court to intervene, it is highly unlikely that the facts of this case would allow the court to do so either.

(b) Implied Term

The second possibility is found in the controversial decision in *Nash v Paragon Finance* (2001). Here it was held that 'the discretion to vary interest rates should not be exercised dishonestly, for an improper purpose, capriciously or arbitrarily' (para 32). By way of example, Dyson LJ suggests that, 'An example of a capricious reason would be where the lender decided to raise the rate of interest because its manager did not like the colour of the borrower's hair' (para 31).[22] But, even if breach is established, it is far from clear how the court would remedy this breach, and what affect this would have on C's current position. Perhaps C would be entitled to an award for damages to compensate her for any loss suffered as a result of the breach of the implied term, but there is no evidence of loss in this case.

(c) Clog on the Equity of Redemption

The first thing to note about the clog on the equity of redemption doctrine is that the judiciary does not appear fond of this rule – *Samuel v Jarrah Timber* (1904), and Lord Mersey in *New Patagonia Meat Company v Kregliner* (1913). *Jones v Morgan* is a rare modern example where an argument based on clogs has succeeded. In that case however the clog was to be found in the ability of the mortgagee to obtain title to the mortgaged property, which is an option not open to B here. The circumstances are very different from that in *Jones*. It seems unlikely that a court would take this route here. Thus, C's best option, it appears, is to argue that the interest rate rise is so capricious that it breaches an implied term of the mortgage agreement such that they are entitled to damages.

The Process of B Going into Possession and Sale

The mortgagee is entitled to take possession 'as soon as the ink is dry' on a mortgage agreement, irrespective of default *Four-Maids v Dudley Marshall* (1957), *Ropaigealach v Barclays Bank* (1998). The Bank's possession was lawful and, as *Ropaigealach* highlights, **s 36 AJA 1970** as amended does not provide protection to the mortgagor if the bank does not seek a court order for possession.

---

21 Although this is a problem question, there is no reason not to question the merits of the rules being applied, as long as you leave enough time to cover all the relevant issues.

22 Where possible the use of quotations, or paragraph numbers, shows that you have revised the detail of cases, as well as the general principles, but an effort to learn quotations should not detract from your overall revision.

As far as the power of sale is concerned, it arises as soon as the contractual date for redemption has passed, or when an instalment mortgage is in arrears (*Twentieth Century Banking v Wilkinson* (1976), **s101 LPA 1925**), as here. It becomes exercisable under **s103**: i.e. when either (i) notice requiring payment of the entire sum has been given and three months have passed since the notice and no such payment has been forthcoming; or (ii) some interest owed under the mortgage is two months in arrears; or (iii) there has been a breach of some other term of the mortgage agreement. In this case it seems likely that the interest under the mortgage is more than two months in arrears. Consequently, it seems likely that C has no recourse in relation to the means by which B took possession. It also seems likely that the power of sale has arisen and become exercisable.

The Sale

When a mortgagee sells the mortgaged property he is under a duty of care in relation to that sale to obtain to the best price reasonably available at the time (*Standard Chartered Bank v Walker* (1982); *Cuckmere Brick v Mutual Finance* (1970)). This duty does not however require that the mortgagee goes beyond selling in an appropriate manner, *Silven Properties* (2003), *Bishop v Blake* (2006). In fact, as *Bishop v Blake* and *Michael v Miller* (2004) highlight, the crucial issue is not the price actually achieved but the steps taken to achieving that price.

In this case, the issue is that the house was purchased by a relative of an employee of the local branch of B. Although there is a strict duty on a bank not to purchase the property itself (*Williams v Wellingborough Council* (1975)) it is possible for an associate of an employee of the bank to purchase the property (*Halifax v Corbett* (2002)), if there was no impropriety in their so doing. If the sale was improper, and P was aware of this, then the sale can be set aside. That does not appear to have been the case here.

It seems then that C's only potential remedy lies in damages. Whether this is because of the breach of the implied term, or (less likely) because of a breach of B's duty of care during the sale, the damages can only reflect what C has actually lost. This will mean, at most, that she is entitled to the difference between the true value of the property minus the money owed at the lower interest rate, and what she has actually received by way of surplus after sale. The sale proceeds would then be divided according to the percentage equitable share. It is highly unlikely that A would be able to set aside the sale given that the Bank's interest had priority over his but he would be entitled to some of the proceeds of the sale.

> ## Common Pitfalls
>
> The danger is that the answer focuses on only possession. As is evident, there are many possibilities here and they should all be dealt with, even if only briefly. Note the role that contract plays in the law of mortgages and do not ignore the initial ownership and priority points.

QUESTION 41

To what extent have recent decisions of the House of Lords clarified[23] the circumstances in which a person may plead 'undue influence' as a defence to a mortgagee seeking to exercise its remedies under the mortgage?

How to Read this Question

The examiner is asking for an analysis of the case law on undue influence. Set out the issue clearly, and then the relevant case.

How to Answer this Question

The following areas are relevant: how is undue influence established (actual, presumed and the meaning/purpose of manifest disadvantage); the consequences of undue influence; fixing a mortgagee with undue influence (agency, notice); how does a mortgagee protect itself? See *Barclays Bank v O'Brien* (1994); *CIBC v Pitt* (1994); *National Westminster Bank v Morgan* (1985); *Royal Bank of Scotland v Etridge* (2002); *National Westminster Bank v Amin* (2002).

Up for Debate

Consider the economic importance of mortgages and whether this led to a rise in undue influence claims. Has the pendulum swung too far back towards lenders?

Applying the Law

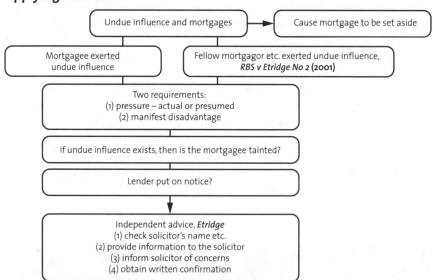

This diagram demonstrates the operation of the rules relating to undue influence and mortgages.

---

23 'Clarified' suggests confusion, so your answer should show the 'path' to the current position for top marks.

ANSWER

The law of undue influence may be called in aid by a mortgagor seeking to avoid the consequences of a mortgagee's exercise of one of its remedies. Often, it is pleaded as a defence to a possession action and, if successful, may prevent the mortgagee realising their security (but contrast *Alliance & Leicester v Slayford* (2001)). Obviously, the defence of undue influence may be raised in a variety of circumstances, although two particular situations are relevant here. First, a mortgagor may claim that the mortgagee (such as a bank) has exercised undue influence over them directly, with the effect that the mortgage is set aside. Such cases are now relatively rare given the regularised lending practices of most institutional mortgagees and the industry's codes of conduct. Second, a mortgagor (often a husband or male partner) may have sought a mortgage from an institutional lender over property that is jointly owned with another person (for example, a wife or sexual partner). Should this be the case, the other joint owner must consent to the mortgage if the lender is to have adequate security (see *William & Glyn's Bank v Boland* (1981) for the consequences of failing to secure consent). Of course, it lies in the power of the joint owner to refuse such consent, but their emotional ties to the person seeking the mortgage might well persuade them to agree, especially if it is to secure finance for their partner's business. If, then, at a later date, difficulties arise such as to give the mortgagee cause to seek possession or sale of the property, the consenting owner may well claim that their consent to the mortgage was procured by the undue influence of their partner

The rationale for the doctrine of undue influence is clear. However, it must be remembered that a vibrant mortgage market[24] – with adequate protection for lenders – is just as important as providing protection for the homes of persons who may have been 'persuaded' to enter a mortgage that they did not really want. A balance must be struck. At one time, the law of undue influence was regarded as a panacea available to most mortgagors at the slightest hint of unfairness in the mortgage transaction. Thus, it was perfectly possible for a mortgagor to avoid the consequences of default by pleading simply that the mortgagee was in a dominant position when the mortgage was made. However, this rather liberal approach was rejected in *National Westminster Bank v Morgan* (1985). In that case, the House of Lords made it clear that two major requirements had to be met before undue influence could be established. First, the mortgagor had to show some victimisation, pressure or unfair advantage by the mortgagee or by a person whose conduct could taint the mortgagee. Second, and more controversially, the House of Lords indicated that even if the fact of undue influence could be established, a mortgage would not be set aside unless it could also be shown to be 'to the manifest disadvantage' of the mortgagor.

As first explained by the House of Lords in *Barclays Bank v O'Brien* (1994) and *CIBC v Pitt* (1994), there are three steps to establishing the defence of undue influence. First, establish the undue influence. Second, ask whether the mortgagee is tainted by it. Third, assess whether the mortgagee has taken steps to prevent its mortgage being voided by the

---

24 Where the 'social' consequences of the rule are important, as in relation to mortgages, it is always good to flag this up to the examiner to highlight that you understand the wider policy framework.

undue influence. As to the first step, these two cases established that undue influence could either be 'actual' or 'presumed'. Actual undue influence arose where the facts established positively the existence of undue influence by the wrongdoer over the 'victim'. In contrast, presumed undue influence arose either where the relationship between the persons was of such a nature that the presumption of undue influence arose automatically (for example, doctor/patient, solicitor/client and parent/child: so-called 'Class 2A cases')[25] or where the substance of the relationship was that one person placed so much confidence in the other that the presence of undue influence should arise (so-called 'Class 2B cases': for example, husband/wife or lover/lover). In addition, manifest disadvantage was required for all presumed cases, but not in actual cases.

The second step was that the mortgagee had to be tainted with the wrongdoer's actions. This would occur if the wrongdoer was the agent of the mortgagee or the mortgagee had 'notice' of the undue influence. Agency will, of course, be very rare as lenders do not usually appoint one borrower to act for it in securing the other owner's consent. However, cases of notice were much more likely as such notice would exist where there was a substantial risk that some form of pressure may have been exerted and the mortgagee was aware of facts that gave rise to that risk. In fact, it soon became clear that such a risk was present in very many cases and lenders soon concentrated on identifying those steps that a mortgagee should take to protect itself in the event that it was on notice of the risk of undue influence. In general terms, these steps boiled down to the fact that the lender should advise the potential victim to seek independent advice and that, if the giving of advice was confirmed (for example, by a solicitor in a letter to the bank), the lender could assume that its mortgage was safe.

All this seemed clear enough after *O'Brien*, but in reality there was too little clarity about the practical application of these principles. The result was a 'bright-line' judgment by the House of Lords in *Royal Bank of Scotland v Etridge*. Once again, the issue can be broken down into three questions.

First, prove undue influence by the 'wrongdoer' over the claimant. If the evidence adduced by the claimant established actual undue influence, then this hurdle was surmounted. Where actual undue influence is established, there is no need to prove that the impugned transaction was to the claimant's 'manifest disadvantage', as such disadvantage only helps to prove undue influence (see below). Undue influence may also be presumed, although this is merely an evidentiary presumption that shifts the burden of proof from the claimant to the wrongdoer. Successful reliance on the presumption of undue influence means that the burden of explaining why the impugned transaction was not caused by undue influence passes to the alleged wrongdoer. When viewed in this light, there is no real merit in adopting the *O'Brien* categories of 'Class 2A' presumed undue influence cases and 'Class 2B' cases. Consequently, two things are now clear. First, that the 'presumption' of undue influence is no more than a tool to explain the shift of the evidentiary burden from the claimant and so 'manifest disadvantage' is necessary as it explains why

----

25 Using recognised labels like this is a good way to avoid unnecessary lengthy repetition.

the burden should shift. Second, the difference between the now defunct Class 2A and Class 2B cases is simply that, in the former, the fact of trust and confidence could not be disputed by the wrongdoer, whereas in the second, it could.

The second issue is whether the lender is put on inquiry. The House of Lords in *Etridge* adopted a robust and blunt determining that a lender will always be put on inquiry (have notice) if a person is standing as a surety for another's debts, provided that such surety is not offered as a commercial service (that is, the guarantor is not charging for the service, as would a bank or other institution). Although this is an extension of the law, it has the great merit[26] of ensuring that lenders do not have to probe the relationship of the parties in order to assess whether they are on inquiry.

Third, if on inquiry, what steps should the lender take to avoid being tainted by the undue influence and risk losing its security? For past cases – that is, mortgages executed prior to the *Etridge* decision – the lender must take steps to ensure that the wife understands the risk she is running and should advise her to seek independent advice. For future cases – that is, mortgages executed post-*Etridge* – the lender must insist that the wife attend a private meeting with the lender at which she is told of the extent of her liability, warned of the risk she is running and urged to take independent legal advice.

It now seems as if *Etridge* has resolved the uncertainties left by *O'Brien*. It even appears to have forced a change in lending practices, but this has been absorbed into the administrative practices of the competent lending institutions.[27]

Common Pitfalls

The question is not just about *Etridge*. It requires an understanding of pre-*Etridge* case law in order to explain how the law developed.

QUESTION 42

To what extent is freedom of contract inconsistent with the traditional view of a mortgage as being the grant of a proprietary interest in land merely as a security, albeit one that deserves special protection from a court of equity?

How to Read this Question

The examiner is expecting a general discussion which balances the rights of the mortgagee with the protection available to the mortgagor, within a framework which recognises the proprietary and contractual natures of mortgages.

26 It is always good to integrate your own analysis of the rules into your explanation of them as it shows that you are thinking independently about the topic under consideration.

27 The answer could be considerably more detailed, but in the examination you may not have enough time to deal with the issue depth. It is therefore important to work out strategies for conveying this information in a shorter space if time requires it.

How to Answer this Question

The answer needs to include the following areas: the nature of a mortgage, but founded in contract; the ability of the mortgagee to impose contractual terms versus the equity of redemption; the mortgagee's contractual remedies modified by statute; mortgages as loan contracts under the **Consumer Credit Acts**.

Up for Debate

To what extent are mortgages financial consumer products that should be protected like any other 'good' that a consumer 'buys'? Is it better to regulate the giving of mortgages, or to reform the law relating to the exercise of remedies?

Answer Structure

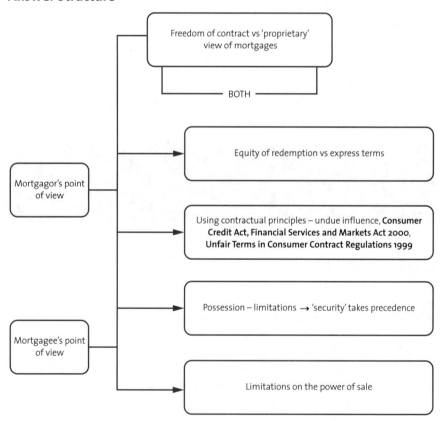

This diagram demonstrates many of the main issues when looking at the question of whether mortgage law prioritises freedom of contract or looks more at the proprietary nature of a mortgage interest.

ANSWER

In one very important sense, this question is misleading.[28] A mortgage is both an interest in land and a contract. It partakes of the attributes of both and in the great majority of situations the dictates of contract and property law are complementary, not mutually exclusive. In other words, just because a contract is at the heart of the dealings between mortgagor and mortgagee does not mean that the mortgage cannot also operate as a proprietary right. Thus, the mortgagee has remedies on the contract (for example, to sue for money due), as well as remedies arising because of their proprietary interest in the land (for example, the right to possession). Likewise, the mortgagor has obligations under the contract (for example, to repay the loan and observe other covenants) as well as rights founded in their equity of redemption, a proprietary right. However, that said, it is true that, in some situations, the nature of a mortgage as a security over land, regulated by equity, can come into conflict with the contract negotiated between the parties.[29]

The most obvious example of this potential conflict arises because of the general rule that equity will safeguard the equity of redemption, sometimes in contradiction of the express terms of the bargain agreed between mortgagor and mortgagee. Thus, an option to purchase granted to the mortgagee in the mortgage deed will be void (*Samuel v Jarrah Timber* (1904); *Jones v Morgan* (2002)) and terms that make the mortgage irredeemable will be struck out (*Fairclough v Swan Brewery* (1912)), even if agreed by the parties. Of course, the court is astute to give effect to the bargain made between commercial parties who are deemed to be able to take care of themselves, especially if they are financing a commercial enterprise (*Knightsbridge Estates v Byrne* (1939)), but that does not allow them to change the essential nature of a mortgage. It is still a security for a loan under which the proprietary interest conveyed to the mortgagee can be recovered on the payment of interest, principal and costs (*Re Sir Thomas Spencer Wells* (1933)). In particular, this emphasis on the equity of redemption has led the court to examine any 'collateral advantages' that are stipulated in the mortgage, being benefits extracted by the mortgagee in consideration for the loan. Originally, such advantages were frowned upon, as constituting a clog on the equity of redemption, but, in recent times, a collateral advantage that is neither harsh or unconscionable nor destructive *in fact* of the equity of redemption will be permitted (*Santley v Wilde* (1899)). Indeed, if the advantage represents the true commercial bargain between the parties and is not void on the above grounds, it will be permitted as an exercise of freedom of contract, even where it continues after the mortgage has been redeemed (as in *Kreglinger v New Patagonia Meat and Cold Storage Co* (1914)).

In addition, it is not only a court of equity that will protect a mortgagor. General contractual principles may also be called in aid.[30] Thus, the general common law doctrine of undue influence may allow a mortgagor to avoid a mortgage contract in much the same way as a party

---

28 Analysis of this sort which questions the 'sense' of the question demonstrates a sophisticated approach to an essay.

29 This is good as it outlines the faultlines of the conflict, giving the examiner a clear understanding of how you are approaching your response.

30 The idea that contract rules themselves limit freedom of contract is separate to the freedom of contract vs property conflict, but a good answer will tease out the ambiguities and contradictions in this 'conflict'.

may avoid any other contract (*Barclays Bank v O'Brien* (1994); *Royal Bank of Scotland v Etridge* (2002)). Again, the **Consumer Credit Act** applies to mortgages as with other loan contracts as does the doctrine of restraint of trade (*Esso v Harper's Garage* (1968)). All of these, and the **Unfair Contract Terms in Consumer Contracts Regulations 1999** (*Falcon Finance v Gough* (1999)), support the court's intervention when seeking to protect the mortgagor's proprietary right in the equity of redemption.

From the mortgagor's point of view, then, both the contractual and proprietary nature of the mortgage can give protection against a mortgagee. When we look at the mortgagee, however, it seems that both statute and general equitable principles do intervene substantially to control (that is, limit) the exercise of remedies under the mortgage contract. In this sense, the contractual nature of the mortgage does take a back seat to its essential nature as a security. Thus, although the mortgagor has a contractual (and proprietary) right to take possession of the mortgagor's property, both statute and equity restrict the full exercise of this right. In the former case, s 36 of the **Administration of Justice Act 1970** (as amended by s 8 of the AJA 1973) gives the court power to set aside the claim for possession in respect of a dwelling house (but note *Ropaigealach v Barclays Bank* (1999)), although only if the mortgagor is likely to be able to meet their commitments under the mortgage and pay off any sums due within a reasonable time (*Bank of Scotland v Grimes* (1985); *Cheltenham and Gloucester v Norgan* (1996); *First National Bank v Side* (1991)). This is supported by s 91 of the **Law of Property Act 1925** (see *Palk v Mortgage Services Funding* (1993)). In the second case, the equitable rule that a mortgagee in possession must account strictly for any income that is derived or could have been derived from the property during his period of possession (*White v City of London Brewery* (1889)) means that most mortgagees of commercial premises will not seek this remedy, although they may rely on the appointment of a receiver instead. Clearly, the court's ability to restrict the right of possession is a firm indication that the nature of a mortgage as a security takes priority over the claims of the mortgagee based on his contract and the proprietary right thereby obtained.

Likewise, the power of sale available to most mortgagees is restricted by the intervention of equity, even though statute (**LPA 1925**) clearly contemplates this as one of the major remedies of the mortgagee. The duty of care owed to the mortgagee to obtain the best price reasonably obtainable (*Standard Chartered Bank v Walker* (1982)) and the trust imposed on any surplus from the sale (after payment of the mortgage) do act as a brake on an eager mortgagee, although, in so far as they prevent fraud on the part of a mortgagee, these principles cannot be criticised. The same is generally true of the mortgagee's power of foreclosure (see s 91 of the **LPA 1925**), although this right – itself stemming from the nature of a mortgage as a proprietary right – is often a weapon of last resort. Technically, such a right arises as soon as the legal date specified in the contract has passed, but in reality the mortgagee often contracts not to exercise the right until some specified breach of covenant has occurred, such as non-payment of interest. This is an example of contract modifying the proprietary nature of a mortgage.[31]

---

31 Introducing the 'mirror image' in this way shows you have considered both sides of the question and demonstrates an imaginative approach to the answer.

To conclude, one must reiterate that which was stated at the start of this answer. The mortgage that springs from contract is effected by means of the creation of a proprietary right in the mortgagee, and partakes of the rules and principles of both contract and property law. It should not be thought that there is a great deal of tension between the two philosophies and even where the equity of redemption is concerned – the most well guarded of the mortgagor's rights – the commercial nature of the mortgage and its role in releasing the economic value of real property has been recognised in the law relating to the mortgagee's remedies.[32] The same is true in such matters as undue influence (*Royal Bank of Scotland v Etridge* (2002)) and human rights (*Horsham Properties v Beech* (2008)). It is illustrated by the fact that the court is only willing to interfere with mortgages on the basis of **s 140A–C** of the **Consumer Credit Act 2006** if it is satisfied that there is an unfair credit relationship between the borrower and the lender.

Common Pitfalls

This is one of the most interesting questions that can be asked on the law of mortgages and so do not treat it as an opportunity to list remedies or list means of borrower protection. You will get more marks if you engage with the question asked. The question also requires some knowledge of how mortgages are created and therefore provides a good test of a student's understanding of this general area of law.

---

32 This is a clear but balanced conclusion and shows what can be done where the question itself is ambiguous or oversimplified.

10 Miscellaneous Problems

INTRODUCTION

The issues considered in this chapter bear no obvious relation to each other and no attempt shall be made to find one. However, they do share one important practical characteristic: they are issues that feature occasionally in examinations in land law, rather than being habitual favourites of examiners. Of course, that makes them no less important, for a well-answered question on say, adverse possession, is worth just as much as a well-answered question on co-ownership. That said, this chapter deals with issues such as adverse possession and fixtures and chattels with no particular attempt to treat them as intrinsically connected.

Adverse possession – or squatting – is a doctrine that truly reflects the feudal origins of English land law and the common law systems based upon it. Behind the ability of a trespasser to actually acquire 'ownership' of land that on paper belongs to somebody else is the concept that, in fact, owners only own 'estates' or titles in the land, not the land itself. Thus, it is perfectly possible for some other person to gain a better title without any formal transfer of 'ownership'. The very idea of adverse possession is based upon relativity of title, not absolute ownership of land. It is now trite law that in England there is no equivalent of the civil law concept of *dominium* and, in practice, this means that one person's title to land is only as good as the absence of a person with a better title. This traditional justification for adverse possession is, however, rapidly becoming an anachronism. Not only were doubts raised on human rights grounds (*Beaulane Properties v Palmer* (2005)) – although in *Ofulue v Bossert* (2008) the Court of Appeal subsequently confirmed that principles of adverse possession were, as a matter of principle, compliant with human rights law – but also, most noticeably, with the coming into force of the **Land Registration Act 2002** the philosophy of a guarantee of title has superseded the justifications behind the rules on limitations. Under this Act, registration as a proprietor is, even with the continued ability to seek rectification of the register, closer to an absolute guarantee of title than has formerly been known in the law of England and Wales. As a consequence, under the registered title scheme, while adverse possession is not impossible to establish, it is, nevertheless, often exceedingly difficult. In addition, squatting in a residential building was made a criminal offence with effect from 1 September 2012 under **s144** of the **Legal Aid, Sentencing and Punishment of Offenders Act 2012**. This is not, as commonly believed, the first time that squatting could trigger a criminal offence (see **s7** of the **Criminal Law Act 1977**) but it indicates clearly a policy move away from old notions of relativity of title.

Checklist

Today, adverse possession is a mixture of common law rules overlain by statute. The student therefore needs to have an understanding of the doctrine of estates in English land law, a working knowledge of the Limitation Act 1980 and a feeling for the purpose behind the principle of limitation of actions. Likewise, decisions such as *Buckinghamshire County Council v Moran* (1990), *Colchester Borough Council v Smith* (1992), *Hounslow LBC v Minchinton* (1997), *Pye v Graham* (2003), *R (Wayne Smith) v Land Registry & Cambs CC* (2010) and *Zarb v Parry* (2012) give considerable guidance on the practical application of these rules. It is also vital that there is a clear understanding of the reforms to adverse possession as it applies to registered land affected by the Land Registration Act 2002 and the way in which these have operated (*Baxter v Mannion* (2010)).

The rules concerning fixtures and chattels are often more important to practising conveyancers than students of land law. Essentially, the question is what, apart from the house/land itself, does a purchaser of property buy on completion of the contract of sale? Does the greenhouse also pass with the title? How about the garden statues and the wall coverings? The answers to these and related questions are to be found mainly in judicial pronouncements, which, while developing a general set of principles, can vary considerably in the confused circumstances of a real case. As with adverse possession, there is no better way to understand the law of fixtures and chattels than a thorough knowledge of case law.

QUESTION 43

To what extent is it possible to define the circumstances in which an occupier of land may make a successful claim of adverse possession against the title holder?

How to Read this Question

The examiner is expecting a thorough analysis of the common law principles whereby title might be established by adverse possession. It also requires some knowledge of recent statutory developments, including the Land Registration Act 2002.

How to Answer this Question

The following areas need to be discussed: the general purpose and role of adverse possession; the concept of limitation – the limitation period; the mechanics of establishing adverse possession; special circumstances – licences, future intentions; stopping the clock; the compromise of disputes.

Up for Debate

Consider whether, as a matter of policy, modern land law should contemplate acquisition of title by mere possession. This was acceptable when title was uncertain, but is it now so under land registration? Note also that landowners and squatters have human rights. How do we manage these competing rights?

Applying the Law

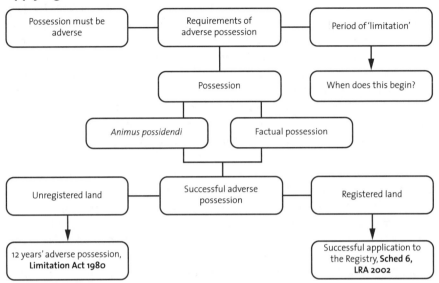

This diagram shows the requirements of adverse possession.

ANSWER

Adverse possession embodies one of the most fundamental principles of English land law: that a person may only own an estate in the land, not the land itself. However, if an estate owner sleeps on their rights, a court will not enforce those rights against the person actually in possession of the land. Adverse possession involves three basic issues: first, after what period of time does a paper owner of land lose their right to sue to recover possession of it for unregistered land? In registered land the question becomes: how long must a possessor be in possession before he can make an application to be registered? Second, when does that period start to run and how can it be brought to an end? Third, what is the effect of expiry of this period, both for the paper owner and the adverse possessor? What must be determined here is the extent to which each of these issues can be defined with precision.[1]

As to the period of limitation, this is the period after which no action can be brought to recover land. In most cases concerning unregistered land, this will be 12 years from the moment of adverse possession by the squatter (s15 of the **Limitation Act (LA) 1980**). There are certain special cases in which the period is different, as where Crown lands are involved (30 years: **Sched 1** to the **LA 1980**) or where possession is alleged to be adverse to a remainderman (s15 of the **LA 1980**). For registered land, the rules are no longer based on the concept of limitation, but an application may be made to the land registry after ten years' adverse possession.

---

1   The use of the words 'extent' and 'defined' here reflects the wording of the question and shows that you are clearly addressing the question set.

Second, at what moment in time does the actual occupation of land by another person become adverse to the paper owner so as to start the relevant period running? The rules concerning this vital question are not to be found in statute: they are entirely judge-made and thus flexible, open-ended and subject to a variety of applications as the circumstances of each case permits. Following a number of cases that illustrated the uncertainties in the law, the House of Lords in *Pye v Graham* (2003) sought to codify, and clarify, the principles of adverse possession and, together with the earlier decision of the Court of Appeal in *Buckinghamshire CC v Moran* (1990), may be regarded as embodying the definitive statement of the modern law.[2] In *Moran*, there was a successful claim of adverse possession by a squatter against the council[3] and the court enunciated the following principles.

First, the adverse possessor should have an intention to possess the land to the exclusion of the whole world, including the paper owner (*Pye v Graham*). So, a belief that possession might become authorised by the paper owner can mean that the adverse possessor fails to demonstrate a *sufficient* immediate intention to possess to the exclusion of all (*Pye*). Second, the squatter must take adverse possession of the land as a matter of fact, either in consequence of the dispossession of the paper owner or following discontinuance by him. Dispossession occurs where the paper owner is effectively driven out by another (*Rains v Buxton* (1880)) and discontinuance where the paper owner abandons the land (*Smith v Lloyd* (1854)). In either case, the loss of possession by the paper owner must be followed by actual adverse possession by the squatter. This will be a question of fact in each case, although it is clear that the degree of physical possession required will vary with the type of land involved. It may well be easier to establish adverse possession over land that is not susceptible to developed use (*Red House Farms v Catchpole* (1977)) and there are some indications that adverse possession is easier to prove in cases of discontinuance as opposed to cases of dispossession (*Red House Farms*). Yet, it is a question of fact in each case (*Powell v McFarlane* (1970)) and there is no requirement that the adverse possession must actually inconvenience the paper owner (*Treloar v Nute* (1976)). But, possession will not be taken from acts equivocal in nature or temporary in purpose, such as growing vegetables or clearing land so as to enable one's children to play (*Wallis's Cayton Holiday Camp v Shell-Mex and BP* (1975); *Techbild v Chamberlain* (1969)), but motive is irrelevant if the acts of the squatter effectively exclude the paper owner (*Minchinton*; *Lambeth v Blackburn*). Of course, the possession must be adverse to the paper owner: it must not be with their consent or permission as that amounts to a licence to occupy and will not start the period of limitation.

Assuming, then, that adverse possession is running against the paper owner, the paper owner may then seek to 'stop the clock' by reasserting their own possession. An action to recover possession of the land necessarily will stop the adverse possession. The same is true of other acts that show an intention on the part of the adverse possessor to

---

2   Extra 'credit' can often be found by mentioning the court in which the case you are mentioning was decided, since this shows that you are aware of the strength of the authority of that case.

3   Remember, you do not need to spend a long time in your response discussing the facts of cases where they do not advance your argument. A brief explanation of the facts can, however, sometimes be useful to put the decision into a context.

acknowledge the paper owner's title, as where the squatter pays rent or by written acknowledgement of title before time has expired (**ss 29** and **30** of the **LA**). However, apart from actually initiating proceedings, it is not clear what other actions by the paper owner will be sufficient to 'stop the clock'.[4] In *Moran*, a letter asserting title was not sufficient, although a letter evincing a definite intention to sue may well be (*Shell-Mex*). Recent guidance has been provided by the Court of Appeal in *Zarb v Parry* (2012). Here the registered owner of the land had attempted to end the adverse possessor's possession by starting to put up a fence. They did not finish the construction of the fence, however, and so the court concluded that although they had started the process that would have brought the adverse possessor's possession to an end, they had not completed it.

Once the relevant period has expired, in unregistered land, both the paper owner's right to sue and their title are extinguished by operation of statute (**s 17** of the **LA**). After this date, the conventional wisdom is that no acknowledgement, written or otherwise, and no payment, can revive the paper owner's title (*Nicholson v England* (1962)), unless the parties can be taken to have settled their ongoing dispute where it would be inequitable to challenge the solution (*Colchester Borough Council v Smith* (1992)).[5] In registered land, expiry of the ten-year period triggers the ability of the squatter to apply under **Sched 6** of the **Land Registration Act**, although this does not mean that they will actually achieve title.

The law of adverse possession also has been clarified in two other ways, one of which has been alluded to already. First, in respect of human rights, in *JA Pye (Oxford) Ltd v United Kingdom* (2007), the Grand Chamber of the European Court of Human Rights held that the **Land Registration Act 1925** was human rights-compliant in that it might deny title to a paper owner, and the reasoning applies also to adverse possession of unregistered land and under the **Land Registration Act 2002**. Confirmation in the courts of England and Wales that principles of adverse possession are, in general, not at odds with human rights law can be seen in *Ofulue v Bossert* (2008).

Second, it is well known that the **Land Registration Act 2002** has effected radical changes in the way modern law approaches claims to title by adverse possession. Thus, under **Sched 6** to the **2002 Act**, a registered owner can no longer lose title simply by reason of the passage of time.

The squatter can apply to the Land Registry to be registered as proprietor of the estate, but notice of this application is then given to the registered proprietor who, save for exceptional circumstances, has two further years to evict the squatter. The exceptional cases – which may be summarised as estoppel, some other right to the land or a reasonable mistake as to boundaries – will enable the squatter to acquire title, but clearly these are of limited effect (see *Baxter v Mannion*).

....

4   The use of the word 'clear' again here ties back to the question, and shows that you have in mind always the specific task set by the examiner.

5   For higher marks, this can be tied to academic commentary on the case, e.g. Dixon, 'Adverse possession: compromises and estoppel' (1992) 51 Cambridge Law Journal 420.

Although in recent years the substantive law of adverse possession has taken on more clarity and certainty, mainly due to the clear exposition in *Moran* and the application in cases like *Minchinton* and *Pye*, the chances of a successful claim being made are falling away because of the impact of the **Land Registration Act 2002**. After, the vast majority of land is now registered. In addition, the introduction of a new criminal offence of 'residential squatting' indicates that policy has turned against squatters. As things stand, the commission of this new criminal offence (**s 144** of the **Legal Aid, Sentencing and Punishment of Offenders Act 2012**) does not mean that a criminal squatter cannot claim title (illegality does not prevent the claim – *Best v Chief Land Registrar* (2014)), but the trend in the law is in favour of formal ownership and away from possessory title.

Common Pitfalls

This is a general question on the law of adverse possession, but a good answer must use a combination of statute and case law. Do not shy away from **Sched 6** to the **LRA 2002** as it fundamentally alters our approach to registered title.

QUESTION 44

In 1990, Ratty purchased an island in the middle of the River Flyte and built a bridge from his adjoining land on the shore. He intended to use the island as a country retreat and throughout 1990–1994 made regular fishing trips. He even built himself a cabin, cultivated a small vegetable garden and laid the foundations for a more substantial house in the future. Unfortunately, in 1994, Ratty became ill and had to leave for the clean air of Austria. Eventually, the vegetable garden became overgrown, the cabin ran to ruin and finally the bridge fell down, leaving the island as isolated as it was before. However, in anticipation of his departure, Ratty had managed to sell the land on the shore to his neighbour Mole, who was enthusiastic about the prospects of establishing a salmon fishery, but had no use for the island. Mole soon set about making enquiries of the local authority for planning permission for his fishery buildings and sought finance from several merchant banks. Again, however, things went awry and Mole could not raise the necessary capital. He resolved to wait until his resources grew and was content to use the land for walking and the occasional spell of private fishing. In 1998, Weasel, the local poacher, decided that the land bordering the river and the island were going to waste and he decided to move in and use the land for his own purposes. Shortly after, he was rowing regularly to the island where he re-established the garden, rebuilt the cabin and began charging tourists for day fishing permits for fishing from the island's shore. This became so successful that he purchased a luxury caravan and parked it on Mole's land, where he began to live. There he also planted a vegetable garden, cleared the land to make way for a dirt road and began keeping horses, also to hire to tourists. Eventually, he had to build a fence to keep the horses from straying. In 2007, Mole became concerned about the extent of Weasel's activities on his land, and although he had tolerated them up to then, having no immediate hope of establishing his fishery, registered his title to the land believing that this would help him in trying to get rid of Weasel. He turned up at Weasel's caravan and began to erect a fence trying to stop Weasel from reaching the caravan. Mole did not finish the fence before he was called away on business. However, in 2010, on hearing (falsely, as it turned out) that Mole had raised the money, Weasel extended the fence and placed a locked gate across the dirt road. In 2012, Mole eventually raised enough money for his project and sought possession of the land. Weasel resisted and when Mole told him that Ratty would also issue possession proceedings, he asserted title to the island as well.

▶ **Discuss the position of Weasel.**

How to Read this Question
In this problem question, the examiner will expect you to state the relevant law of adverse possession and then apply it to the precise facts.

How to Answer this Question
The answer needs to deal with the following issues: the intention to possess; discontinuance, dispossession and adverse factual possession; implied or actual permission given to the squatter. Also, the difference between registered and unregistered land in application of the rules of adverse possession.

Answer Structure

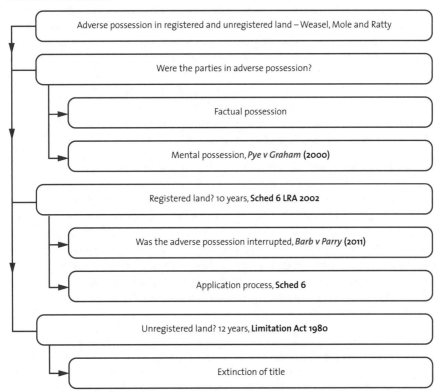

This diagram shows how to apply the rules of adverse possession in registered land to the problem of Weasel, Mole and Ratty.

ANSWER

This question requires discussion of the law of adverse possession, for this is at the root of any case that Weasel may have to resist the claims of possession of both Ratty and Mole. In order to establish adverse possession, it is clear from *Buckinghamshire CC v Moran* (1990) and *Pye v Graham* (2003) that Weasel must establish a number of things: first, that he had an intention to possess the land; second, that he possessed the land following a discontinuance or dispossession of the paper owner; third, that that possession was adverse to the paper owner. In addition to proving adverse possession, Weasel must also show that this adverse possession has been sufficient to entitle him to resist possession proceedings. In relation to unregistered land then, he must have been in possession for the 12-year period of limitation specified by **s 15** of the **Limitation Act (LA) 1980**. For registered land, he would have to show ten years of adverse possession as well as that the procedural steps in **LRA 2002, Sched 6**, had been taken.[6]

(a) The Island

The position in respect of the island seems relatively straightforward. There is no doubt that from 1990–1994, Ratty was in possession of the island and his activities there clearly demonstrated his ownership, backed as it was by paper title. However, in 1994, Ratty was forced to leave the country and the following events tend towards the conclusion that he abandoned or discontinued ownership. This is supported by the implication that Ratty wished to sell all his property but, except for the land on the shore, was unable to find a buyer. He appears to have no future plans for the island such as would indicate continued interest. Indeed, there seems to be positive proof of abandonment in that the bridge falls down and is not rebuilt, as in *Red House Farms v Catchpole* (1977). Of course, Ratty may argue that he was unable – as opposed to unwilling – to continue possession of the land as his emigration was forced through ill health. However, this is unlikely to rebut the presumption of abandonment so clearly indicated by the facts we are given. In such circumstances, it seems that even very slight acts by a trespasser will be sufficient to constitute adverse possession of the property (*Wuta-Ofei v Danquah* (1961); *Red House Farms*).

Second, does Weasel make use of the land as if he were owner, combined with an intention to assert ownership? Remembering that this is a case of discontinuance, the re-establishing of the vegetable garden and the rebuilding of the cabin may well suffice but, even if these are regarded as equivocal (*Powell v McFarlane* (1970)), the fact that he charges tourists for fishing rights clearly manifests both an intention to possess and sufficient acts of possession. He is, in fact, treating the land as if it were his own (*Hounslow LBC v Minchinton* (1997)). In such circumstances, assuming that Ratty has done nothing in the intervening period to stop time running, the paper owner's title will be extinguished some 12 years later, around 2010 (**s 17** of the **LA 1980**). Thus, he obtains title by statutory conveyance (*Central London Commercial Estates v Kato Kagku* (1998)).[7]

---

6 Where there are many different issues to be discussed in a problem, it is good to use the introduction to give the answer shape. Here, the most important thing to notice is that the two plots of land must be dealt with very differently, since one is registered, the other not.

7 It is a good idea to outline the consequences of the law you are applying in one sentence at the end of a section – this makes your conclusion easier at the end as it will save time when you are looking back over your answer to summarise your findings.

(b) The Riverside Property

First, we should note that title to this land is registered and since Weasel was not in possession for 12 years prior to the coming into force of the **LRA 2002**, this issue will be dealt with under **Sched 6** of the **2002 Act**. Clearly, on the facts of the case, Mole has not abandoned the property. He has a clear, future use for the property and is actively seeking the money to finance it. It is necessary, therefore, for Weasel to establish that he has dispossessed the paper owner and followed this by his own adverse possession, uninterrupted, for ten years, and that the procedures outlined in **Sched 6** have been followed.

(i) The Position up to 2007

Originally, Mole had a clear, future intention to use the land and that, as a matter of fact, the acts of the trespasser were not inconsistent with this intention. Formerly, under *Leigh v Jack* (1879), these facts would have justified the implication of a licence in favour of Weasel issuing from Mole. The effect of this licence – or permission – would have been to remove any possibility that the possession of the occupier was adverse to the paper owner. However, following *Moran* (and confirmed in *Pye*), it is clear that the existence of future intentions cannot, of itself and without more, justify the court in implying a licence in the actual possessor's favour.[8] So far, then, as a result of *Moran*, Weasel's claim is not defeated. However, it is still necessary for him to establish his own possession of the land following dispossession of the paper owner. In this respect, the acts of Weasel may be too equivocal to count. Thus, the planting of the vegetable garden (*Powell*) and the keeping of animals (*Techbild v Chamberlain* (1969)) may not be sufficient. Likewise, the building of the fence seems designed as much to keep the animals in as to keep the world at large out. This is also equivocal (*George Wimpey v Sohn* (1967)). On the other hand, the clearing of land for the driveway may amount to an act of ownership (*Williams v Usherwood* (1981)). The establishment of the caravan is also important, but again it does not necessarily evince an intention to exclude the world, merely to occupy the land. It is therefore likely that Weasel has not been in adverse possession, but it is possible that the clearing of the land may provide the necessary factual possession.

(ii) The Events of 2007

If Weasel has indeed been in adverse possession, since Weasel had been in adverse possession for only nine years to 2007, the outcome of the events of 2007 are crucial for any potential adverse possession claim. The key events were (a) Mole's decision to register his title to the land and (b) the attempted erection of the fence on the shore land. Both of these events will potentially have significant consequences for Weasel's claim in adverse possession.

First, in relation to the registration of title, the effect of this is that although Weasel's possession commenced whilst the land was unregistered, registration at any point before the required period of possession is up, will result in the issue being dealt with as a matter of registered land (**Sched 6, para 1(4) LRA 2002**). Second, as far as the erection of the fence is concerned, the question is whether the erection of an incomplete fence in this way can bring Weasel's possession to an end. It seems likely that it would not have had this effect, as

---

8 Referring to the older case law rules in this way is a good technique for showing off your knowledge of the topic without going too far off track in a problem question answer.

a result of the decision in *Zarb v Parry* (2012) where an incomplete fence was considered not to have brought adverse possession to an end. Thus we can conclude that the fence did not 'stop the clock' and so the question will now turn on the application of **Sched 6, LRA 2002**.

(iii) Schedule 6, LRA 2002

Schedule 6 determines when an adverse possessor of registered land will be successful in obtaining title to that land by virtue of his possession. It outlines, that where the adverse possessor has been in possession for ten years, as Weasel has, he must make an application to become registered proprietor **(para 1(1))**. Since Mole has not abandoned his land, it is likely that if his contact details are up-to-date, he will object to this application, **(para 3(1))**. The result of this is that the application will be dealt with under **para 5** and Weasel will only be able to be registered proprietor if one of the exceptions in this paragraph applies. The only potentially relevant exception is the boundary exception, but, crucially, it is clear that Weasel does not reasonably believe that the land belonged to him, and so this exception will not assist him. As a result, Weasel will not be registered as proprietor, even if he were to apply before Mole brought his possession proceedings.

Thus, although Weasel is likely to be able to resist Ratty's claim for adverse possession, he is probably unable to do so in relation to the shore land. This conclusion fits in fact with the justifications for adverse possession since although Ratty has abandoned his land, putting it to no economic use, Mole has active plans for his land. As a result, if adverse possession is seen as a way of ensuring that land is put to good use, then the way the rules apply in this scenario seem to suggest that a good balance is being struck.[9]

Common Pitfalls

It is crucial to understand that the **LRA 2002** kicks in whenever 12 years' adverse possession is not completed under the old law. The point of the question is to highlight differences in the regimes.

QUESTION 45

Some years ago, when Hannibal arrived back in the country from a long stay overseas, he sought your help in finding a quiet secluded property for his family as well as an office in town from which to run his optician's business. Unfortunately, the first house that he purchased proved too small for his needs and after several years he wished to move to a larger house. Hannibal experienced great difficulty and delay in selling his previous house but, finally, last month he went to view Roman Villas, an old property on the edge of town. After some doubt, he has just completed the purchase of Roman Villas from Vesuvius. Unlike the situation with his house, Hannibal had not, however, had any difficulty in finding suitable office accommodation and had agreed with Pontius, the freeholder, for a seven-year lease of

---

9 In a question where there is little analysis to be found as the answer to the problem is going along, one way to bring analysis in, is to question at the end whether the rules as applying in the problem meet with the aims behind those rules.

suitable premises in a good location. He soon installed his equipment in the premises, fixing lights to the ceiling and a suitable chair to the floor and, in order to make the place more welcoming for his customers, he refitted one room with oak panelling and a large wall-mounted fish tank. Four years ago, on the expiry of the lease, he and Pontius had agreed a further four-year term. Now, on the purchase of Roman Villas, Hannibal has decided to work from home and has removed all the equipment, including the lights and chair as well as the oak panelling and fish tank. He moves them to Roman Villas, only to find that Vesuvius has removed the greenhouse, the rose bushes, the garden ornaments, the television aerial and some antique banisters, all of which Hannibal greatly admired when being shown around the property before contracts were exchanged.

Hannibal comes to you for advice as to whether he should sue Vesuvius for the return of items, only to find that you have been instructed by Pontius to sue him (Hannibal) for the recovery of the equipment removed from the office in town, as it seems that Pontius had arranged to let the premises to a new optician.

▶ Discuss.

How to Read this Question
This problem is on a marginal issue: the nature of fixtures and chattels and who may be entitled to the various items of property. The examiner expects a significant amount of case law.

How to Answer this Question
The following areas need to be discussed: the nature of fixtures and chattels; the relevance of the distinction – s 62 of the **LPA**; the way to make the distinction – *Holland v Hodgson* (1872); *Elitestone Ltd v Morris* (1997); *Botham v TSB Bank* (1997); *TSB v Botham* (1996); *Chelsea Yacht and Boat Club Ltd v Pope* (2000); tenant's fixtures.

Applying the Law

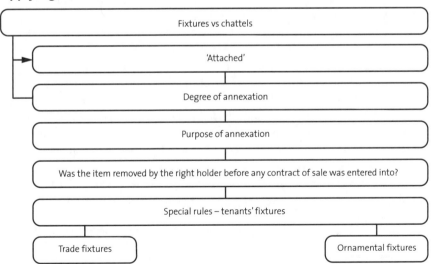

This diagram shows the how to determine whether an item is a fixture or a fitting.

ANSWER

It is a general principle of land law that what becomes attached to the land becomes part of the land – these are fixtures (*Minshall v Lloyd* (1837); *Elitestone v Morris* (1997)). In practice, this has important consequences. First, it means that when one person conveys land to another, they will also convey all 'fixtures', save those that have been expressly excluded from the conveyance or can be removed by the vendor by virtue of some exceptional right (see **s 62** of the **Law of Property Act 1925**).[10] Second, it means that should one person affix articles to land owned by another, those articles fall into the ownership of the landowner, as where a tenant affixes articles to the land they are leasing so that at the end of the lease they fall into the ownership of the landlord. In our problem, although there are two separate factual situations to consider, the essential points at issue are the same: first, whether the articles that are removed from the land by Hannibal and Vesuvius are fixtures so as to make them presumptively liable for such removal; second, if they are fixtures, whether removal could be justified by exceptional circumstances.[11]

(a) Roman Villas

The general rule in relation to the Roman Villas is clear enough. All articles that, at the date of the contract, can be regarded as fixtures will belong to the new purchaser (Hannibal) on completion of the contract (**s 62** of the **LPA**; *Phillips v Lamdin* (1949)). If Vesuvius, the vendor, is to have good title to any of the articles he has in fact removed, he must show either: (a) that he removed them before the contract was signed; or (b) they are not fixtures at all but chattels personally owned by him; or (c) that, if they are fixtures, his removal was by virtue of some exceptional right.

First, a freehold owner may, at any time before they contract to sell, remove any item from their land as this is part of their normal rights of ownership (*Re Whaley* (1908)), but there is nothing here to indicate that has occurred. Second, are the items fixtures or chattels? Chattels are personal goods, not forming part of the land and, therefore, not conveyed as such to a purchaser of it. The general test as to whether an item can be regarded as a fixture was summarised in *Holland v Hodgson* (1872), while the most detailed recent discussion of what could be fixtures in the context of ordinary household goods is found in *Botham v TSB Bank plc* (1997). Consideration must be given to the *degree* of annexation to the land (the primary test) and the *purpose* of annexation to the land. Thus, generally, a fixture is something attached to the land in some substantial way, even though it could be removed quite easily (*Culling v Tufnal* (1694)). However, the *purpose* of annexation can override 'annexation' where affixing is necessary for the proper use of the article (*Leigh v Taylor* (1902)). Conversely, items intended to enhance the value of the property may be fixtures even though resting on their own weight (*D'Eyncourt v Gregory* (1866)). All in all, everything turns on the particular facts of each case, bearing in mind the nature of the property, the use of the articles and the physical relation of them to the land itself.

---

10 Even when making general statements, it is always good practice to back up your statement with statute or case law.

11 In problem questions, use your introduction to help outline your structure. This will help in the exam as it shows the examiner what to expect from your answer, but also keeps you disciplined to ensure that you address all the relevant issues required in the time allotted.

(i) The Greenhouse

If the greenhouse is fixed to the land, it will be a fixture, as with the temporary sheds in *Webb v Frank Bevis* (1940). However, there is clear authority that a free-standing greenhouse is to be regarded as a chattel (*HE Dibble Ltd v Moore* (1970)) and a 'Dutch barn' was still a chattel even though it was founded in sockets in the land to give it more support (*Culling v Tufnal*).[12] Probably, Vesuvius was entitled to remove the greenhouse as a chattel provided that it was not actually affixed to the land in a permanent way or was not part of an ornamental garden designed for the betterment of the land as a whole.

(ii) Garden Ornaments

Prima facie, the garden ornaments are chattels as they are, in all probability, free-standing and not attached to the land at all: *Berkley v Poulett* (1976). However, it is clear from *D'Eyncourt v Gregory* that, if garden ornaments are part of a general garden design created to enhance the particular house, they will be regarded as fixtures that pass with the land. Once again, then, presumptively these will be chattels unless the ornaments are integral to the property. They can be removed by Vesuvius.

(iii) Television Aerial

This article to consider is clearly designed to facilitate the use of another article (a television), which is so obviously a chattel. However, it is quite common that television aerials are attached to property (for example, on the chimney) and, if this is the case, the presumption will be that it is a fixture. This is reinforced by the fact that the aerial can be detached from the television and is not an integral part of it: cf. *Jordan v May* (1947). Note, however, that in *Credit Valley Cable v Peel Condominium Corp* (1980) a television cable was held to be a chattel, being for the better use of a television and not better use of the land. Perhaps the only solution is to revert to the basic *Holland* test: the degree of annexation. If this decrees that the aerial is a fixture, it is no reply that it thereby confers a personal benefit on the new owners of the land.[13]

(iv) The Bannisters

The banisters appear to be affixed to the land in what is intended to be a permanent fashion. If fireplaces can be regarded as fixtures (*Buckland v Butterfield* (1820)), surely so must banisters. Vesuvius is not entitled to remove them any more than he would be entitled to remove the floorboards.

(v) The Roses

Here, the position is clear. Roses, as with other trees, shrubs and flowers growing on the land are part of the legal definition of the land within **s 205** of the **LPA 1925**. Thus, they belong to the estate owner and were conveyed to Hannibal when he purchased the land. Vesuvius is not entitled to remove them.

---

12 Use similar factual cases to draw parallels.

13 If there is no clear case on point, then you can make your argument from first principles.

(b) The Office

A tenant who brings articles on to the land and then fixes them to it effectively passes title to those articles to the landlord. They cannot, therefore, be removed at the end of the lease unless some special rule so provides. In our case, there are the lights, the chair, the oak panels and the fish tank.

There is a general rule that a tenant has a right to remove certain types of fixture from the land at the end of the lease – that is, that even though in law they are fixtures and within the title of the landlord, the tenant may reassert ownership for special reasons. One important category of such fixtures is 'trade fixtures', which may be removed by the tenant during the continuance of the lease or (probably) within a reasonable time after its end (*Poole's Case*). This right is lost if the tenant does not remove trade fixtures during the term (or just after), but it is clear that the tenant does not lose the right to remove fixtures attached during one lease that then ends, if that lease is immediately followed by a new term in continuation of it (*New Zealand Government Property Corp v H and M Ltd* (1982)). This is the case here and it seems certain that the lights and the chair can be removed by Hannibal as trade fixtures when he quits. Of course, if they are not fixtures, he can remove them anyway.

Further, assuming that these are not necessary for his trade, can it be said that either the oak panelling or the fish tank are fixtures or are they merely personal chattels? There is authority that panelling (*Buckland v Butterfield*) and even tapestries (*Re Whaley*, but contrast *Leigh v Taylor*) are fixtures because of the degree of annexation to the property. If this is followed, the oak panelling is a fixture and must remain. The fish tank might be different, as Hannibal could claim that it is fixed to the wall for steadying purposes, not as an attachment per se: see also *Viscount Hill v Bullock* (1897), in which a collection of stuffed animals nailed to the wall were held to be chattels. In any event, however, even if the fish tank is a fixture, Hannibal can claim that he has a right to remove it under another exception – namely, the right of a tenant to remove ornamental fixtures during his lease so long as this can be done without damage to the building (*Martin v Roe* (1857)). Indeed, one case (*Spyer v Phillipson* (1931)) suggests that even panelling (assuming it is a fixture) may be removed under this general heading, although it will be rare that this can be done without damage to the premises.

All in all then, the chair and lights can be removed whether they are fixtures or not (the trade exception), the fish tank may not be a fixture but, if it is, could be removed under the 'ornamental/domestic' exception, and the oak panelling is probably a fixture and could be removed under the 'ornamental/domestic' exception only if there is no damage to the premises.[14]

Common Pitfalls

This is a relatively straightforward question, hence the examiner will expect to see significant case law. The danger is that the answer will use just *Holland v Hodgson* and this will cause a low mark.

---

14 In problem questions where time allows you should always reach a clear and reasoned conclusion, just like an essay.

Index